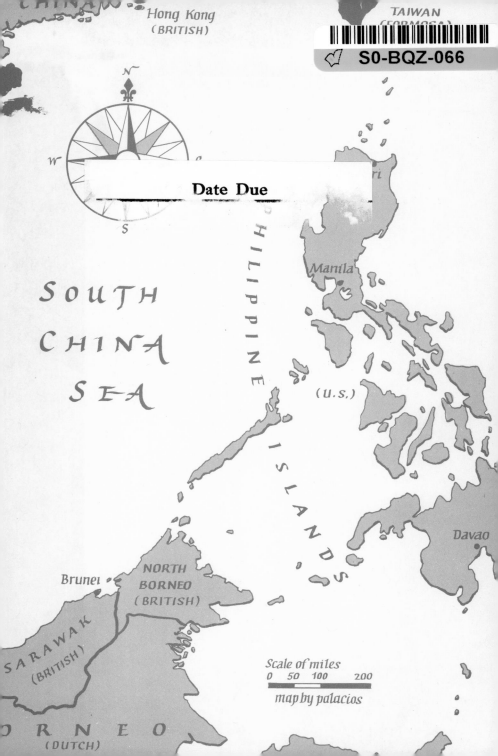

CHINA

Hong Kong
(BRITISH)

TAIWAN
(FORMOSA)

N

W   E

S

Date Due

SOUTH

CHINA

SEA

P H I L I P P I N E

Manila

(U.S.)

I S L A N D S

Davao

Brunei

NORTH
BORNEO
(BRITISH)

SARAWAK
(BRITISH)

Scale of miles
0   50   100   200

map by palacios

B O R N E O
(DUTCH)

SOMEONE HAD BLUNDERED

SOMEONE
HAD
BLUNDERED

The Story of the "Repulse" and the
"Prince of Wales"

BERNARD ASH

DOUBLEDAY & COMPANY, INC.
GARDEN CITY, NEW YORK
1961

Library of Congress Catalog Card Number 60–13724
Copyright © 1960 by Bernard Ash
All Rights Reserved
Printed in the United States of America
First Edition

PREFACE

A BOOK OF THIS SORT—IF IT IS TO BE MORE THAN AN ABstract of official papers and other works already published
—depends to a high degree on personal recollection and on
the author's luck in running to earth people who have personal contributions of value to make. Only a few of the many
people who have helped me with this book appear in it by
name, for the smaller contributions have become absorbed
into a larger picture; moreover, as the personalities of the
two ships began to emerge and the pattern of events in
which they were involved began to become significant, individuals tended inevitably to fade into the background.

I am profoundly grateful to all who have sent or given me
information: to some I owe a special debt. Pride of place
among these must undoubtedly go to Slinger Wood of the
Repulse, followed closely by Alf Tudor of the *Prince of
Wales*. There was a point at which the book almost became
the story of Slinger Wood, not only because he was an able,

enthusiastic, and well-balanced informant, but also because there was a thread in his own life, as the reader will find, that ran curiously close to the life lines of the ships. For that reason he "appears and disappears" (as Mr. Churchill might have said) more often than any other of the characters who are mentioned by name and becomes, perhaps, in the end almost a symbol of the ships and their companies. I am particularly indebted also to Marine J. E. Garner, Stoker Albert Dick and Chief Petty Officer F. G. E. O'Rorke of the *Repulse*, to Cyril Williams and F. V. Seddon of the *Prince of Wales*.

I owe at least as much as anyone who researches into naval matters to the kindness and co-operation of the Admiralty librarian and his staff. I owe thanks to Captain J. W. C. Dendy, R.N. (ret.), *Repulse*'s commander, for technical help on the damage situation in both ships in the final action. It was inevitable that I should seek the aid of *Repulse*'s last captain and the senior surviving officer of Force Z, Admiral Sir William Tennant: his help and advice have been readily given and most valuable. It is impossible not to comment on the respect and affection with which he is invariably spoken of by survivors of his ship's company. For her help in tracking down survivors of the ships, I am grateful to an old and sturdy friend and fellow townsman, Bessie Braddock, M.P.

A short bibliography will be found at the end of the book. While the responsibility for my facts is spread over many sources, both human and documentary, responsibility for the conclusions I have drawn from the facts lies upon my shoulders alone; neither those mentioned by name above nor anyone who has helped me in any degree can fairly be charged with any part of them. This is the more important because my conclusions will be unpopular at least in some quarters—though I cannot help it if they are. I have no axes to grind, nor do I seek a little ephemeral publicity through Churchill-baiting. I have tried to write as honest a history as

I could, and on the basis of the facts, insofar as I was able to come at them, my conclusions appeared to me inescapable.

To all those who have helped me and to the memory of two great ships and their companies my book is dedicated.

SOMEONE HAD BLUNDERED

CHAPTER
1

ON THE MORNING OF DECEMBER 10, 1941, JAPANESE airmen, flying north over the Gulf of Siam, looked down at a calm sea and saw what they had been sent to find. They saw two great ships steaming at speed with three attendant destroyers. They knew that the ships were the *Prince of Wales* and the *Repulse*. They knew which was which and they knew precisely the armament and the armour of each. They knew what they had to do.

These two ships should not have been there.

Because they were there, they were bombed, torpedoed, and sunk. Many hundreds of men lost their lives, some of them trapped within the battered hulls of their ships, others in the oily water. With this disaster the control of the whole South China Sea passed beyond possibility of dispute into the hands of the Japanese—who already, after the virtual extermination of American sea-power at Pearl Harbour, held mastery over the rest of the Pacific Ocean. Hong Kong was isolated, Singapore exposed, the way into the Indian Ocean laid open. In the whole of World War II no more bitter, sudden, or decisive blow fell upon Britain and her allies.

This is the story of those two ships and of their passing; of the long sea ways that took them to their doom; of how they came to be there, and why they should not have been there. It is a proud story, not without glory. It is also a story of failure and folly. It is a story which men will remember, and about which they will dispute as long as there are ships to sail the sea or men to sail in them.

Two ships . . . two very different ships. Both proud ships, but very different. One, a ship almost of another age that had known royal occasions, even been dubbed the "Royal Yacht," steamed an immense tale of miles in many waters, sought the enemy indefatigably in fair weather and foul, never lost a ship from any of her convoys, yet came in the end to be H.M.S. *Anonymous*. The other a new ship, dubbed in her turn "Churchill's Yacht," planned for the contingencies of modern war and known to some as H.M.S. *Unsinkable*, which is always a dangerous thing to call a ship. She had known enemy fire before she left the dockyard of her birth, and controversy raged about her from her cradle to her watery grave. The few short months of her life were crammed with history. One man in this story helped to lay her keel and, struggling in the water, a survivor from the *Repulse*, watched his handiwork drown.

To the eye H.M.S. *Repulse* was a most handsome ship, to those who lived on her a comfortable one. Before Slinger Wood discovered that if you lost your "breathing permit" you could not, in fact, breathe; before Stripey Shatwell menaced Mess 46 with the threat of the scran-bag; before the days of Leading Seaman Bigmore, Ginger Devine, Chicken Howe and the rest, a generation of ratings had found her messes spacious, airy, and well-arranged as messes go. In wartime, of course, with hundreds of extra hands to be crammed in somehow or other, they became overcrowded, as did the messes on all ships; nonetheless, by lower-deck standards, she wasn't a bad ship to live on. She was fast: on her trials she had comfortably exceeded her contract 31½ knots, and even in her old age (without being re-engined, as her sister-ship *Renown* was) showed a clean pair of heels. She was efficient and well-officered; her whole company was profoundly convinced that its gunnery was the best in the Fleet, and that Six-Gun Coney, their gunnery officer, was the best shot on the seven seas. Many fights in clubs, pubs, and canteens were waged in support of this contention.

Yet *Repulse* had an Achilles heel—an Achilles heel in the most literal sense. For she belonged to the vanishing race of battle-cruisers and therefore, in a sense, to a conception of naval warfare which became obsolete not long before she received her first commission—back when the *Queen Mary* and the *Invincible* blew up with appalling loss of life at the Battle of Jutland, just as the *Hood*, greatest of all the battle-cruisers and the British Navy's biggest ship, was to blow up in the *Bismarck* action twenty-five years later. In the age when the capital ship queened it over the world's oceans, the task of the battle-cruiser was to seek out by superior speed and destroy or cripple by superior gun-power—precisely the role which was assumed by the torpedo-bomber in World War II. She was not intended to swap blow for blow in a stand-up action; least of all was she designed to meet any menace from the air. So *Repulse* was lightly armoured —so lightly armoured that, in the light of the Jutland disaster, she was modified after her completion in 1916 before going into service. She was modified again in 1919, when her armour belt was extended and torpedo bulges fitted, and again in 1932, though she was never modernised to the same extent as the *Renown*. But to the end of her days her armour was far too light, and she was vulnerable not merely to air bombardment but also to the plunging fire of shot aimed at her from ranges of 13,000 yards or beyond.

It was out of this very weakness that her beauty came— out of her function, her need for speed. It was the need for speed that endowed her with her shapely hull with its pronounced sheer. The rest of her build, her well-proportioned upper works, completed the picture. At last in her and in her two surviving sisters, *Renown* and *Hood*, the capital ship had emerged from the incredible ugliness of the slab-sided, top-heavy monstrosities of the late Victorian and early Edwardian years that had made men hark back nostalgically to the sweeping lines of wooden hulls, the towering symmetry of masts and shrouds. At last sheer function had created loveliness out of a mass of steel, an accumulation of machinery. To this day, those who saw the *Repulse* steaming at speed remember the sight with a catch in the throat.

For the technically minded, she displaced 26,500 tons, was 794 feet long, ninety feet in the beam and twenty-seven feet in draught. Her turbines gave 112,000 horse-power to four shafts, she had forty-two boilers, and carried 4,200 tons of oil. She mounted six fifteen-inch guns in her three turrets fore and aft, fifteen four-inch guns, eight torpedo tubes; but for air defence she had but six obsolete four-inch high angle guns, with small-bore weapons and a couple of pom-poms. Eager hands and skill made the most of these, but she was no match for the Imperial Japanese Air Force or any other air force.

In the 1920s she carried Edward, the Prince of Wales, on his tours to South America and South Africa; in 1939 she was to have carried the King and Queen on their visit to the United States. These were her days of pride, her summer days. She represented a Navy that ruled the seven seas, a vision of imperial majesty that was already gone from the face of the waters by the grim spring of 1941 when the *Prince of Wales* left her fitting-out berth to be precipitated into the throes of a war for very survival—the latest and greatest of battleships, already a legend in her lifetime.

One of the best impressions of the *Prince of Wales* as she

appeared to the beholder against the taut, emotional background of those times has been left by H. V. Morton, one of the two journalists who accompanied Prime Minister Churchill on his journey in her to meet President Roosevelt at Placentia Bay, Newfoundland.

> We saw [he wrote] *a giant among giants, the splendid ship that was to be our home, her great guns pointing fore and aft, her crew drawn up on deck. How beautiful she looked that morning as she appeared out of the mist, full of power, strength and pride. As we approached her . . . we slowed and swung round to her and as we did so, we saw that the battleship, which from a distance had looked so graceful and so lithe, now towered above us like a mighty hill of steel. Far above us the fifteen hundred odd members of her crew stood mustered on the decks, the bosuns stood at the gangway, the Officer of the Watch with his telescope, the Captain, the Royal Marines with their band upon the quarterdeck . . .*

General C. E. Percival watched her arrival with *Repulse* at Singapore barely a week before her end and wrote of ". . . the thrill it gave us all as we watched those majestic ships steaming up the East Channel of the Johore Strait and coming to anchor." Alfred Duff-Cooper (sent to administer a territory of whose appalling perils both he and those who sent him there appear to have had singularly little idea) chronicled her arrival as an impressive and reassuring spectacle. Churchill boasted to Stalin that she was able to hunt down and destroy any unit of the Japanese Fleet; and even the men of the *Repulse*, disgruntled and bitter as many of them were at being reduced to the role of H.M.S. *Anonymous*, could not restrain grudging admiration of her, steaming past them to take up her station ahead as Force Z sailed out to its doom—and even as the signal was made from Changi Point that there would be no fighter cover for the ships.

"Just look at her, boy," O'Dowd Gallagher reports them saying, "Churchill's Yacht . . . the Glamour Ship. Look at her!"

Yet all was not well in the midst of all this admiration, through no fault of either her captain or her crew. Those fourteen-inch gun turrets that appeared so overwhelming to Morton had her in trouble from first to last. She fought the *Bismarck* with half her heavy armament out of action—in the words of an Admiralty observer, with one hand tied behind her back. Her anti-aircraft armament, though immeasurably more than that of the *Repulse*, was still below the needs of modern war, so that additional pom-poms had to be loaded on to her at Colombo, for fitting after her arrival at Singapore. And though her crew were keen, ship-proud, and trained to the peak, though they had already given good account of themselves, she never had a real chance to "shake down."

She was laid down in 1937 at Cammell Laird's dockyard on the Mersey, in the same ways which the *Rodney* had left more than a decade before—and no battleship had been laid down since either there or anywhere else, while the might of the Axis grew and the menace of war again descended on the world. She was shorter than the *Repulse* by a good fifty feet, but thirteen feet wider in the beam, and nine feet deeper in draught; her displacement was 35,000 tons. Her silhouette was described as differing from the traditional British "look" and was closer to that of the later German battleships, which points to nothing except that, in similar circumstances, naval designers tend to think alike. While *Repulse*'s lack of armour endowed her with a vulnerability that belied appearances, *Prince of Wales* and her four sister-ships of the *King George* V-class were more heavily protected than any battleships yet built. She had a sixteen-inch waterline belt with an "advanced system of underwater protection and defence against air attack, a good distribution of side and deck armour and elaborate subdivision." Her armour weighed, in fact, no less than 15,000 tons, and though it had to be paid for both in gun-power and in speed (for with roughly the same engine power she rated three knots less than *Repulse*), it stood her in good stead, both in the *Bismarck* action and in her final struggle against impossible odds. But alas, even the most heavily armoured of ships cannot escape having rudders and screws, and one lucky torpedo was enough to put her completely out of control and seal her fate.

Churchill thought she, too, had an Achilles heel as far as her armour was concerned. The aircraft hangar in the midst of her citadel, he insisted, left a gap in her protection and made her more vulnerable than she need have been. In this he was wrong, for her deck armour ran uninterrupted from stem to stern, hangar or no hangar, and the siting of the hangar made not one iota of difference to it, but the great man remained unconvinced and unrepentant. Where he was right—utterly and horribly right—was about her guns, and her guns became a sort of obsession with him. In memorandum after memorandum he harped on them, even while admitting that the issue was academic, because the guns and the turrets were there and nothing could be done about them. In the very midst of battering down, with the dogged insistence that he brought to every task, the Naval Staff's resistance to sending this ship out East, he still went on about the guns.

Now to put the reader thoroughly in the picture, the *Prince of Wales*'s armament consisted of ten fourteen-inch guns, sixteen 5.25-inch guns, sixty two-pounder ack-ack guns and numerous smaller guns, including 40mm. Bofors and 20mm. Oerlikon. It was the fourteen-inch guns that were the trouble. They were a new type, smaller in bore than the fifteen- and sixteen-inch guns of other years and other nations but designed for greater penetration and a higher rate of fire. She was originally intended to have had twelve of them, but two were sacrificed for greater weight of armour, making her broadside less weighty than had been intended. The turrets as well as the guns were new in design and even their arrangement was novel—two quadruple, one foreward, one aft, weighing 1,400 tons each, with a smaller, two-gun turret superimposed above the forward four-gun turret only. Had it been thought for a moment that both guns and turrets would have to be proved in war instead of experimented with in peace, things might have been done differently, but Hitler's affairs were more pressing than her designers, busy with drawing-board and theory, imagined. Not only was the weight of the *Prince of Wales*'s broadside less than that of older ships with fewer guns, but mechanical trouble with the new machinery dogged her brief existence. It was not until over a month after she joined the Home Fleet that her last turret was accepted from the contractors. She sailed to meet the *Bismarck* with more than a hundred civilian contractors still aboard (something that must be almost unique in naval history, and a pretty poor view the contractors' men took of it), and before the brief minutes of that action had run their course, mechanical breakdown had silenced five of her ten big guns. It is to the endless credit of the ship and her company that in the face of that tremendous handicap she succeeded in doing *Bismarck* damage that ultimately led to her undoing, and there is nothing meaner in the whole web of rumour, surmise, and sensation-hunting that is woven round any war than the attempts which were made at the time to deprive her of that credit. It can be taken that the Japanese, who knew more than we had the wit to realise, were not ignorant of these matters, and that the arrival of the *Prince of Wales* in Eastern waters was not so terrible to them as the Foreign Office, the fools' paradise of Singapore, or even the Prime Minister himself supposed. Someone had blundered . . . This was the first of many blunders.

Yet there is more to ships than metal, machinery, and guns. Ships must be manned by men, and here is something which neither naval contractors nor strategists can blunder over. There were no two finer ships' companies in the Navy than the companies of these two, and the warmth with which their survivors speak of them, even after the passing of the deadening years and the fading of young men's fire and brightness, is spontaneous, unmistakable, and sincere. Stronger, perhaps, in the case of *Repulse*, because her people had been together longer, had been—the bulk of them—a ship's company in peace as well as one at war, had steamed a quarter of a million blacked-out miles together, had known frustration as well as joy—stronger, perhaps, in her case, but strong in both. Happy ships, both of them, well commanded. Captain William Tennant of the *Repulse* survived, to become an admiral and earn a knighthood. "We didn't make things easy for them," was the only comment he would make on being confronted with the spontaneous tributes of his men, but then fighting men don't ask to have things easy. Flag-Captain John Leach of the *Prince of Wales* was drowned together with his Admiral, Tom Phillips (better known to the lower deck as Tom Thumb, which any photograph will explain), and of Leach survivors have said that he always wore a smile upon his face: heaven alone knows he often had precious little to smile about. Leach's running commentary over the ship's loudspeaker system during the *Bismarck* action (when he had plenty of other things to do) was so clear and vivid that men still speak with remarkable unanimity of what went on in that battle; and Tennant's handling of his ship under the overwhelming assaults of the Japanese bombers and torpedo-bombers reads like the pages of a naval instruction manual. Had we still been living in an age when ships laid alongside one another and fought their battles by sheer guts and spirit, these two ships' companies would have proved unbeatable. But nothing could beat the blunders that led them into the South China Sea, committed to an impossible task, devoid of air cover, without refuge or means of retaliation. They shot down seven bombers. They could have shot down seven hundred: they still would have been sunk. Had they survived that day, they would have been sunk the next day, or the day after, or the day after that. Once they were there, nothing could have saved them; and their being there was the last of the worst of the blunders.

CHAPTER

2

SLINGER WOOD WAS LUCKY TO HAVE A JOB. NOT SO VERY MANY years before, Cammell Laird's shipyard and all the other shipyards of the Mersey had been silent; and those who have known what silence means on a great river where the clang and clamour of the pneumatic riveters should be echoing ceaselessly from shore to shore pray they may never know it again. The great graving docks and fitting-out basins had been deserted, the long slipways tenanted only by the ghosts of the proud ships of war and merchant ships innumerable that had taken shape upon them. The Great Depression had closed them down.

There had been no Great Depression in the shipyards of Germany, Italy, and Japan, which were building modern ships of war as fast as they dared and merchant ships as fast as they could, till in every harbour of Europe the crooked cross of the Nazis, fluttering from the jackstaffs of serried ranks of loading and unloading tramp shipping, had almost

ousted the red ensign from the quays. In those years Japan
had had her Manchurian adventure; Italy had laid her bloody
hands on Ethiopia, and finally, much nearer home, the grim
rehearsal for World War II had begun in Spain; so that at
long last there had been some sort of awakening. Ships were
being built once again and, by a strange paradox, the coming
of the war that was to bring disaster and death to so many of
them put work into the hands of people like Slinger Wood.

As a matter of fact, Slinger Wood should not have been
in Cammell Laird's shipyard at all, but in Birkenhead Park
High School, to which he had won a scholarship at the age
of eleven. That meant an outlay of nine pounds on a school
uniform: in those years of bare feet and bare bottoms on
Merseyside, it might as well have been nine hundred. A year
before that his mother had died in childbirth of her tenth
child. His father, an ex-Regimental Sergeant-Major who deserved better than the dole, taught the boys to darn and
sew their own clothes, and mended their boots with bits of
old motor tyres, but darned breeches and patched-up boots
weren't the uniform at Birkenhead Park High. Someone had
blundered about this sort of thing as well, and in the event
it might be said that Slinger Wood and thousands like him
gave their country better service than it had a full right to
expect.

So he left school at fourteen, became an errand boy, and
in 1936, the year that the Berlin-Rome-Tokyo Axis was
forged, was lucky enough to find himself a job as an appren-
tice driller at Cammell Laird's shipyard. He worked first of
all on the *Ark Royal*, the aircraft carrier whose planes were
to put paid to the *Bismarck* long after Lord Haw-Haw had
consigned her to the bottom of the sea; and after *Ark Royal*
was launched, in the following year, he worked on the keel
of the *Prince of Wales*, which was then not the *Prince
of Wales*, but only a number. As the hundreds of compartments which were to make up her double bottom took

shape, he and his fellow-workers marvelled. "When one got inside with a drilling machine," he writes (and truly, if he'd have been able to take advantage of that scholarship, he would have made a much better job of this book than the present writer), "there wasn't room to turn round. We used to swear that she would be unsinkable when she was finished . . . little did I realise that what my own eyes were to witness in only four or five short (or were they long) years' time."

So even as she lay upon her very cradle the legend of this ship's invincibility was born—a legend which was to send Singapore happily back to its flesh-pots and even coloured the better judgment of the Prime Minister himself. A fine thing to be building a great ship, but a finer thing still to sail on one! To Slinger and his mate, as they worked in the narrow compartments, came the vision which had come to generations of Liverpool lads before them, calling them away from the mean streets, the crowded little homes, the dole queues, the shifts and contrivances. Both their brothers were doing a China commission on H.M.S. *Emerald*: all of Wood's mother's family had been connected with the sea, and her uncle was one of the first secretaries of the Seamen's Union, while his father and grandfather had been soldiers, and the old man had many a tale to tell of the South African War. These were worlds beyond the shipyard, the docks, the wide estuary with its swirling tides.

"Come over to Canning Place and join up," said Slinger's mate.

To cut a long story short, they did.

Not long after the Munich crisis, Slinger finished his boy's seamanship course and passed out of H.M.S. *Wildfire* at Sheerness with the Captain's Prize, for which he chose a cigarette case and a wrist watch. Both these now lie in his ditty box at the bottom of the China Sea. And by way of the Royal Naval Barracks at Devonport, known to the lower deck as Jago's Mansion, he found himself posted on his

eighteenth birthday, January 16, 1939, to H.M.S. *Repulse*,
which was fitting out in the dockyard for yet another royal
tour—the tour of the King and Queen to the United States
and Canada. There was not a man in the whole of the Navy
who did not yearn for such a posting at this time. *Repulse*
was the most envied ship in Pompey—albeit a Devonport
ship at that—and there was a lot of heartburning about these
postings. Stoker Dick, who arrived on her about the same
time, found much bitterness and jealousy in the town, for it
was argued that the job belonged by rights to a Portsmouth
ship, manned by Portsmouth men, not a ship from the
other place, full of Scouses, Geordies, and other miscellaneous breeds, some of whom didn't even have a seaport in their
ancestry at all. There were what sailors politely term "differences of opinion" about it—and not a few bloody noses.
A very far cry indeed from those other days, not much more
than two short years ahead, when this same proud ship was
to find herself at Singapore in the role of H.M.S. *Anonymous*, poor relation of the Glamour Ship, the *Prince of
Wales*, whose decks swarmed with pressmen of all nationali-
ties, whose crew were feted by the town, while the erstwhile
Royal Yacht lay forgotten and despised astern of her. There
were reasons for this, but they were bad ones, and the bitterness has even now not yet passed for many survivors of the
Repulse, Slinger Wood himself among them.

But however much *Repulse*'s company and Pompey in
general might be preoccupied with preparations for the Royal
Tour, they were not the sole preoccupation of the Admiralty. Hitler's New Year Message, as well as certain sections
of the British press, had made it quite clear that there was
to be no war this year. But those concerned with the realities
of life found themselves by no means so certain that the
next autumn crisis would end in a Munich, complete with
the then-unfamiliar spectacle of an airborne Prime Minister
bearing an umbrella in lieu of a pipe of peace. Roughly
coinciding, in fact, with the arrival on the *Repulse* of Slinger

Wood and Stoker Dick, the Navy's first war plans had been issued to the Fleet. The detail of them is unimportant for this narrative, but the background to them is of the utmost significance. For in the first place, they showed a clear understanding of something which too many people in high places found it easier to forget in the years to come, or when they remembered it, speedily devised reasons why it should once more be forgotten. We must, declared the Admiralty very clearly, be prepared for the active intervention of Japan against ourselves and France. The forces at our disposal in the foreseeable future, moreover, would not allow us to wage war at sea simultaneously in the Atlantic, the Mediterranean, and the Pacific. An effective fleet in the Far East could only be provided by withdrawal from the Mediterranean—the containing of the Axis forces wherein would have to be left, in that eventuality, to the French. What the plans did not foresee (and what no-one who wished to continue to think himself sane could foresee) was that the collapse of France would not only remove the French Fleet from the Mediterranean, but would shortly thereafter give the Japanese air bases in French Indochina within striking distance of Singapore and the whole South China Sea, but not themselves within striking distance of the scratch, short-range American fighter aircraft with which our forces in that area were to find themselves equipped. Japanese air power, indeed, was accorded very little thought at all. The Japanese "were not very good at aircraft." They were not very good at anything in particular, and moreover, with the long war in China and one thing and another, their resources would already be stretched to the limit. They would starve; they would run short of oil; they would run short of everything. Remember that at the same hour we were comfortably reassuring ourselves that German mines were made of cardboard, the ignition cables of their armoured fighting vehicles insulated with ersatz rubber which would not keep out the wet and so on—why, even their soapless detergents wouldn't wash! All these legends were part of the blunder which led the Royal Yacht, for postings to which men ached so bitterly, and the Glamour Ship that was yet to be, to their destruction in the Gulf of Siam in a December morning in 1941—and they were legends that were to die hard.

All this was fortunately unknown and almost unsuspected to some hundreds of young men just back from Christmas leave and on top of the world, who left Devonport on a special train on a cold, wet morning and who, just before dark, found themselves alongside the *Repulse*, which was sitting on the blocks in dry dock and didn't look in the least like a royal yacht, or even very big. Among them was Slinger Wood, who was now a fully-fledged Ordinary Seaman, and who had met, on his leave, the girl who was to be his wife. He had not so far, however, been to sea on anything bigger than the Woodside Ferry, or known the ocean beyond New Brighton Pier. He found himself issued, in common with generations of seamen before him, with a station card, known in the Navy as a "breathing licence." It bore his name, his mess number, his religion, his part of the watch, and some other details, and it was about one-and-a-half inches square. It seemed an insignificant trifle to add to the mass of kit with which he was already burdened on a long and complicated journey through a ship which he suddenly discovered to be very large indeed: as, moreover, she was in dry dock and on shore supply, which was very short, she was also extremely cold, and every watertight door that could be closed was closed as tight as possible, making things more confusing still and enlivening their progress with roars of "Shut that bloody door!" From the quarter-deck, via the half-deck, the torpedo flat, the marines' mess deck (where the first Japanese bomb was later to fall), past the bookstall, through the canteen flat, these sorry sailors struggled. How familiar is that sight of soldier, sailor, or airman staggering weary and strange to the complications of a new berth or billet! Round B Turret barbette, through a hatchway in the armoured deck, down into the mess-deck space between A and B Turret barbettes which was to be his home from that moment until *Repulse* went down in the China Sea. And as he deposited himself and his belongings more or less upright at the bottom of the steel ladder, he heard for the first time the voice of Stripey Shatwell, whose welcome consisted of telling him to put his hammock straight in the hammock netting with the name showing, and not to leave anything lying around—ever.

"Or into the scran-bag it goes," declared Shatwell with conviction, and he was always as good as his word, from that moment until the ship went down, for he remained mess-deck dodger during the whole of that time. Men speedily learned that it was better to use their soap for washing their towels and other similar matters than to pay an inch a time of the bar to retrieve them from that same scran-bag—and not to leave anything about. All this is not irrelevant: multiply the image of Stripey Shatwell by as many messes as *Repulse* contained, and you have an image of the spirit and the smartness of this ship. You have an image of what sort of men manned her, and you begin to regard her as something more than a pawn in the game of naval warfare; you begin to realise indeed that something more than a hull, some guns, and a miscellaneous collection of machinery was lost when she sank to the bottom of the sea because someone had blundered.

"We didn't make it easy for them . . ." Which of them ever wanted to have it easy? Not Stripey Tom Murch, not Reg Slatter, not Cowin Webb, nor Chicken Howe. Not even Ginger Devine, the Scot, who believed in spending as little time as possible on board when there was a pub near enough to get to. Not Mess 46 or any other mess.

Slinger's next duty was to report to the leading hand of the mess, Leading Seaman Bigmore, and never a man was better named, for he was one of the biggest men on the ship, and when he required something done there was no

argument. He ruled his mess with a rod of iron and a heart of
gold, and was a father to the younger men, as well as the
hardest of taskmasters. What he required just now was
Ordinary Seaman Wood's breathing licence, and it was at
this point that the breathing licence was discovered to be
missing. Ordinary Seaman Wood literally had no right to
breathe. There followed a nightmare journey back to the
Regulating Office through all the complications of a ship
that now seemed very big indeed, an outraged broadside from
the Regulating Petty Officer, and his first visit to the Commander's table the following morning. The only time thereafter that the precious square of cardboard was not in the
pocket of his waistbelt was when he was on leave or under
punishment—which, for the time being, was to be pretty
frequently.

A book could be written about Slinger Wood's progress
from being a green new hand to a working member of
Repulse's company who knew exactly what was required of
him and who could do it quickly, keenly, and efficiently,
whether the ship was on a peace-time exercise, rolling and
pitching in the anxious darkness of the wartime North
Atlantic, or in the relentless inferno of the Japanese bomber
attack. Seamen of only a few generations before had learned
their trade in a different way, by a three-year cruise round
the world under sail alone in an old three-decker of the
Flying Squadron: now there was no sail, no Flying Squadron,
and certainly not three years to spare, but Stripey Shatwell,
Leading Seaman Bigmore, Stripey Murch, the petty officers,
the chief petty officers, the First Lieutenant, the Commander, the Captain himself—all knew their trade through the
long chain of command. There is no more vital thing either
for men or for ships than this process of "shaking down."
Once a ship's company is knit together in this way, hell-
fire itself can barely undo it; once interrupted in the
knitting, it is never accomplished to quite the same degree. It is only when this is understood that it becomes

clear what a shocking blunder it was completely to disorganise the *Prince of Wales* (which had already had to fight a major action when barely out of the dockyard) by choosing her to be Churchill's Yacht for the journey to Placentia Bay —and in what peril both Churchill and all the Chiefs of Staff were placed by the same token.

It is a pity that there is neither room nor very much excuse to follow Slinger Wood through his individual process of shaking down, for it is the shaking-down of a ship in miniature and contains quite as many hair-raising incidents. The highlight of it was undoubtedly a matter of falling forty-five feet into the stokehold by way of an air intake through which the dockyard mateys had been lowering firebricks, and on which they had inconsiderately omitted to replace the cover; and it is quite typical of the ship, her discipline, and her sense of humour that when he returned to her later after six weeks in Haslar, he was on Commander's Report for not falling in with the duty watch after he had fallen down the stokehold. He was still on light duty when the ship sailed for Gibraltar, and on her second or third day out, she made a rendezvous with the Home Fleet, in or near the Bay of Biscay. The Bay was living up to its unenviable reputation, and filling both Ordinary Seaman Wood and some scores of other dry-land sailors with amazement at the antics which a big ship could peform and with agonised apprehension at what was clearly happening inside them. *Repulse* was a lively ship in a good sea—Scouse Garner was to make the same discovery when he joined her eighteen months later.

It was dawn when Slinger decided that he might feel better on the upper deck. When he arrived there he found himself not the first to come to such a conclusion, and there were plenty of others already hard at it. But what he saw (coupled, perhaps, with the cold, clean air), drove all the seasickness out of him. The rendezvous had taken place during the night and now, in the strong wind and heavy sea, they steamed in good order in as mighty a company of great ships of war as a man could wish to see, a sight which will never be seen again on the seas of the world. In the van, the *Nelson*, wearing the flag of the Admiral of the Fleet; with her, *Rodney, Resolution, Revenge, Ramillies, Repulse, Ark Royal*, the other ship he had helped to build; most of the City class cruisers, all the new Tribal class destroyers, and a host of others besides. Still the greatest fleet in the world, unchallenged for a century in its mastery of the sea—full of precision and power, the capital ships almost contemptuously shouldering their way through the steep and stormy waters, the others keeping station with them almost as far as the eye could see. What need to remember that more than one of these ships was old, nearly all of them lacking in some degree or other their full equipment for defence or attack, the whole company of them inadequate in numbers for the tasks that were shortly to be demanded of them? Just as the folk of Singapore were to gaze on the *Prince of Wales* and the *Repulse* and see in them a whole mighty fleet which was to be their salvation, so young Wood and his fellows could gaze upon these ships and have no thought except that this was a Navy that ruled the ocean and would always rule the ocean. What price Germans, Italians, Japanese? It was this that had called in the clamouring shipyard, across the sandy flats of the Mersey, above the narrow, mean streets of Liverpool and Birkenhead. This was glory and they were the inheritors of it.

The bad weather that had brought Slinger out on deck persisted (though he never felt like being seasick again) and cut down the exercises that had been intended. Nonetheless, they did a "throw-off" shoot with their fifteen-inch guns against *Rodney*, and *Rodney* returned the compliment: she was only just visible on the horizon, but her shells were landing very close to *Repulse*'s wake, several hundred yards astern, as the method was. It was during this exercise that Lieutenant Commander Coney, *Repulse*'s gunnery officer, earned his name of "Six-Gun Coney," with Lofty Waters in the rangefinder. "Nobody in the Fleet," declares Slinger, "could have convinced us that *they* had a finer or better shot than our Six-Gun Coney." If gunnery alone could not prove it, it was proved in the fist fights ashore, and in the pubs and canteens. A feeling of confidence filled the whole ship, and they never lost it, right up to the end. They were eager to have a go at anything or anybody.

It is a matter of history that *Repulse* never took the King and Queen across the Atlantic. From that last of all her peace-time exercises with the Home Fleet she went to Gibraltar, and there her crew painted her from stem to stern, made everything spick and span for her assignment as Royal Yacht; but when she arrived back at Pompey, gleaming as surely no ship had ever gleamed before, there was a grievous disappointment in store for her. The year in which there was to be no war was already proving so dark and disastrous before it was half over, that the Admiralty had decided no ship could be spared from home waters for such a length of time. The *Empress of Australia* was to take their Majesties instead—it was still before the days when Royalty could sail the seas in a converted cargo liner—and *Repulse*, together with the cruisers *Southampton* and *Edinburgh* could escort them half-way across the Atlantic, no more. The spick-and-span ship remained spick-and-span, the Queen's boudoir remained untenanted. Later (still decorated for the use for which it had been intended) it became an upper-deck wardroom, while the King's quarters reverted to the Captain. But Captain Tennant seldom used them, preferring his sea-cabin.

Regretfully the *Repulse*'s crew (all those arguments and bloody noses had been in vain after all) dressed ship and saw the Royal party leave them. They took back with them the Royal mail; in getting it aboard the Commander and a party of men were overwhelmed by a green 'un which wrappd them round Y Turret, and a lot of profane remarks

were made about His Majesty and his mail. His Majesty saw
nothing of this, and made a signal ordering the main brace
to be spliced. The bunting-tosser missed it and was never
forgiven, although the double issue was made good later.
Slinger Wood got his share. He was well under age, but by
now had good friends on the mess deck. In the weeks of hard
training that followed, he found himself assigned to the forward starboard triple four-inch turret, almost abreast the forward funnel. These old-fashioned triple mountings (a nov-
elty in their time) were cramped as well as complicated, and
it took a lot of training before a crew could work smoothly
in them, especially at night when they were liable to be
blinded by the flash of the guns. As rammer on the centre
gun he was equipped with a sort of mop about seven feet long
and a tub of water in which he splashed it, being careful not
to step into the recoil of one of the other guns, and endeavouring to get in no-one else's way if possible. When the
breech of his gun was opened, it was his duty to souse it
(and everyone else within reach) with water, to cool it as
much as possible.

"What'll you do," he asked Stripey Shatwell, who happened to be breech worker of this same gun, "if I shove the
head of the rammer in your face?"

"Shove all your kit in the scran-bag," replied Stripey
Shatwell.

Through these summer days the shadows of war were
creeping up about them, and about a whole island which
had already forgotten that Munich was peace in our time,
or even that there was to be no war this year. Ships were
ordered to their home ports, to give their crews summer
leave a month earlier than usual, and on their way 'round to
Plymouth, the mess deck debated furiously whether this was
going to be another September crisis or the real thing. They
were not as well-equipped for the real thing as their sister-
ship *Renown*, now nearing the end of a major refitting in
which she had not merely been completely re-engined but

had her high-angle guns replaced with ten twin four-and-a-half-inch turrets—twenty new guns for anti-aircraft work where *Repulse* still had only her six four inchers of World War I pattern. But they bragged of the drogues they had shot down and disposed of Hitler's navy. He hadn't much navy anyway—only submarines, and the asdic equipment of the new destroyers would soon take care of those. By the time they made port they had sunk the lot, forgetting (as gentlemen in high places, prone to blunders, were wont to forget) that a torpedo may be launched from an aircraft as well as a submarine, and neither knowing nor thinking anything about Japanese torpedo-bombers at all.

There are those in Liverpool who still remember the arrival of the *Repulse's* leave party (Slinger Wood among them) at Lime Street Station—about three hundred of them who owned to the soubriquet "Scouse." It was July 12, the anniversary of the Battle of the Boyne, when all good Orangemen march to their day's outing in honour of the good King William and the Protestant cause. The train bringing the Orange Lodge home had pulled into the station a few minutes before them; the Lodge had formed up ready to march out of the station, and the fine weather had brought out an impressive crowd to greet them—to cheer or jeer, according to denomination, Billies or Paddies. The band struck up "Heart of Oak," and at that moment, down the centre of the roadway which the police were keeping open for King Billie's Navy, out charged three hundred men of the real Navy, fit, full of themselves, and all agog for leave. The crowd went wild, Billies and Paddies together. Who could have wished for a better reception?

Beyond the city, across the turbid river where it widens out into the great, sandy lagoon of the upper estuary, the hull on which Wood and his mate had once worked towered immense amid its confining scaffolding, still not yet a ship. A quarter of a million miles of water still separated the *Repulse* from her rendezvous with the *Prince of Wales* off

the coast of Ceylon; and from that rendezvous all too many
of the bluejackets charging out of the station to the plaudits
of the crowd would not return. Give them their hour: they
deserved as much.

CHAPTER

3

ON THE MORNING OF SEPTEMBER 3, 1939—A SUNDAY MORN-
ing—people in Britain waited in a curious state of suspense
for the declaration of war. It was already two days since Hitler
had invaded Poland, but the last act of the tragedy was being
played out in the same atmosphere of indecision which had
permeated every grim and darkening movement of its
course. Some still hoped against hope for another Munich,
another miracle which would bring yet another interlude of
specious peace; others hoped that the long suspense would
be over at last, that the fears would be ended, that we might
know the worst. It was commonly expected, remember, that
the moment war was declared, the sky would be dark with
bombers, that all the terrors of the textbooks would descend
on London, and probably every major populated centre in
the land. There were to be no cheering crowds in the Mall
this time, no wild enthusiasm, no overwhelming certainty
of power and victory.

Chamberlain made his speech, and almost immediately

the sirens sounded—a false alarm, a prelude to the "Phony War."

There was no uncertainty aboard the *Repulse*, for which the war had already started. On August 31 she was at Scapa Flow, forming with *Hood*, the largest capital ship in the world, the battle-cruiser squadron of the Home Fleet, commanded by Admiral Forbes. On September 1 she was at sea near the Skaggerak, on Germany's very doorstep, and her crew was quite convinced that if any major units of the German Fleet ventured out, the shooting would start without further formality. Furthermore they had no doubt of what the issue would be, with their fifteen-inch guns against the eleven-inch guns of the *Scharnhorst* and *Gneisenau;* although in the light of the subsequent fate of the *Hood*, the situation takes on a somewhat different colour. On the day war was declared, the two ships were sweeping away to the north in search of the *Bremen*, which was somewhere on her way home to Germany from the United States. But the *Bremen* fled to Murmansk and eluded them, as so many other things were to elude them in the endless combing of the seas in the coming months and years. Then came a report that the German Fleet was leaving Schillig Roads, and away they went through the Fair Isle Channel, plunging after phantoms through the grey northern seas. East of Orkney they groped, now in thick fog. On the morning of the 6th they were back in Scapa Flow. On the 7th they were away again, patrolling the Norwegian coast to intercept enemy shipping which did not materialise.

The ships were blacked out at night now, and if Slinger Wood and his fellows listened to one lecture on how far a cigarette-end could be seen in the darkness, they must have listened to a dozen. Life had changed very much for them, especially for the crews of the four-inch guns and the main armament. It became a regular thing, after dusk action stations, for the close range weapons to go into four watches, which meant that every fourth night they had no watch at all; but those on the fifteen-inch and four-inch turrets and the torpedoes remained in two watches, and there was no such luck for them. All very well for those on the main turrets and the torpedo tubes, for they were under cover! Wood and his mates on T-1 were in the open. Under these circumstances the long woollen pants which had caused so much innocent hilarity on the mess deck when they were first issued, ceased to be funny. They were worn with gratitude.

Two things became important to them in the long, dark, cold hours of these watches: cover and cocoa—the thick, greasy-looking "pusser's kye," of which a huge vat was left in the galley every night, and which became very palatable after the addition of a great deal of condensed milk and a great deal of sugar. Slinger Wood and Chicken Howe, who were usually the fetchers and carriers of the cocoa, became thieves, vagabonds, and liars in their endless quest for a sufficiency of both these commodities, and many a laugh they had quietly up their sleeves when Petty Officer Cory praised the generosity of the cooks, not knowing the sugar had come out of his very own mess's tea chest.

As for cover, they would spend hours huddled up against the forward funnel, swapping lies, living their good times over again with interest, until the cold, the darkness, the sea, the war, the *Scharnhorst*, and the *Gneisenau* receded. Leading Seaman Davey in particular could have licked the hide off Barnacle Bill himself, especially with his yarns about the China commission from which he had not long returned, and Stripey Shatwell, who had been in the Navy since Adam was a lad, was not far behind him. No-one believed these stories any more than the primitive Greeks probably believed the heroic feats of Homer's heroes, but belief was a thing that bore no relation to them: the important thing was that they took the listeners away into another world where chill winds, damp, and discomfort did not exist; and there they squatted in comparative comfort in the lee of the roaring funnel while the ship beneath them, black as the night but vibrantly alive with her humming machinery and the thrust of her screws, drove on, pitching and rolling through the sullen, sinister seas.

When submarines were rumoured, the ship zig-zagged, driving them at intervals from one side of the funnel to another, and sometimes all this circumnavigation would fail to give them shelter from sea, wind, and spray. Then they would sneak into the captain's sea cabin flat—usually to be evicted wrathfully by one of the duty Petty officers. Some of these were new to the ship, having joined when she was made up to her wartime complement, and their severities were less lightly taken than those of the PO's the men knew. One of them was a gunnery instructor, who won for himself the enviable title of Spit and Whistle.

October—a whole month of war and still nothing but empty seas and grim northern weather, with the dubious delights of Scapa when in port. These included a canteen which was not yet finished, football pitches which were being laid out by reservists not yet posted to ships (how they must have loved it!) and the northern lights, which palled rapidly. But on October 8 an aircraft patrolling the Norwegian coast sighted German ships near the Lister light, steering north in murky weather, identified them as the *Gneisenau*, the cruiser *Köln* and nine destroyers. Here was a break-out, here was action at last! Flogging her old engines to the full, *Repulse* set out in high hopes, with the *Hood*, the cruisers *Aurora* and *Sheffield*, and the four destroyers which now were all that could be spared for a screen with the heavy demands of convoy duties. Alas, the seas were still empty. The German ships had reversed course under cover of darkness, re-entered the Kattegat, and were safely home in Kiel long before the hunt was called off. They never had any intention of breaking out: the thing was a snare, intended to draw the Fleet within the range of air attack—and not even that materialised. The initiative was with the hunted, who could choose their time and place to sally out, to feint;

the hunters had all the wide wastes of the ocean to cover with too few ships, and naval intelligence was not yet equal to coping with the enemy's moves. *Repulse* returned to harbour disgruntled. Six weeks of war and not a shot fired in anger, not so much as a glimpse of the German Fleet that had already been consigned to the bottom of the sea. Spirits began to flag.

Far to the south in Cammell Laird's, the dockyard workers strove against blackout and earlier autumn sunsets to complete the *Prince of Wales*. There was still a year's work and more to be done on her, and the beginning of her war was to be a different matter. Two years were to pass before her meeting with the *Repulse:* if Lord Haw-Haw was to be believed, the meeting would never take place, for he had already sunk the *Repulse* more than once.

But don't imagine for a moment that the *Repulse* was a dispirited and disillusioned ship. For one thing there was too much hard work to be done. H. V. Morton, writing later about the *Prince of Wales*, gave the world a very odd impression of life in a battleship at sea on a wartime ocean:

> *While Nelson's seamen, stripped naked to the waist,* [he wrote], *manhandled their tethered guns and lit them with fire, the modern gunner picks up a telephone and presses a button. No more physical effort is involved in firing a broadside . . . than in ringing the vicarage bell.*

Friend Wood and his shipmates, slopping and sweating in the confined space of their triple turret, could have given the world another story, much closer to Nelson's navy and certainly very far removed from the vicarage! Indeed that was one thing: for another, it only needed the merest hint of unusual movement, the slightest mess deck "buzz," to make them forget the weary weeks at sea and the dubious delights of Scapa Flow. Was it the *Hipper?* On the mess deck the *Hipper* was critically examined, assessed, disposed of, and sunk. Was it the *Scharnhorst?* The *Gneisenau?* They too, in turn, were speedily consigned to the bottom of the sea. Was it a matter of destroyers? Certainly the matter of destroyers might give anyone to think, for now the urgent need of escorts for the Atlantic convoys had skimmed their destroyer screen to the bare minimum and below. The four-inch and the close-range weapons would, they decided, cope with the destroyers. The main turrets wouldn't have all the shooting when the big gun battle came on. And the destroyers in turn were sunk. Captain Spooner, and for that matter, my Lords of the Admiralty, would have given the world for such a wealth of confidence.

In the middle of October they went south to Rosyth for a boiler-clean. They had been at the degaussing range at the Kirkwall end of the Flow the previous afternoon, testing the degaussing equipment that had been hurriedly fitted when Jerry came up with his latest wonder-weapon, the magnetic mine. They'd passed within a cable's length of the *Royal Oak*. They always passed within a cable's length of the *Royal Oak*. She was as much a part of the scenery as the *Rodney* was to become before long in those days when a member of *Rodney*'s crew was alleged to have had his romantic passage with a sheep. When the radio told them that the *Royal Oak* had been sunk, and sunk by a submarine at that, they wondered momentarily whether Lord Haw-Haw had taken over the BBC. But sunk she was. The mess deck decided that, after all, the safest place was at sea.

But it was the high angle guns that fired their first shots in anger, and that, above all places, from the very dry dock where their boiler-clean was in progress, with half the ship's company on five days' leave. Jerry chose this moment to stage an air-attack on the fleet. The cruiser *Southampton* and the destroyer *Mohawk* were damaged. *Repulse*'s after H.A. guns alone would bear from where she was lying, and they opened up with gusto. They had barely fired a dozen rounds when they found that with the best gunnery in the world, their chances of hitting Jerry or the Forth Bridge were just about equal. Out of respect for the Forth Bridge they gave up.

Barely a week after that they were at sea again, this time with the aircraft carrier *Furious*, and they were at sea in a hurry. The *Scharnhorst* and the *Gneisenau* had broken out, made the northern passage undetected, and were at large in the sub-Arctic mists. This time there was no trailing of coats: it was commerce raiding in earnest. And there was a Halifax convoy already at sea.

They found their convoy, and escorted it safely to port, the first of the many convoy jobs that were to be so much of *Repulse*'s history. The pocket battleships did not find them: equally, they did not find the pocket battleships, and patrolling thereafter to the south and east of Newfoundland, storm-tossed, drenched and cold, they still did not find them. It was the armed merchantman *Rawalpindi* that found the *Scharnhorst* and, after a brief, unequal battle, went down fighting. *Repulse* and *Furious* were at Halifax refuelling. They put to sea in the teeth of a gale which might have been whistled up by the German Admiralty to conceal the movements of its ships, a gale through which even battle-cruisers and aircraft carriers could not steam at speed unscathed. *Repulse* suffered damage severe enough to make it impossible for her to carry on, and an aircraft carrier on its own was no match for pocket battleships. Both ships put back to Halifax.

On their next patrol, the battleship *Resolution* joined them. The stormy sea was still empty, and even submarine alarms seemed to be mythical. In the beginning the sound of depth-charges had been enough to send men scrambling from all directions to the upper deck in the hopes of seeing a kill, but they had scrambled so often with so little reward that they had given up wasting their energy in this way. However, in the dark, early hours of the morning, no more than a day's steaming from Halifax, it seemed as though the real thing had come at last. Slinger Wood, being off watch

at the time, was sleeping on a mess stool. The mess stool
was about nine inches wide and the ship was rolling and
pitching in her usual heroic fashion. (He often wonders now
how he managed to anchor himself so successfully to so
narrow an object with all that motion going on, and furthermore to relax while doing so.) Into the soundness of his
slumbers came action stations, and he had barely blinked
himself awake before the mess deck was empty. He got up
to the gun deck as quickly as he had got up to the gun deck
in his life, and when he got there it was obvious that this
was not one of the periodic exercise alarms whereby the men,
however browned-off by their lack of success in finding the
enemy, were kept on their toes. T-2 was already closed up,
loaded, and trained. In a matter of moments T-1 was likewise.

Was it the *Scharnhorst*, the *Gneisenau,* or some other of
the mythical raiders they had searched so many leagues of
sea to find? It was, at least, a ship, a shape that emerged, an
infinitesimal fraction darker than the darkness as eyes became accustomed to the night. Moreover, it was only a
thousand yards or less away, and they were closing it broadside on. The range was short enough even for the close-range
weapons: the squeeze of a gun-layer's fingers could let loose
anything on the target, fifteen-inch, four-inch, torpedoes,
even pom-poms. And the target didn't seem to be aware of
their existence.

As Woods and his mates waited, tense with excitement in
the triple turret, *Repulse* suddenly flashed her challenge, and
even as it flashed, wondered whether the retort would be a
blaze of fire. One second, two, three . . . the retort was nothing.

The challenge was repeated, and still there was no reply.

Then the *Repulse*'s searchlights stabbed out into the
night, over the white crests and the wrack of the stormy
water.

"Cripes! It's a liner!" said someone.

Liner it was, and on a parallel course to their own. In fact, it was the *Duchess of Richmond*, and she was packed full of evacuees bound for Canada—many of whom were probably, at that moment, saying their prayers pretty hard. In a matter of seconds the *Duchess* had lights on all over the place, so that the astonished men of the *Repulse* thought she looked as though she was on a peace-time cruise: in a matter of less than seconds, the signal deck was telling her to get them out again and take up station astern of the battle-cruiser. One can be forgiven for thinking that there was some degree of slackness, followed by a considerable degree of panic. Daylight showed her keeping station nicely with the *Repulse* ahead of her and the *Furious* astern, and no doubt by then the landsmen on board her felt that nice glow of safety that always comes of being convoyed by a capital ship; but there must have been a nasty moment.

Did somebody blunder? Whether *Repulse* expected to meet the *Duchess of Richmond*, or the *Duchess of Richmond* the *Repulse*, cannot be known without the help of records that will not be made public for years, if ever; and by then the matter will have lost such small importance as it still has claim to. What evidence there is tends to the conclusion that the meeting was unexpected, and that the liner came within an inch of being blown out of the water by everything the *Repulse* possessed. At this period of the war, such escapes were not uncommon, and there may even have been a few tragedies that have not yet been revealed, for the Admiralty, in a praiseworthy quest for perfect security, was overdoing things and still had lessons to learn. There were too many watertight compartments; the movements of ships were not universally known to each other. On the very return voyage to England with the Canadian convoy, the *Furious* and the *Aquitania* were in collision with the *Samaria*, outward bound—fortunately without serious damage to any of them—and the official history admits that naval control at Liverpool did not know the movements of the *Samaria*.

It is easy enough to pass strictures after the event. In the last resort the culprit was the war and its exigencies: even rookies sometimes damage themselves with their own weapons.

A few days later the *Repulse* and the other two ships were on their way back to the Clyde with a very precious convoy indeed—five large liners carrying the First Canadian Division, the first Dominion troops to reach England, and the first of *Repulse*'s troop convoys. They themselves were not empty-handed: the hangars and every bit of spare space on board were crammed with flour and food and stores of all descriptions. People at home might not be feeling the pinch very hard as yet: to American commentators and the world at large it was still a phony war—but every sack of flour and every tin of food was vital to the island that had not fed itself for generations, had found it more profitable to buy food beyond the seas, and let its own farmland go to rot. Another blunder? At every turn there was a blunder, a blunder of long or short standing. A battle-cruiser at war was stuffed as full of men as a hive is stuffed with bees, or an anthill of ants, but still room had to be found for food.

Still their luck held, and they delivered the Canadians to the Clyde: the only untoward incident was the collision already referred to. Then it was back to the Home Fleet again, still based at Loch Ewe instead of Scapa, where work to ensure that the *Royal Oak* episode could not be repeated was still not finished. Back to the Home Fleet and back to those endless patrols. Bitter they were now. The northern winter seemed to have no end, and the shelter of the forward funnel was little comfort indeed to Slinger Wood and his mates. Elderly ladies (and not so elderly ladies) knitting comforts at home have always seemed slightly funny—heaven knows why, because the men of the *Repulse* would have been hard put to it without their help, and now, years later, feel that they never expressed their gratitude enough. Two pairs of socks, scarf, gloves, and two balaclavas were the minimum needed (on top of woollen underwear and everything else provided in the way of issue) to stop a man from turning into a human icicle, and they were donned as soon as the ship cleared harbour, not to be removed till she returned.

So, three days after Christmas, they were steaming, rolling, pitching, and freezing in company with the battleship *Barham* (a new companion for them) and five destroyers. The crew of the triple four-inch guns had just decided for the hundredth time that it couldn't be long now: all they had to do was patrol the seas, keep the Jerries out of the convoy routes, polish off such odd surface raiders as the *Scharnhorst*, the *Gneisenau*, the *Hipper* and the rest—Jerry hadn't a fraction of the ships he'd had in the first war, as the recalled veterans reminded them again and again. Then, in the spring, the Army would get moving, and before you could say "knife," it would all be over and back to peace-time sailoring. It all sounds very silly, but how many well-informed landsmen with ten times as much knowledge about the war as the men on the mess decks of the *Repulse*, succeeded in convincing themselves in these months that the war was only beginning, would drag on for year after weary year, that unimaginable disaster lay only a few short months away, that disaster would be repeated again and again and again, first in Europe, then in Africa and Asia, then in the Far East, until the tiniest island of the Pacific was not out of the range of war? Singapore, at ease behind its impregnable defences, Hong Kong with a few old destroyers, good enough for a station remote from the battle area of the Atlantic—who gave a thought to these or imagined that they in their turn would be overrun, engulfed in the day of reckoning for blindness and blunders? The Admiralty had warned of the active intervention of Japan. Who, even at the Admiralty, actively remembered—or had the ships or the resources to do anything about it if they did?

Anyway, the crew of the triple four-inch had settled the

war for the hundredth time, and it was at this point that the torpedo hit the *Barham*, which was just astern of the *Repulse*. No-one had spotted the submarine—there had been no alarm. So much for that utterly fool-proof asdic, with which Mess 46, on a summer evening not so very long ago, had consigned every German submarine that dared venture within its range to the bottom of the ocean! Stoker Dick has told the author quite categorically that the torpedo was intended for the *Repulse*, missed and hit the *Barham* instead—on no authority whatsoever except that, when a ship like the *Repulse* was sitting in the periscope sights, who would waste torpedoes on the *Barham?* The funny thing was that after it was all over, the Liverpudlians in *Repulse*'s complement were envious of the *Barham* because, being far from mortally wounded, she limped in to the Mersey and was there in dock for three months, while her crew got leave. Just now, however, the destroyers were charging furiously about the area and depth charges were throwing up mountains of water in all directions, hammering on the hulls of the other ships under water as depth charges will; and *Repulse* was best out of it. Her long hull quivered and rose to the seas and she put on speed until she looked more like an outsize destroyer than a capital ship herself. She raced into the Clyde and up the Clyde, nearly washing away the boom defences, boom vessel and all in the process. A battle cruiser left unescorted with submarines on the warpath was in no condition to think about her dignity.

Now *Hood* became their companion again, but only for a little, because she was badly in need of a refit—the mightiest battle cruiser in the world could raise no more than twenty-five knots. After her, *Renown*, *Repulse*'s sister-ship, re-engined, re-equipped, and very pleased with herself indeed. January, February—the endless North Atlantic winter still dragged on—and in March, Scapa Flow became their base again. The *Royal Oak* was gone, but the battleships *Nelson* and *Rodney* were bidding fair to take her place as permanent features of the uninviting landscape. Every time the *Repulse* returned from patrol, the two great ships were still there, swinging at their moorings. Some said, in fact, that they swung no longer—that they were aground on a mountain of food tins accumulated beneath their keels. The joke was an old one, even then, but Mess 46 relished it nonetheless for that, and lost no opportunity of rubbing it in on the battle-ships' men when they got a little canteen leave. At the same time they admitted magnanimously among themselves that it wasn't their fault, that there was nothing much they could do about it, and that they probably didn't get much joy out of being stuck there for weeks on end. And yet, after all, it was to be *Rodney* that was in at the kill of the *Bismarck*, and not *Repulse*. In the event, *Rodney* laughed both last and longest, and no amount of ba'aa-ing from the *Repulse* could make up for it.

The long, dreary months of the phony war were drawing to a close. Any time now would come the Allied spring offensive on the Continent: then there would really be action instead of all these dreary sea-miles and all these chases after phantoms. Then *Repulse* would come into her own—even *Rodney* might get off her shoal of food-tins. There was an offensive, all right, but it was not the offensive the men of the *Repulse* or, for that matter, the whole of the English-speaking world had been looking forward to. For Germany struck first. Before unbelieving ears could take in the news, Denmark was overrun, Norway invaded—a seaborne invasion by a power whose navy had seemed beneath consideration.

"Every ship in the Skagerrak will be sunk," cried Churchill desperately, and hearts lifted momentarily with the hope that the damage could be undone. It was a vain cry. Where were the great ships to do the sinking, the destroyers to escort them, the carriers to give them fighter cover? Where were the heavy, long-range bombers, or for that matter, the heavy bombs with which to arm them? Great ships, desperately needed, still building, destroyers stretched out over an ocean too vast for their numbers . . . capital ships too few, too slow, keeping the sea for months, and some of them now urgently in need of refit. And phantoms breaking out everywhere, the initiative still always with the besieged, the besieger trying to stop a hundred holes at once.

The *Repulse* was at Scapa when news came of Norway on April 7. At dusk that day came the order to raise steam, and less than three hours later the whole fleet was making for sea at top speed. Far away to the north the little destroyer *Glowworm* had run full tilt into the *Hipper* and was fighting it out as best she might against impossible odds. As the *Repulse* drove, pounding and straining into a full north-north-west gale, Captain Spooner told his men over the loudspeakers of the situation, and had desire been steam or prayers propellers, she would have moved as a battle-cruiser had never moved before, and skimmed the towering seas like a veritable Flying Dutchman. All through the night they wrestled with the gale as *Glowworm's* reports came in; but before nine the following morning the reports had faded. *Glowworm* was gone and her men were heroes. *Hipper* was gone, the seas were empty again.

Further north they went, where Admiral Whitworth was pursuing their old quarries, the *Scharnhorst* and the *Gneisenau*, with their sister-ship *Renown*. There was no sign of either when *Repulse* joined Whitworth the following day. *Renown* was to distinguish herself against the *Gneisenau* later—but without the aid of the *Repulse*.

"I think we could sail this bloody ship into Bremen without meeting a Jerry," commented Stripey Shatwell in disgust —and he didn't seem far from the truth, for before long they found themselves at the entrance to Narvik Fjord, which was certainly full of Jerry ships and Jerries too. Their destroyer escorts, *Hardy*, *Hunter*, *Havock*, *Hotspur* and *Hostile* went in and rattled up a hornet's nest. *Repulse* was about to go in after them when she was ordered out, and the *Warspite* went in instead. There was good reason enough for it:

Warspite had eight fifteen-inch guns against the *Repulse's* six; her guns had greater elevation to deal with German gun positions on the cliffs, and she had more secondary armament as well, which she used to good purpose, but the battle-cruiser's men could be forgiven for thinking that the other ship had stolen their thunder. *Warspite* went in and got her name in the news bulletins; the *Repulse* stayed outside on guard. Eighteen torpedoes were fired at her; all missed, so that at least she could be considered lucky, but it was a different sort of luck that Mess 46 asked for. Maybe they ought to have been grateful, but then they weren't that sort of men, nor was the *Repulse* that sort of ship. It is difficult for civilians, difficult even for men in middle age to look back on a war they took part in twenty years ago, to realise that men really pray for death and glory. It was the *Rawalpindi's* sort of luck they wanted, the *Glowworm's*, the luck of Warburton-Lee and his immortal destroyers, the luck of *Glorious*—that sort of luck, not the luck of standing by with guns that had never fired a shot in action, while others went in.

Sometimes her frustrations had their humours. It was not long after the Narvik business that the *Repulse* and the *Renown* together were ordered out of Scapa in a hurry to the aid of the cruiser *Suffolk*, which had been bombed. Speed was all important and the *Renown* was told to make what speed she could with her fine new engines, so that the business took on some of the atmosphere of a race. Superhuman efforts in *Repulse's* engine room produced a few cables' lead to start off with, but her sister-ship soon closed the distance and was slowly forging ahead along the *Repulse's* port side, with money, rum, and every other imaginable thing being wagered, when the lookouts reported aircraft on the starboard beam. Slinger Wood and his mates, reluctantly withdrawing their attention from the race, pronounced them German: the air defence position was just as sure that they were friendly—RAF planes going to the assistance of the *Suffolk*.

"Friendly aircraft!" disputed Leading Seaman Slatter, with heat. "They're Heinkels . . . 111s. And here's some friendly bombs, by God," he added. "Look out!"

They dived for cover as the bombs came tumbling out like tennis balls, and in the same moment the AA guns opened up. The ship, still at full speed, heeled over under full starboard helm, and the next instant a wall of water rose up solid from the sea, to rear down again and drown the decks. On the *Renown*, they could see nothing but water—it looked as though the *Repulse*'s last moment had come. But she came steaming out of it without a scratch, and the only thing that was very much shaken was her crew's confidence in the air defence position. The air defence officer was christened "Friendly Aircraft"—a less complimentary title than the gunnery officer's "Six-Gun Coney," but it stuck just as hard.

The *Suffolk* was located, well down by the stern, and it was a slow convoy back to port, but there were no more Heinkels.

Now came the invasion of the Low Countries: the hard-won gains in Norway had to be abandoned, and all the heroism was in vain. Out of the host of blunders came the *Repulse*, shepherding a slow convoy carrying evacuated stores from Harstad—precious stores indeed, with the immense loss of equipment that was to follow in France, but not a glorious operation. Came Dunkirk, and a tremendous feeling of helplessness, while even the smallest unarmed motor-boats were playing a desperate game in the English Channel. And there began to dawn a realisation that the war wouldn't be over soon, that the lords of the contemptible German Navy were masters in Europe and would be masters for many a day, even if we managed to keep them out of England. All the wiseacres of the mess deck had been wrong —politicians, service chiefs, wishful thinkers and war correspondents had been wrong. There was no foreseeable end to it now, and what the way might be out of all the blunders, even the mess deck couldn't guess.

In particular, they couldn't guess that it was the happenings of the last few weeks that were to lead them to their end in the South China Sea. For the defeat of France took away the French Navy, on which the Admiralty had depended for the holding of the Mediterranean when war brewed up in the Far East: indeed, the Admiralty was (in the very words of the official historian) now at its wits' end for ships, even for the tasks of the moment. But the fall of France also meant the neutralising of French Indochina, and worse was to follow: for the Vichy government was presently to cede to the Japanese, air bases in that territory, and those air bases, while themselves out of range of such aircraft as we had in Malaya, were to be just (albeit only just) within striking distance of Singapore. What matter? The Japanese weren't very good at aircraft, they had no more than eighteen months' reserves of oil, they wouldn't risk an attack upon the Western Powers. The politicians carefully assessed the evidence, proceeded to their conclusions, and blundered. The reckoning for their blunders was still eighteen months or more away, and in the meantime the *Repulse* could go on steaming her endless miles, searching forever for phantoms, and never coming to grips with them. She was to come to grips in the end—with phantoms at whom she could not strike back effectively.

It was just after Dunkirk that Captain Tennant took over the ship from Captain Spooner. He knew her well—he had been her navigating officer fourteen years before. He took over a good ship: it is no slight to Spooner to say that he made her an even better one.

Look at the ship for a moment through the eyes of a young marine, John Garner, who joined her not long after this, together with two comrades, Marines Stocking and Claxton. He was barely eighteen, had just completed his recruit's training, and the *Repulse* was his first ship. He had originally been drafted to the cruiser *Devonshire*, but for some reason or another was unable to join her, but he never had any regrets about the *Repulse*. He had seen the ship only once before, in Plymouth, and the old soldiers had filled him and his youthful fellows with dread tales of how "pusser's" she was. They were undeterred—they couldn't get aboard quick enough. Vividly and easily over the years he recalls his shipmates, Loot Lissaman, Dusty Taylor, Scouse Johnson, Paddy Drake, Butcher Lovedon, each of whom could have written a book about his experiences; the Captain of Marines, Captain Lang ("Old Joe") and his second-in-command, Lieutenant Davies, who was to lead the marine survivors in their jungle days after the ship was lost; Sergeant Major Parsons, known (not to his face) as Jan.

"Later," writes Garner, "as was usual, we met the Skipper, Captain William Tennant. The Skipper was a man who had the affection and the loyalty of every man aboard the ship, and I think it was his handling of the men that made the ship the happy community she was."

Neither sailormen nor marines, nor any other sort of servicemen pay that sort of tribute out of politeness. Tennant may protest as vehemently as he likes (although he is not a man given to vehemence) that he didn't make things easy for them. He made things easy for them in a way that sailors and soldiers understand, by running an efficient and well-disciplined ship. And the ship lives on in the memories of those who served in her.

Garner was assigned to the after four-inch handing room and later became breech worker on T-3 gun—originally T-4, but re-numbered when the original T-3 was taken out and replaced by a multiple pom-pom. This was a marine's gun, with Corporal Mick McKillen as its captain, and on it he was to become a neighbour, in a manner of speaking, of Slinger Wood, to whom the fitting of the pom-pom was presently to bring release from the cold watches of his triple gun deck and the eternal dodging round the forward funnel.

For the arrival of the extra pom-pom and some half-dozen additional Oerlikons (how slender the ship's resources in these weapons still were!) created a shortage of AA gunnery ratings, and over a ready-cut wool rug with which Slinger happened to be giving him a hand, Leading Seaman Slatter, whose business up to that time had been .5 machine guns, put it to him that it might be a good thing to volunteer for the instruction class.

Presently, therefore, he found himself on the after pom-pom, M.3. with Slatts in charge of his watch: that was advantage number one because the close-range weapons, as we already know, were divided into four watches instead of two. The other advantage was that just behind M.3. were the engine-room air exhausts which poured out a constant stream of hot air, and this was very welcome, indeed, after all those frozen nights of dodging 'round the funnel. Unfortunately it wasn't quite so welcome when, with the widening of the theatre of war, the ship found herself in the tropics; but then it would have been too much to expect everything.

The way the pom-pom was handled was typical of the way most things were handled on the *Repulse*. On the somewhat slender excuse that he was a bit rusty on pom-poms (slender, because he never really gave evidence of being rusty on anything to do with the Navy) Slatts insisted on stripping and cleaning one or two of the guns every watch—never, of course, having more than one gun out of commission at a time, so that if necessary, fire could always be opened with the other seven. In the course of a couple of weeks both Slinger and any of the other ratings could have stripped, cleaned, replaced, oiled, and re-loaded any one of the guns blindfolded on a dark night; just for a change they would take down, clean, grease, and re-place the hundred rounds of ammunition on each gun's tray.

Slatts very rarely let up. One of the few occasions when he did was on New Year's Day of 1941, when the ship was at anchor in Scapa. Scapa was full of ships and a batch of mail had arrived. Slatts decided to answer his letters, Slinger Wood buried his head in a cowboy book, Seaman Brown did likewise, and Kenny, the other member of the watch, got busy with a Hank Jansen. It was a general make and mend throughout the Fleet, with a low cloud ceiling, and everything was nice and peaceful. It was at this precise moment that an aircraft chose to make its presence obvious above the cloud base and outside the safety lanes. Wood drew Slatts' attention to it, and Brown reported it to the Control, but before anything further could happen the plane's engine noise seemed to rise as though it were going into a dive. Slatts yelled at them to open fire and in the same instant the eight guns were each pumping out their one hundred thirty-five shells a minute. The whole Fleet followed suit; but in the next instant Slatter was yelling to Wood to cease fire and throwing the gun off the target. He had realised that the plane was a Fairey Fulmar off course: it dived and twisted away over Flotta and there was a lot of explaining to do, as well as four hundred thirty-five empty cartridge cases to deprime, the guns to clean, sponge out, and re-load, and in general quite enough work to keep them occupied until the next watch took over. Down on the mess deck they found themselves distinctly unpopular, and M.3. gun deck appeared to become a rendezvous for inquisitive visitors including the Fleet Gunnery Officer. However, nothing more was heard of it.

There was a later occasion in Freetown when, owing to one of the tappets becoming jammed in the firing position after testing the circuits, M.3. sent seven two-pound shells sailing over the quarter deck of the aircraft carrier *Furious* at zero altitude. Nothing was heard of this either: the mess deck noted, however, that their mail suddenly started arriving promptly—they had been missing it through leaving harbour at inappropriate times. Whether this was pure coincidence, or whether someone in authority thought the ship was on the verge of mutiny, is another of those things which will never be known. Had some newspaperman of the baser sort been lucky enough to get hold of the story, we should probably have had a legend of mutiny on the *Repulse* as well as on the *Prince of Wales*.

All this is anticipating the course of events a little, but it would be fruitless to attempt to continue to follow the movements of the *Repulse* in detail for the rest of 1940. There were more false alarms and more phantoms to chase. There were more Halifax convoys and convoys further afield. There was what Captain Tennant christened, in his own words, "the Watch on the Bay"—still against the breakout of the *Scharnhorst* and the *Gneisenau*. There was another episode similar to the episode of the *Duchess of Richmond* when the *Alcantara*, bearing a load of evacuees from the Middle East, failed to answer a challenge until the third attempt, and came within an ace of getting herself blown out of the water in her turn. But it was mild stuff after the way in which their sister-ship *Renown*, leaving her destroyer escorts behind and steaming twenty-nine knots into a shocking sea, caught and severely mauled the *Gneisenau*. In October the *Scheer* broke out and found a convoy escorted by the armed merchant cruiser *Jervis Bay*. But for a combination of circumstances the *Repulse* would have been escorting that convoy, and she would have made a better match for the German raider: as it was, ablaze from stem to stern but with her guns still firing, the *Jervis Bay* steamed to her end and into history, saving her convoy and leaving the men of the *Repulse* once more to bemoan the chance that had been denied them. In December the elusive *Hipper* broke out again, but was back in Brest long before the *Repulse* and other units had given up the search for her. In January the *Scharnhorst* and the *Gneisenau* again . . .

Yet all those sea miles, all those alarms and excursions, all those convoys from which never a ship was lost, could build a ship up to a peak of efficiency in which every man and his job fitted with perfect ease and certainty into the complicated jigsaw which makes up a great ship of war—even to Stoker Dick, whose job as freshwater tanky was to start the pumps for the pom-poms fore and aft every time the alarm went up. He started them time and time again, but apart from the escapades of M.3. there was very little to show for it. A ship could build up to a peak of efficiency like this: it seemed such a waste to have nothing to use it on.

The blitz was causing the men a lot of worry now—especially the Merseyside men, of whom there were so many aboard. It was easier for them in their interludes in Scapa, when the mail came regularly and leave could mostly be got somehow if the worst happened; but it was often very bad when they were on the other side of the Atlantic or in Gib or Freetown, where the shore lights still blazed across the harbour on the hot, humid nights, making blackout and blitz seem unreal. To Mess 46 it often seemed at this time that it was safer at sea than at home.

Slinger Wood's grandfather died at this time, taking all his memories of the South African War to the grave with him. It was a pity he couldn't have lived just a little longer to wonder at his grandson being regaled with a pep talk by General Jan Christiaan Smuts at Durban, and wonder at the strange way in which things turned out.

In October there was a dry-docking at Rosyth, and the ship's company all got leave in one go, with the exception of a small nucleus for necessary purposes and emergency defence. Most of these were volunteers, including Slinger, Slatts, Chicken Howe, and Ginger Devine. Slinger didn't do badly out of that, for apart from other considerations he spent a weekend at Ginger Devine's home in Belshill from which the pair of them returned like two walking barrels of beer. He got his leave from Scapa in November and during that time he took an important step in a man's life: he got engaged to be married. When he returned from that important event, the ship was at sea, and it was the only time in her whole commission that he missed a trip. She came back from Iceland with a bunch of German scientists, whom she had been sent to scoop up from an enemy meteorological station: it seemed a pretty humdrum job for a battle-cruiser.

So came the end of 1940—a long, long way removed indeed from the previous winter of the phony war, and from the days when Mess 46 confidently waited for their chance to polish off the little German Navy and hold the seas until the Army moved to its great offensive in the Spring. It had been a year of blunders and of penalties for blunders. *Repulse* herself had suffered from some of the blunders—the blunders of faulty intelligence that had sent her chasing phantoms, the blunders that had left the Navy at its wits end to carry out all its tasks at sea, the blunders that had closed the Mediterranean and the Suez Canal, and left only the long sea route round the Cape to be covered by too few merchant ships and too few escorts. Another year was yet to pass before the full consequences of all this were truly felt, before the Far East was aflame, the war world-wide, and the *Repulse* herself at the bottom of the South China Sea. The Japanese menace still lay, in Churchill's words, "in a sinister twilight," and nearly everyone, from that great man down to Mess 46, was busy blundering over it.

The great ship's last year was dawning. For the *Prince of Wales*, life had not yet begun. She still lay in the fitting-out basin at Birkenhead, baptized by the fire of the blitz before she could seek the enemy in her own element. She was near completion: the *King George V*, first of her class, had already appeared at Scapa Flow before the eager and critical appraisal of the Fleet—bristling (or so it seemed) with AA guns and every modern device, more heavily armoured than any ship afloat, the shape of battleships to come.

Across the narrow sea the *Bismarck* was also nearing completion.

CHAPTER

4

WHEN ALF TUDOR FIRST SET EYES ON THE "PRINCE OF WALES" at the end of a long and dreary train journey north from Devonport, he said to himself "Tudor, son, you won't settle on that one." Alf was a regular sailor and a small ship man. He had gone down with the destroyer *Brazen* off Dover and been fished out of the sea, which was the reason for his posting—he was to be fished out of the sea twice more before his war was over. In fact, he did settle in the *Prince of Wales* and, before a short space of time was out, would not have dreamed of wishing himself in any other ship.

To young Cyril Williams and something like a hundred other boy seamen she was the most tremendous thing they had ever seen, and like Marine Garner on the *Repulse*, they couldn't get aboard her quick enough. They, too, found themselves on a happy ship and led their own peculiar and intense life on the boys' mess deck forrard.

To the Navy at large she was H.M.S. *Unsinkable* which, as we have already noticed, is a dangerous thing to call a ship. To the world of soldiers, civilians, and other shore-bound individuals, she was a vast floating mystery replete with every device for attack and defence known to man. To the Prime Minister she was something almost magical, regardless of his just condemnation of her main armament, and his misgivings about the apparent gap in her armour caused by the aircraft hangar.

She had finally been completed at Cammell Laird's dockyard in spite of the difficulties of blackout and blitz at the end of February 1941; and fortunately the blitz had caused her even less damage than we were liable to inflict in our desperate bombing attacks on German battleships in harbour.

Five weeks before her completion—on January 18—Frank Seddon, who was to be a member of her communications branch from that moment until her end, joined her in the dockyard; and he is a useful and reliable witness to many happenings, for he had a signalman's view of all the events of her short and stormy life, and still has a signalman's memory. He was seeing his second war; he was another representative of the people over whom Britain blundered in the years between his two wars, for his tale was not unlike the tales of Slinger Wood's father and his grandfather. He had joined the Navy at Devonport as a boy of fifteen, and his first ship had been the old battleship *Albion*, guard-ship at Scarborough—he had his first taste of fire there in 1916 when the Germans were shelling the East coast. After that he'd gone to the 4th Battle Squadron in H.M.S. *Collingwood*, then to destroyers. He was discharged to the Reserve in 1920, but soon found work in the dirt and stench of Fairrie's Sugar Refinery a different life for a man than the Navy. He had tried to get back but there was no getting back, and if it hadn't been for his second war he would never have got back at all.

Seddon was on her when she left the dockyard, and her beginning was lacking in dignity, for at the very outset of her first short voyage her condensers were found to be thoroughly bedevilled with Mersey mud, and she had to anchor while things were put right. At least no-one is to blame for this except the strange and sinister genii who brood over the mud banks of that turbid estuary.

That first voyage should, in fact, have only taken her a matter of a couple of miles down river to Gladstone Dock to collect her stores; but the bombers that had failed to do the ship any material damage had succeeded in destroying the stores completely, and they were not there for collection. Escorted therefore by four destroyers, she set out for the Clyde. There were still a large number of dockyard civilians aboard her, and some of them were to stay aboard her for longer than they bargained for because this ship was having more than her fair share of teething troubles, and it is doubtful if she ever had time to get the last of her troubles out of her system.

Now any ship—let alone a ship with such an infinity of mechanical complications as a battleship—is liable to trouble in her early stages, and we must be cautious of making too much of the troubles that beset the *Prince of Wales*. The overwhelming number of these can be put down to no more than the normal difficulties of getting new machinery run in, and new equipment into smooth working order. In peacetime they would have been disposed of one by one in a lengthy period of working-up, and modifications would have been made where necessary. Certainly there was an immense amount of trouble with her radar (or RDF as it was called in those days) but perhaps even of this too much can be made, because this equipment was still barely out of its experimental stages and the number of hands in the Navy thoroughly skilled in its use were very, very few. We know that both her search radar and her gunnery radar had been tested and found working in experts' hands a short time before she left to meet the *Bismarck*, and while there are some contradictions in the evidence, as we shall see, it is pretty evident that neither yielded any help worth talking about in that action.

But the really serious trouble—especially for a ship liable to be pitchforked into battle almost as soon as she joined the Fleet—was the trouble with her main armament, the fourteen-inch guns. Here there was an endless and exasperating series of mechanical breakdowns. The design was new, the type of turret was new, everything was new. Whether there was similar trouble with the *King George V*, the *Duke of York* and other ships of her class, is a matter on which, at this moment, there is no available evidence—nor is there any evidence as to whether the modifications made to the turrets after the *Bismarck* action were also made to her sister ships. The fact is that it was only at the end of April—a few weeks before she sailed to intercept the *Bismarck*—that the last of her turrets was accepted from the builders. It must have been even then accepted with some reserve, because we know that this was one of the things that kept the civilian dockyard workers aboard, and we also know that this turret broke down at an early stage of the action. Even later that summer, when the Admiralty was fighting a rearguard action against Mr. Churchill's determination to send the ship to the Far East, one of the specific points made was the necessity for the ship to be kept within as easy reach as possible of dockyard services.

If the main armament had been so overwhelmingly superior in fire power to anything the enemy could bring against it, there would at least have been a reasonable pretext for a ship being involved in such unnecessary difficulties in the middle of a war, but it wasn't. The idea behind the whole thing had been to equip the ships of this class with a slightly smaller calibre gun capable of a rapid rate of fire; the reduction in calibre was to be more than compensated for both by this rapid rate and by the fact that they were to carry twelve guns instead of eight. But at a later stage a fatal compromise was indulged in: the weight of the pro-

tective armour was increased and two of the fourteen-inch
guns were sacrificed to allow for this. With only ten guns,
even allowing for the rate of fire, the broadside was inferior
to that of older ships and certainly inferior to the massive
broadside of the *Bismarck*. Mr. Churchill told Stalin that
the *Prince of Wales* was capable of hunting down and sinking anything the Japanese possessed; but there is very little
doubt that she would have been outgunned by the Japanese
just as she was by the *Bismarck*. All this we shall have to
take into account when we come to consider the final
blunder that sent her out to the South China Sea in a role
which it was virtually impossible for any battleship to fulfil—
even had she displaced a hundred thousand tons and been
equipped with as many guns as Field-Marshal Montgomery
at the crossing of the Rhine. So much for the theory, so
much for the facts. And on top of the facts the thing that
is above dispute—the turrets were always in danger of failure
and did fail in her one encounter with a major enemy unit.

Could a change have been made in mid-1939 when it was
seen that an early war was unavoidable, that there would be
no time to trifle with the temperaments of experimental
equipment? Who is to say, with a great mass of the records
and evidence on these matters still not available to the public,
and the memories of those who were concerned with them
still bound by the Official Secrets Acts? Certainly the
Admiralty were disillusioned on this topic by the time the
Vanguard was laid down because the *Vanguard* carried eight
fifteen-inch guns of more conventional pattern.

Obviously the whole tale of troubles was not known to
the *Prince of Wales*'s complement although there can have
been few of them unaware of some of them. Captain Leach
was undoubtedly aware of all of them and that is why it is so
surprising to be told that he always wore a smile upon his
face. This mannerism is described repeatedly by a number of
people: perhaps, indeed, it was only a mannerism; perhaps
under the circumstances he found the smile particularly

necessary. Seddon describes him as a fine, upstanding, and quiet man: he had much to be quiet about. One thing is certain: with all the difficulties of working-up under wartime conditions added to the difficulties created by the special problems of his ship, he succeeded in a very short time in producing a happy ship's company and, under the circumstances, a surprisingly efficient one. On the whole he got little credit for it at the time, and even Admiral Tovey seems automatically to have echoed Rear-Admiral Wake-Walker's assumption that there could not possibly be anything to be said in favour of the *Prince of Wales.*

It was a very diverse ship's company, as wartime ship's companies were liable to be. In age alone it spanned the distance between the boys' mess deck and reservists who themselves had sons older than the boys aboard. Its HO personnel ranged from characters such as Esmond Knight, who later fought his way back to fame as an actor while still blinded from the *Bismarck* action; and Empire Boxing Champion Johnny King, who became a particular member of Alf Tudor's circle—and a very useful friend too, both in differences of opinion aboard, and in scrounging free entertainment in Singapore and elsewhere. Their hobbies were as diverse as themselves, ranging from the differences of opinion already referred to (to be settled finally in the approved fashion on the forecastle) to leather work and mat-making. Seddon applied himself enthusiastically to the latter: he had sent several completed works home before he started on his masterpiece, the *Prince of Wales's* Feathers in gold on a blue background. This one went to the bottom of the China Sea.

However, there was not too much time for hobbies. Captain Leach kept his ship's company hard at it, trying all he knew to make them as efficient as possible in the brief period before he must report that she was fit for service with the Fleet. She would go on working-up, of course, and working-up on active service had plenty to be said for it as long as it did not include an engagement which would subject to the

very severest of strains a new ship and a new ship's complement. The landsman who sees a great ship and admires its
power and majesty is in the happy position of not needing to
pause for a moment to consider the vast amount of organisation that knits the endless complications of its equipment,
and the vast number of its personnel, into a thoroughly
efficient whole that can be depended on to function under
any circumstances. There is infinitely more to it than that
button-pressing H. V. Morton found so impressive. The
complement of such a ship alone is many times larger than
that of an infantry battalion, and apart from the skills of seamanship, practically every trade recognised by all the three
Services finds its place aboard. Difficult enough to organise
this so that every man knows his job and his place, and the
equipment he is handling in a calm sea under peace-time
conditions; but a battleship must be capable of going into
action in fair weather or foul with all these complications,
of suffering damage, light or severe, and still being able to
carry on. It is a tremendous credit to the memory of Leach,
his officers, and men that they were able not merely to survive their first action so soon after being commissioned, but
that they came out of it still efficient in spite of severe damage and were, moreover, able to inflict wounds on the enemy
that led to his ultimate undoing.

As one of those evils necessary under the circumstances
they were inspected by a number of people of varying degrees
of importance. They were inspected by the Commander-in-
Chief, Home Fleet, Admiral Tovey. Finally they were inspected by the King.

"I trust you have been to sea before," he said to Alf Tudor
and his adjacent shipmates.

"Are you kidding?" thought Alf while assuring his
Majesty that he had.

Was it one of that conscientious and well-loved monarch's
less apposite remarks? Was he pulling Alf Tudor's leg? Or
was he (being in an exceptionally good position to know

what manner of things were in store for them) genuinely concerned about their welfare? After all, the King *had* been to sea!

While Captain Leach was desperately making the most of every available moment to get his command into fighting shape, another ship was finishing her working-up on the other side of the narrow seas; and about her working-up there was no life-or-death urgency, for her job was to be efficient beyond any possibility of failure before she embarked on her first mission. This ship was the *Bismarck*, the flower of the new German Navy, and there is no reasonable doubt that at that time she was the most formidable fighting ship in the world. Slinger Wood's messmates on the *Repulse* could dispose of her as much as they liked—she would not be disposed of that easily. Landsmen, civilians, war correspondents, and wishful thinkers could still bandy the word "ersatz" about—a convenient word—but the meaning had rather gone out of it since the battle of France and the decisiveness with which German arms and equipment had won the mastery of Europe. There was nothing ersatz whatsoever about the equipment of the *Bismarck*, and there was certainly nothing ersatz about the quality of her complement or its training. Everything of which Germany had been starved in the years leading up to the war had gone into this ship: a nation had been combed for its finest men and nothing had been spared for their indoctrination and their morale. They were the New Germany, the masters-to-be of the world for a thousand years; and unlike the ships of the hard-pressed Western Powers, desperately put to it to keep the seas, to protect the precious convoys, and to watch every bolt-hole from which the enemy might issue forth, they were not going to put their noses outside their protected seas until they were absolutely certain that they were fully efficient in every possible detail for the job.

On May 21, Captain Leach piped all hands and told them over the loudspeakers that he had reported to the

Commander-in-Chief that his ship was ready for service. He had, in fact, made this report on the 17th. It was not understood by this, any more than it was meant to be understood, that the ship was a fully effective fighting unit in every respect. She was no more than reasonably fit for ordinary service operations with the Fleet, and neither her Captain nor Admiral Tovey, who commanded the Home Fleet, had any illusions about it. Unfortunately neither they nor the ship's complement had any choice in the matter. In a very short time they, and all the world, were to know what at that moment was hidden from them—that three days previously the *Bismarck*, in company with the cruiser *Prinz Eugen* had left Gdynia and was at that very moment steaming as hard as she could for the north-about passage by which they would break out into the Atlantic and wreak havoc among the convoys. Their crews had no dreams of knightly battles between ship and ship; they would show their metal to any ship that opposed them, and there was no ship on the seas that could face them single-handed; but their job in the first place was to destroy, to cut the lifelines between the old world and the new, by virtue of which Britain narrowly survived.

Almost immediately, therefore, after their Captain's announcement—or so it seems in the memories of the *Prince of Wales*'s survivors—came an order from the C.-in-C. for steam at one hour's notice, and every man aboard knew that there was a "flap."

At this stage nothing was known of the whereabouts of the *Bismarck* except that air reconnaisance had shown her and her consort missing from every harbour where they could possibly be. Weather conditions were poor with wind and a heavy sea; far to the North, on the escape route out into the Atlantic, there would be "rainstorms, snowstorms, icefloes, and mirage effects," to quote Admiral Tovey's later report. Through it all the German ships would be steaming at their best speed, which was at least as good as that of any battle-cruiser we possessed, and action to head them off was urgent. At midnight, therefore, the *Prince of Wales* was sailed for Iceland in company with the *Hood*, under the command of Vice-Admiral Lancelot Holland, as the Battle-Cruiser Squadron of the Home Fleet. *Prince of Wales*, in other words, acting for the nonce as a battle-cruiser, was sailing with the *Repulse*'s old companion in the role in which *Repulse* had sailed with the *Hood* so many times—a search for yet another elusive phantom in the Northern mists. The *Hood* had only recently rejoined the Fleet from the dockyard, and had already been out on convoy duty before she had had time to regain her full efficiency. The whereabouts of the enemy were not yet known. We were, as our first move, to head him off, throwing into the battle, in the words of the official historian "one twenty-five year-old ship, one so new that her armaments had not yet been fully tested, nor her ship's company adequately practised in their use." In the words of Leach's report on the action, his men were "immensely keen and well-drilled, but inexperienced."

At this point the *Repulse*, instead of being in company with her old comrade was preparing for another of her never-ending convoy jobs—convoy WS 8B, crammed with troops and about to leave the Clyde on the long voyage to the Middle East around the Cape. With her was the aircraft carrier *Victorious*, herself almost as new as the *Prince of Wales* and able to put no more than a handful of Swordfish torpedo-aircraft into the air, flown by pilots who had next to no experience of active service. Both these ships were detached from their convoy and ordered to rejoin the Home Fleet: the convoy sailed naked and defenceless and probably the greater majority of those who made that voyage on the crowded troop decks still do not realise that in that state they steamed right through the battle area and crossed the track of the *Bismarck* twice. It was as well that they did not know about such things, for it is bad enough to be a helpless soldier on a troopship without being aware that one is in the middle of a major naval engagement and wide open to the largest and nastiest battleship in the world.

But the *Repulse* and the *Prince of Wales* were not yet to meet.

CHAPTER

5

MAKING THEIR BEST SPEED IN VERY HEAVY WEATHER, the *Prince of Wales* and the *Hood* steamed together on a course for Hvalfjord. Through the racket of the storm and the pulse and vibration of machinery there was tenseness and quietness among the men. Once they had cleared harbour they had been told whither they were bound and why. For men like Seddon, for men like Alf Tudor and his mates, it was a familiar feeling. For the boys and for so many of the newly-joined ratings, not to speak of the civilians who had never expected to go into action at all, it was a hastening into the unknown. For Leach and his officers, possessed of all manner of knowledge which was denied to their men, it was a time of tremendous testing.

Far away in the northern mists for which they were heading, not far from the ice edge in the Denmark Strait, Rear-Admiral Wake-Walker with his two cruisers, the *Norfolk* and *Suffolk*, was keeping watch on the northern passage—a difficult and exacting watch. On the evening of the 23rd, look-outs on the *Suffolk*, dimly and only for a few moments, sighted a large and a smaller ship steering south-east at speed. There could be no doubt what ships they were, and she immediately made her sighting signal. This was never received by the Admiralty but shortly afterwards, at 8:32 P.M., *Norfolk* in her turn sighted them and made a report which was received. The hunt was on and the *Prince of Wales* was in the forefront of it: she and the *Hood* with their six accompanying destroyers altered course to intercept. Watching the destroyers, the men on the bigger ships thought they would never be able to remain in company; but they held on, and the fact that in the course of that night they were parted from the *Hood* and *Prince of Wales* was not their fault but Admiral Holland's—a poor reward for all their tenacity.

At the same time, now that the whereabouts of the quarry was known, Admiral Tovey left Scapa with the Home Fleet. The *Repulse* had sailed from the Clyde at 7:10 that morning and, with her three destroyers, came up with him northwest of the Butt of Lewis. This was better than convoys, even than a W.S. convoy. She was back where she belonged, and all that could be hoped for was that the battle-cruiser squadron would leave enough of the *Bismarck* and her consort for them to get their teeth into.

Far ahead of them Admiral Holland had certain special problems in the action which was now almost inevitable. His adversaries were two ships whose object was to break out into the wide spaces of the Atlantic, and which by now had only to complete their passage of the Denmark Strait before they would do so. One of them was an immensely powerful and formidable ship, faster than his own ships, but also more heavily armed. His own ship, the *Hood*, was the British Navy's greatest ship, but she was a battle-cruiser and in common with all battle-cruisers, including the *Repulse*, was thinly armoured and especially weak in her horizontal armour. She was therefore safest at ranges of less than thirteen thousand yards, for beyond this range the trajectory of shot begins to plunge steeply towards its end. The *Prince of Wales's* situation was precisely the opposite: the horizontal armour was exceptionally strong, for she had been built to survive aerial bombing attack. She therefore was merely subject to the ordinary consideration that the closer she got to the enemy, the more the enemy's shot would hurt. This matter was so obvious to Admiral Tovey that he had thought of ordering Admiral Holland to send the *Prince of Wales* in first, but considered it unwarranted to draw the attention of so senior an officer to so obvious a situation. Whether Admiral Holland thought of it or not, the world will never know, for he went down with the *Hood*. All that can be said is that he led the way into action himself. His intention was to make contact at daylight on a favourable gunnery course.

Now the gunnery officer's ideal is a situation in which he himself is broadside on to the enemy, so that as many as possible of his guns will bear, while the enemy is bows on to him, giving a margin of error in the fall of shot of a whole ship's length: in the case of a capital ship, a matter of the greater part of a thousand feet. Such a perfect situation can never be realised completely in practice; commanders make the best approach to it they can, and a ship which is increasing its advantage in this way is said to gain bearing, while one which is losing it is said to lose bearing.

Admiral Holland's original course was an excellent intercepting course. He expected to make contact in the northern twilight any time after 1:40 A.M., and shortly after midnight, the *Prince of Wales*, plunging furiously along on the *Hood's* starboard quarter, was closed-up for action. But even as the men hurried to their stations, something happened twenty miles or more away which upset all calculations: the shadowing cruisers lost touch, and as a result of this Admiral Holland made the first of a series of fatal blunders. He assumed that the crusiers had lost touch because the *Bismarck* and the *Prinz Eugen* had altered course. He reasoned that they had altered course to escape into the northern mists, and he himself therefore altered course from north-west by west to due north, reducing speed at the same time.

Why should the enemy have altered course? It is almost impossible to follow Holland's reasoning, although it is easy to criticise—with time for calmer reasoning and full knowledge of the whole story—decisions made in the heat of an emergency. It also goes against the grain to criticise the decisions of an officer who cannot answer back because he lost his life in the action which was about to take place. But the object of the *Bismarck* was to break out into the Atlantic; being bottled up in the northern mists was the last thing she desired. She knew, admittedly, that she was being stalked by the cruisers and would assume the cruisers had called down the hunt upon her; but she was completely unaware of the presence of the battle-cruiser squadron and therefore could not possibly have been trying to escape it. If, moreover, it came to escaping it, she had both superior speed to run, and superior armament to fight it off while still continuing towards her objective. All this is confirmed by what we know after the event of the decisions made aboard the *Bismarck* that night: she held on her course to the south-west and all Admiral Holland was doing was to lose bearing, putting his gunners at a disadvantage, and his ship in the direst peril.

In a moment the whole picture—with the battle-cruisers on an intercepting course, the Home Fleet hastening up in support and ships over a wide area being redeployed towards the scene of the coming action—was broken like a frustrated jigsaw puzzle. At 1:40 A.M. the *Prince of Wales* prepared to catapult her Walrus into the air to search, for twilight in those latitudes at that time of the year should last all night. But this night was unusually dark, and the attempt was abandoned. It was this particular aircraft's last chance of doing anything useful; for not much later, it was damaged by shell splinters and jettisoned. At two o'clock, long after he should have made contact, the Admiral turned south but left his destroyers to continue on their northerly course. This again was a decision which as the official historian would say "calls for consideration." The destroyers could do nothing against the *Bismarck* themselves, but by thus being separated they lost the chance of weighing in with their torpedoes while the big gun battle was in progress and, in fact, only arrived on the scene in time to search for survivors from the *Hood*. At the same time, the *Prince of Wales* was ordered to search an arc of the horizon with her gunnery radar, but it would not cover the arc and Captain Leach requested permission to use his search radar. The official history says this was refused, but Admiral Tovey refers to the mysterious appearance on her radar screen of three echoes where it was known there were only two ships. Maybe, as he suggests, the *Bismarck* threw up two echoes, maybe the equipment was playing tricks. Used or not, it gave little or no help in the course of the action.

It was after two o'clock when the frantically searching cruisers picked up their contact again, and Holland immediately made his final change of course to intercept; but it was a course that would make the gunners tear their hair with frustration when they in turn got their first sight of the enemy. At this time visibility began to improve and the men on the *Prince of Wales*, who had been closed-up and tense now for nearly two hours, were able to see a little more of what was going on—those of them, that is, who were in a position to see; for the fact is that very few of those engaged in a naval action in a capital ship ever got much of a view at all. For this reason one finds that the memories of even the best of people are often confused; their timings, in particular, go astray, and events are telescoped in recollection into a much shorter period than they actually occupied. It has been the writer's experience in talking to survivors that for the first time after all the years they were able to get a whole picture of this and other battles straight, things fell into place which they had never probably understood before —light dawned. It is odd for one who was never nearer than many hundreds of miles from the *Bismarck* and who was, in fact, on dry land at the time, to find himself explaining to the people who took part in one of the most important naval actions of the War, exactly what went on under their noses.

There was, in any case, very little to be seen except the same expanse of stormy ocean they had seen the day before —if anything a little stormier—with the *Hood* pitching and rearing her way along perhaps half a mile ahead of them on their port bow and their own ship carving her way at thirty knots through the heavy weather, repeatedly taking the sea green and flinging great sheets of spray over the forward turrets and the upper works. It continued to clear fast until visibility was twelve miles or more.

It was 5:35 A.M. when the enemy was sighted. In the twenty minutes that were still to pass before the range closed sufficiently to open fire—while the last urgent preparations for battle were being made—Captain Leach surveyed in his mind the state of his untried ship and crew. He had done everything a commander could do in the time allowed him. He had told his men what was expected of them, kept them informed, minute-by-minute, of the scene which he and those around him could see while so many of them could not. Something still seemed to be lacking——there was still something to be done. H. V. Morton got the story from the Padre, the Rev. W. G. Parker, of how the Captain sent for him and told him that he wanted him to read a prayer to the ship's company.

"Can you remember," he asked, "a prayer which begins, 'Oh God thou knowest how busy I am . . .'?"

"It is Sir Jacob Astley's prayer before the Battle of Edgehill," said the Padre, "and I have the words in my cabin."

"Fetch it quickly," said the Captain, "There's not much time."

And so through the loudspeakers all over the ship, in the midst of all the business of war, in the midst of the tenseness, the anxiety and the fear which comes before action to the bravest of men, there came the calm voice of the Chaplain. The words he spoke were the words of men in another age, fighting quite a different sort of war for quite different reasons, but their age was the age which created the Book of Common Prayer and shaped the language of prayer for the whole of the English-speaking world for countless generations to come:

"Oh Lord, Thou knowest how busy we must be today. If we forget Thee, do not Thou forget us; for Christ's sake. Amen."

It was all there was time for, and all there was need for. Men bowed their heads briefly in their turrets, amid the roar of the machinery in the bowels of the ship; and the preparations for battle went on.

There must have been something approaching consternation in the *Prince of Wales*'s gunnery control when the course on which they were approaching the enemy became apparent; for the German ships were almost dead ahead, or at least fine on the starboard bow, so that it was touch and go whether the after turrets would bear on the target at all. The range-finders in the after turret were useless while those in A and B Turrets were obscured by spray: moreover, owing to the speed of their end-on approach, the range was difficult to determine in the extreme. In the event, we are told, fire was opened on a range obtained from a small auxilliary range-finder in the control position. The gunnery radar was in theory useable for obtaining ranges, but either through defect or through the inexperience of the half-trained operators it was, for all practical purposes, useless throughout the action. On the German ships, of course, the situation was exactly the opposite: the battle-cruisers were approaching them at a point only a little forward of midships, bows on to them, and they could hardly have been better placed for opening battle.

This was the situation into which Admiral Holland's blunder of the night before had led them. It must be taken into consideration in passing judgment on the performance of the *Prince of Wales*; it must be taken into account when reading Rear-Admiral Wake-Walker's dispatch and Admiral Tovey's dispatch, which was based on it, and in correcting the very poor opinion they obviously had of Captain Leach's ship. It must be taken into account in passing judgment on the cruel and senseless rumours which were bandied about after the action, and in asking ourselves why nothing was ever done about them. It is only long, long afterwards, in recent years, that the facts have become public property and even so, as we shall see, some sections of the press could not resist raking up the ugly rumours all over again.

It might be thought that nothing could now be done to make the situation worse than it already was for the *Prince of Wales* and the *Hood*. In fact, something was. The unfortunate Holland now proceeded to make his biggest blunder of all. During the night the two enemy ships had changed station and the *Prinz Eugen* was now leading the line, dead ahead of the *Bismarck*. It is true that the silhouettes of the two ships were remarkably similar, although it is equally true that the *Bismarck* was many times larger than the cruiser; it is also true that conditions were not ideal and that the relative sizes of ships at sea are often difficult to determine. Whatever allowance we may make for all the circumstances, there is no escaping the fact that Holland mistook the *Prinz Eugen* for the *Bismarck*, and ordered both his ships to open fire on the leading vessel. In the *Prince of Wales*'s control position the mistake was immediately realised and fire was opened on the right-hand, not the left-hand ship. The evidence now is overwhelming that the *Hood* never fired a single salvo at the *Bismarck* and this conclusion is supported both by the official history and by Sir Winston Churchill's *Memoirs*.

At 5:53 A.M., after the endless hours of suspense, the guns at last spoke. Both the German and the British ships opened up almost simultaneously. The range was twenty-five thousand yards and closing rapidly. The *Prinz Eugen* took the *Prince of Wales* for her target while the *Bismarck* concentrated the full output of her massive fifteen-inch broadside on the *Hood*, especially vulnerable at this long range. Clearly the German ships were well informed about their adversaries and how to deal with them. Their equipment was first class and the men who handled it trained to the peak, so that they were able to make the most of their favourable position. They found their target rapidly. Against them were the fifteen-inch guns of the *Hood* and the fourteen-inch guns of the *Prince of Wales*. *Hood* was firing at the wrong target and there is no evidence that she found it in the few salvoes she got off. The *Prince of Wales* did not cross her target until the sixth salvo, and in view of both her difficult position and the lack of training of her men, it is much to her credit that she did not take longer. On top of all this, one of her forward guns failed after firing one single round, while a few salvoes later Y turret broke down completely and became useless.

What happened now was engraved for the rest of their lives on the memories of those aboard the *Prince of Wales*—both those who saw it and those who could only hear what was going on. Boy Williams in P.3. high-angle turret heard the commentary coming over the loudspeakers amid all the din of action: first salvo in the wake of the *Hood*, second salvo between the *Hood* and *Prince of Wales*, third salvo closer still to the *Hood*. At this point he looked through the periscope and was in time to see shells from the fourth salvo hit the *Hood* somewhere about the after turret. Immediately a mass of flame engulfed the quarter-deck and seconds later the whole mighty ship erupted in a single titanic explosion. Seddon saw it also from the bridge: momentarily to him and to other watchers the forecastle of the *Hood* showed at a crazy, impossible angle, and then the whole ship completely disappeared from the face of the waters to rain down in wreckage on the sea and on the decks of the surviving vessel. So, in almost an instant, perished the British Navy's greatest ship, leaving the *Prince of Wales* alone against the enemy with only five out of her ten main guns serviceable. It was Jutland all over again. It was a fierce reminder of the chances of battle-cruisers in any action between capital ships—a fierce reminder for any battle cruiser, including the *Repulse*. And no doubt the Japanese as well as the Germans took note of it.

All over the *Prince of Wales* there went up the cry "The *Hood*'s gone!" and following on it came the voice of Captain Leach telling them that they must do what they could by themselves.

The range was still closing rapidly: the 5.25's were now in action, as well as the main guns. *Bismarck* immediately switched her target and switched it with devastating effect. Boy Williams's turret was put out of action by a shell that hit the working space below it but did not explode——miraculously the only casualty was the seaman torpedoman, who had his hair singed. In the course of the next few minutes the *Prince of Wales* received direct hits from four fifteen-inch shells and three eight-inch shells. She was holed below the waterline aft and soon had a good four hundred tons of water aboard. Her radar room was wrecked, her foreward funnel shot nearly in half. Both her foreward H.A. directors and her after starboard director were put out of action and there was an infinity of minor damage. At two minutes past six Seddon, still at his post on the bridge, heard a crash above him like the end of the world, as one of *Bismarck*'s shells hit the compass platform, carrying part of it clean away and killing and wounding practically everyone upon it. The only unwounded survivors were—miraculously—the Captain, the Chief Yeoman, and Leading Signalman Willey, who is deaf to this day from the blast. The Captain came staggering down to the bridge. He seemed dazed but was in full possession of himself.

"Clear up the mess," he said.

Almost immediately he turned his ship away, making smoke, to open the range. He needed time to recover from the shattering blows which had been dealt him.

The damage control parties went to work, and all men not otherwise engaged were put to cleaning up. Alf Tudor, emerging from his turret, was astounded at the damage and the change in the appearance of the ship for, with all the racket of the main and secondary armament firing, he had not realised how many times she had been hit or how hard. The foreward funnel was a caricature of a funnel, the compass platform was a ruin, the air reeked with high explosive and there seemed to be casualties lying around everywhere— one of them he recognised was Esmond Knight. The battle ensign was in shreds and when he got up on to the compass platform the wreckage was literally spattered all over with flesh and blood.

Boy Williams was having a similar experience, he and those around him having been set to work on what was left of the after radar room. Here there were bits of complicated equipment all mixed up with bits of human beings. It was no baptism for a boy, but with the others he got on with it. Seddon, in a note of his experiences at this time, compasses a laconic and almost Pepysian phrase. It was, he says, "not to our liking."

Unknown at this time to any aboard her, the *Prince of Wales* had in fact scored three hits on the *Bismarck* which set into motion the train of events that led to her ultimate destruction. They had been seen aboard the *Suffolk*, nearly fifteen miles away, but not by Wake-Walker's people in the *Norfolk*. They had not caused major damage to either ship or machinery but they had holed one of her fuel tanks, causing her both to lose oil and contaminating the rest of the supply in the tank with salt water. It was this that changed the whole of the *Bismarck*'s plans, stopped her from breaking out into the Atlantic (which she was now other-wise in a position to do long before the Home Fleet came up), and caused Admiral Lutjens to decide to part company with the *Prinz Eugen* and make for St. Nazaire. In short—and we shall hear more of this later—in spite of all her appalling handicaps, and in spite of the blunders that had put her at an even greater disadvantage than she would already have been, she had accomplished sufficient of her mission to earn boundless credit for a newly-commissioned ship in trouble with her most vital equipment and with her crew half-trained. What she got instead of the credit that was her due we shall presently see.

Had those who were busy trying to make things as ship-shape as they could out of twisted steel, wrecked equipment and shattered bodies known all this, it would have done them a power of good; for it can readily be understood that their morale had been dealt a serious blow. It did not interfere in the slightest with the job on hand—at least it does not appear to have done so. Perhaps there is nothing that puts the training and co-ordination of a ship to a greater test than the kind of situation with which they were now coping. On a ship something less than half worked-up conditions could well have become chaotic. What did happen was that at 7:20 A.M.—no more than an hour and seven minutes after the brief action was broken off—the ship was being conned once more from her normal position, two guns of Y turret were serviceable again, and Captain Leach reported himself able to make twenty-seven knots. However, Rear-Admiral Wake-Walker of the cruiser squadron, under whose command the *Prince of Wales* fell automatically when Vice-Admiral Holland went down with the *Hood*, ordered him not to re-engage. Disconsolately she followed in the wake of the cruisers, which had now come up with her and were still stalking the *Bismarck*.

It was only forty minutes later that Admiral Lutjens signalled his intention to make for St. Nazaire. If only they had known of it!

Now, at the moment the battle-cruiser squadron opened fire on the *Bismarck*, the *Repulse* was pounding and thundering along with streaming decks in company with the Home Fleet three hundred miles or more from the scene of the action. With her were Tovey's flagship, the *King George V*, the new carrier *Victorious*, the cruisers *Galatea*, *Hermione*, *Aurora*, and *Kenya*, and seven destroyers. It had been a hectic and hurried departure from Greenock, and the mess deck had been alive with "buzzes" of every description, all on the best authority (this was regular routine) until once harbour had been cleared, Captain Tennant broadcast to the ship's company and told them what they were about. The favourite "buzz" in Mess 46 had been that they were going to the rescue of a convoy which was being attacked off Northern Ireland. There was a convoy all right, for they steamed through it at twenty-eight knots, leaving their wash behind them, but the truth was much more acceptable. At speed in that heavy sea, the ship was putting on one of those displays of acrobatics that had so upset Slinger Wood on his first trip through the Bay, long ago in a world of peace—she was taking it green as far aft as B turret. Nonetheless, Slinger and his mates settled down to plan out the campaign. They did not realise that the battle-cruiser squadron would go into action long before them; they visualized a concerted attack on the *Bismarck* by the whole of the Home Fleet together. Long before they turned in that night—if the term could be used for a night of action stations, with most men trying to get some sleep alongside their guns, down shell rooms and magazines, and in all manner of other unlikely places—the *Bismarck* was at the bottom of the sea, as the U-Boat fleet, the *Scharnhorst*, and the *Gneisenau*, and every other unit of the German Navy had been before them. There was utter confidence everywhere, the confidence of a good ship, which these men never lost. Scouse Garner remembers discussing the limitations of their guns against the *Bismarck*, but also remembers the marines deciding that their gunnery would make up for it.

Early in the morning a bridge messenger, a boy seaman, came running through the marines' barracks.

"The *Hood*'s gone!" he cried, bursting with the importance of his news.

A marine corporal grabbed him.

"What's that?" he demanded.

"The *Hood*'s gone," repeated the boy. "Sunk by the *Bismarck*."

"I've a bloody good mind to run you in," said the corporal. "Spreading buzzes like that."

"It's true. Honest it is," insisted the boy. "She's gone."

The corporal let him go reluctantly and he disappeared into the racket of the driving ship. The marines looked at each other, unwilling to believe. Ten minutes later Captain Tennant piped all hands and told them over the loud-speakers, and then they knew it was true, whether they wanted to believe it or not. It was the same for Slinger Wood and Mess 46—it was the same for all of them. It wasn't just that the Navy's greatest ship had gone to the bottom of the sea, sunk literally in seconds after firing no more than a few rounds at the enemy. It was much more than that: *Hood* was almost their sister-ship, they'd sailed together so many times, shared so many of those grinding searches and abortive chases. They'd friends aboard the *Hood*, many friends. They weren't the first friends they'd lost in the war, any more than the *Hood* was the first ship to be lost, but this was something different. They burned with revenge, every one of them. They wanted to get at the *Bismarck* and get their own back. Six main guns and twelve four-inchers regardless, they wanted to get at the *Bismarck*. They'd have wanted to get at the *Bismarck* if they'd been in a trawler equipped with no more than a popgun.

But where was the *Bismarck*? All through the day they stormed along, the weather getting worse rather than better.

They knew now that the mighty *Prince of Wales* had been battered into breaking off the action, they knew that in a matter of hours the *Bismarck* would be out in the Atlantic, loose among the convoys, and that finding her would be like looking for a needle in a haystack. The hours seemed interminable, the seas through which they crashed their way, endless.

Captain Tennant had his own anxieties. All this high-speed steaming was using up oil at a frantic rate—as it also was for the other ships—and if the chase went on too long their tanks would be empty long before they came to grips with the enemy. The lesson of the *Hood* had also not been lost upon him: he knew quite clearly and dispassionately that one plunging shot in the right place on his horizontal armour would do to him exactly what such a shot had done to the *Hood,* as well as to the *Queen Mary* and *Invincible* a quarter of a century before. There was precious little he could do about either. As to the former, he must take his orders from the Commander-in-Chief and steam as long as he could; as to the latter, it was just one of the risks of the business, and there was an end of it. It was one of the risks which he and other people accepted when they joined the Navy.

Far ahead of them, all through this day, the *Prince of Wales* steamed in company with the cruisers, alongside the *Suffolk* and on the *Norfolk*'s port quarter, shadowing the *Bismarck*. The German ship was twisting and turning now: she seemed to be trying to shake them off and might well do so. The need to slow her was desperate, yet further engagement might drive her beyond their reach. Shortly after midday she turned south and reduced speed to twenty-four knots. There was a brief exchange of fire: the two surviving guns of Y turret immediately broke down again. The admiral ordered Captain Leach to fire no more unless himself fired on.

This was, in fact, the moment when Admiral Lutjens parted company with the *Prinz Eugen* and laid his course for France, the course that was to lead him into the net of his destruction. The *Prince of Wales* was responsible for it. The *Prince of Wales* still didn't know. And the rest of the world was not to know for years.

The day wore on with Tovey's ship steering a converging course, in the hope of bringing Lutjens to action at first light the following morning. He ordered *Victorious* to close to a hundred miles of the quarry, and fly off the few Swordfish planes that were operational, in the desperate chance of being able to slow the German down; but the planes were too few, the conditions too bad for their inexperienced pilots. Alf Tudor, Johnny King, and the rest of them aboard the *Prince of Wales* saw the aircraft go over: it heartened them to know that the Home Fleet was getting near. What would have heartened them still more would have been to have known that one of the pilots, mercifully scraping home at dusk on to a wildly plunging flight deck, had reported that the *Bismarck* was leaving an oil track behind her. It was the first indication anyone had had that she had suffered any damage at all. It was automatically assumed that the damage had been done by the *Hood*, because it was taken for granted that the *Prince of Wales* was incapable of hitting anything.

By morning the *Repulse* had been steaming at high speed for the greater part of two days, and the fuel situation was becoming critical. Already, if everything went according to plan and contact was made with the *Bismarck* at daylight, she had enough to last her for no more than a short sharp action. Then she would have to break off and make for the nearest port at as economical a speed as she could compass. Just a few salvoes—surely this ship had it owing to her to try her metal against the enemy just this once!

It was not to be. There was to be no action for the *Repulse*. She and the *Prince of Wales* were not yet to meet. For in the early hours of the morning, the cruiser squadron blundered.

Through the dim twilight of the northern night, they had been shadowing their quarry by radar. The *Prince of Wales's* radar was, as we know, unreliable, and the *Norfolk*'s was an early installation which would only cover a limited sector. *Suffolk*, having the best radar of the three, had been ordered to keep in touch and act independently. The *Bismarck* was zig-zagging; so was *Suffolk*, for there had been a submarine report. At the end of every leg of her zig-zag, the *Bismarck*'s echo disappeared from her screen: regularly, as she made good on her new course, it came back. She grew over-confident—that is the charge laid against her by the official history—and there came a moment when the *Bismarck*'s echo did not come back. By pure bad luck, at the very moment when she was invisible to the radar as well as to the naked eye, the *Bismarck* had changed course. It was 3:20 in the morning, the Home Fleet was still a good four hours' steaming away, and the *Bismarck* was lost.

Admiral Tovey split up his ships and proceeded to quarter the seas as best he could, but the area to be covered was a wide one, conditions were still bad and the *Bismarck* might have turned in any direction. An examination of the official chart of the action shows, after the event, that the direction in which she had turned was the one direction he did not cover: she had laid a straight course for St. Nazaire. Roughly about the time Admiral Tovey had hoped to engage, the German ship passed a hundred miles astern of him.

With the splitting up of the ships, the *Repulse* found herself alone and the amateur tacticians aboard her had to revise their plans completely. Even such optimists as Slinger Wood, Chicken Howe, Slatts and the rest could not blind themselves to what had happened to the *Hood* as they hammered it out at their action stations. They thought perhaps they might at least be able to hold the *Bismarck* at bay until K.G.5 and the others came up, if they were lucky enough to find her: they had an idea also that there were other heavy units on their way. In this they were perfectly right, for the Admiralty had whistled-up Force H from Gibraltar, and all other units with the remotest chance of getting there on time—but all these were still a long way away.

"I wish we had the bloody *Rodney* with us," Slinger remembers someone saying. "They don't know there's been a war on yet. All that time swinging around a buoy and now they're going to the States for a bloody refit."

For the last time they had seen their friend, the *Rodney*, that (to them) permanent ornament of Scapa Flow, her decks had been stacked with wooden cases of spare parts, and she had been all set for departure to an American dockyard. Many a true word is spoken in jest; wooden cases and all, it was the *Rodney* that played a major part in the last scene of the *Bismarck* drama, battering her into silence after she had been finally slowed down by the *Ark Royal's* torpedo bombers, till the *Dorsetshire* could be left to finish her off with torpedoes. Wooden cases and all, after all those months of sitting on those empty tins, the *Rodney* got the chance that the *Repulse* had steamed her never-ending miles of ocean and failed to find.

Before eleven o'clock that morning the *Repulse's* fuel supplies had been reduced to a point that made action out of the question and even made it doubtful whether she could make port. She was detached to Newfoundland, and when she arrived at Conception Bay it was touch and go whether she would have to be towed into harbour. She had also suffered damage battering her way at high speed through the storm. Much of it was trivial, but some of it was at least uncomfortable—her forward breakwaters, for instance, were flat on the deck. She was in need of repairs as well as fuel.

Some four and a half hours before that, Admiral Tovey had signalled to the *Prince of Wales* to join him, but now the *Prince of Wales* was in the same predicament as the *Repulse*. She, too, had to withdraw for fuel. Burying her dead on passage, she arrived at Hvalfjord in Iceland on the 27th, and from thence went to Rosyth for repairs in her turn.

The rest of the *Bismarck* chase was, therefore, no concern

of either the *Repulse* or the *Prince of Wales*, and there is no
point in retelling a story which has already become history.
But there was a dreadful moral about the end of the *Bismarck*
which people in high places as well as amateur strategists
would have done well to mark. If ever there was a ship that
was "unsinkable" it was the *Bismarck*: she was at least as
unsinkable as the *Prince of Wales* and perhaps had an even
better claim to the title. She had demolished the *Hood* and
crippled the *Prince of Wales*, while herself suffering damage
that certainly caused her to abandon her raiding mission,
but which only affected her endurance without affecting
either her speed, her seaworthiness, or her fighting strength.
Turned into the pursuers' net by this, she yet out-distanced
them all and came within an ace of finding safety under the
protection of the Luftwaffe. Only one thing stopped her: that
one thing was that the *Ark Royal*'s Swordfish (string-bag,
antiquated-looking planes to many eyes)—flown off under
well nigh impossible conditions—found her, blasted her
steering gear, and wrecked her propellers. How much more
easily were modern torpedo-bombers of long range, flown
from shore bases, to find and cripple the *Prince of Wales*
and the *Repulse* over a calm sea with excellent visibility,
away on either side of the world! After Taranto, after what
had happened to the *Bismarck*, could responsible people still
think of battleships as unsinkable? Could they still dream of
capital ships dominating any area of sea to which they might
be sent? Or did they, like Slinger Wood and his pals, think
of the Japanese planes as made of rice paper and put together
with string and glue?

There yet is one more thing about the *Bismarck* action of
which we must take notice, for it, too, has a bearing on the
end of the *Prince of Wales* and the *Repulse*. In this action
we see for the first time the "working-up" of the Admiralty's
own war machine accomplished and perfected: from it
emerges a very different picture from that of the days of the
phony war and the *Repulse*'s endless phantom chases after

adversaries who were discovered too late, or were never in the places where they were reported to be. Intelligence was now excellent, appreciation and decision rapid, co-ordination in the concentration of forces over a wide area outstanding. There could no longer be any doubt that the Admiralty knew what it was about and its views and appreciations were worthy of respect. That the Admiralty's views were not respected in the long drawn-out battle of words which was shortly to commence over the dispatch of the *Repulse* and the *Prince of Wales* to the Far East, was one of the biggest blunders of the war.

In this now-perfected web of command and control there was inherent a factor which was not only of paramount importance in sinking the *Bismarck* but also in finally winning the war at sea—the training and experience of subordinate commanders which made it possible for them, under conditions of radio silence, to act correctly and promptly in the way that the overall plan of action clearly demanded. Nearly two years of unremitting warfare at sea had been the school in which this accurate and intelligent use of initiative had been learned. Luckless Admiral Holland, unfortunate in his decisions, was an exception. In the words of Captain Roskill, the official historian, "the instinctive manner in which every commander in every class of ship had guessed and correctly interpreted the wishes of the Commander-in-Chief proved the soundness of our basic Naval training and traditions." And with justifiable pride Admiral Tovey, in his report of the action, declares that "the co-operation, skill, and understanding displayed by all forces . . . gave me the utmost satisfaction. Flag and commanding officers of detached units invariably took the action I would have wished before and without receiving instructions from me."

At the very centre of this web of trained and instinctive command, at the Admiralty in London, was working one Rear-Admiral Tom Phillips, Vice-Chief of Naval Staff and right-hand man of the First Sea Lord, later to command

Force Z at Singapore and drown with his two capital ships, the *Repulse* and the *Prince of Wales*. In that last action, as we shall presently see, he in his turn reacted instinctively to intelligence that was passed to him and took it for granted that those who passed him the intelligence would foresee his reactions without him breaking radio silence. They did not do so because they had had neither Admiral Phillips's training nor his experience of such battles as the battle of the Atlantic and the chase of the *Bismarck*; and we shall have to ask ourselves whether he could in all fairness and justice be blamed for that.

CHAPTER

6

THE FACTS ABOUT THE "PRINCE OF WALES'S" BRIEF EN-
counter with the *Bismarck*, related in the last chapter, are
those which are now generally accepted by people best quali-
fied to judge: among these, the greatest weight must be given
to the official history of the war at sea because its author,
Captain Roskill, points out (a little smugly, perhaps), in
his preface to it, that many of the official records from which
it is compiled will not be accessible to the general public
for years to come. But they are supported in addition by the
memories of the ship's survivors who either observed shot
strike on the *Bismarck* themselves or were told so by their
Captain in his running commentary over the loudspeakers;
the latter is also the evidence of the Captain himself. And
they are confirmed by German sources. These were not the
facts accepted at the time, and under the cloak of the wartime
security blackout on information, sinister rumours circulated
about the *Prince of Wales*. She had "run away," or to use
the phraseology of more exclusive circles, she had "with-

drawn somewhat precipitately from the action." How strong the rumours were, or to what extent they were believed, is difficult at this distance of time to say: some of the *Prince of Wales*'s people admit rather guardedly to having heard them or heard about them, to finding a certain coolness in the canteens and pubs. On the other hand, others disclaim all knowledge of them. It is quite certain that hasty and cruel remarks were made to Captain Leach by certain people in high places, who were afterwards obliged to apologise for what they had said; but for him the wound was never quite healed in the short spell of life left to him.

These rumours bubbled evilly in the lower strata of the press, sensation-starved and prevented by wartime restrictions from letting the stuff out into the open air. God knows, there was enough copy for the press in those times without hunting for this sort of dirt, and the greater majority of decent newspaper men who knew their business had no truck with it. In 1948, when the official despatches on the action were first published, one "naval correspondent," at least, was at pains to drag it all out and turn it into a running commentary to the despatches, together with the story of the *Prince of Wales* "mutiny" and a lot of other nonsense which would best have been left in oblivion.

How did all this start? In official circles, at any rate, it cannot but have started with Rear-Admiral Wake-Walker's report. His view of the action was from the cruiser *Norfolk*, fifteen miles away in fair visibility but stormy weather. He states that he observed no hits or damage on the *Bismarck*—although we know in fact that the hits were observed from the *Suffolk*, which was in company with him. He goes on to say of the *Prince of Wales*:

"I had seen her forced out of action after ten minutes, at the end of which her salvoes were falling short and had a very large spread indeed. She was short of one gun and her bridge was wrecked. I did not and do not consider that in her then state of efficiency the *Prince of Wales* was a match for the *Bismarck*."

He adds that re-engagement would only have resulted in further failures and damage to the cruisers in return for little damage or loss of speed to the *Bismarck*. Admiral Tovey's fleet, he points out, was coming up—and demonstrates his own accuracy and efficiency by miscalculating the estimated time of Tovey's arrival by no less than five hours—a fact which appears to have been overlooked in commentaries on his report.

Well, Admiral Tovey was coming up—to be robbed of his chance of engagement when almost within sight of the enemy by a blunder on the part of one of Wake-Walker's own ships, now set down to over-confidence. There is no criticism of the *Suffolk* in either Wake-Walker's or Tovey's despatches—at least in the form in which they were made public after the war, yet it was this blunder that robbed the *Repulse* of her long-awaited battle, robbed the *Prince of Wales* of the chance of vindicating herself by re-engagement, and caused the fuel supplies to Admiral Tovey's other ships to be so severely eaten into as to jeopardize the rest of the action.

Tovey's own account is coloured inevitably by Wake-Walker's bias, since he had to depend upon Wake-Walker for his facts. Of the beginning of the action he says, "the shooting of both the *Hood* and the *Bismarck* was excellent and both scored hits at once." Yet we know now that *Hood* was not firing at the *Bismarck*, and if the hits are admitted, they must have been from the *Prince of Wales*'s guns. Tovey's authority for the hits is apparently from observation from the *Suffolk*. He says, in fact, elsewhere that the *Suffolk* reported three hits on the *Bismarck*, but that Wake-Walker on the *Norfolk* did not observe them, although black smoke was seen at times.

Captain Leach's own statement is factual and logical. It contains no criticism of other units nor any criticism of his superior officer, who was drowned and could not answer for himself. Neither does it contain any criticism of the manner in which he was led into action on a course which would have made gunnery difficult for any ship, let along a newly-commissioned ship with her obvious troubles. This is what he says in his own despatch:

"Some explanation remains to be made as to my decision to break off the action after the sinking of H.M.S. *Hood*—a decision which clearly invites the most critical examination. Prior to the disaster to the *Hood* I felt confident that to-gether we could deal adequately with the *Bismarck* and her consort. The sinking of the *Hood* obviously changed the immediate situation, and there were three further considerations requiring to be weighed up, of which the first and second had been in my mind before action was joined.

"(a) The practical certainty that owing to mechanical 'teething trouble' a full output from the main armament was not to be expected.

"(b) The working-up of the ship had only just reached a stage when I could report to the Commander-in-Chief, Home Fleet, that I considered her reasonably fit to take part in service operations. This was the first occasion in which she had done so . . .

"(c) The likelihood of a decisive concentration being effected at a later stage.

"In the circumstances, I did not consider it sound tactics to continue single-handed the engagement with two German ships, both of whom might be expected to be at the peak of their efficiency."

This cool and calm reasoning is accepted and supported by Admiral Tovey, although in all the dark rumour and surmise that followed not one hint of it (suitably vetted to meet the requirements of security) was allowed to escape. It shows quite clearly that Captain Leach, in spite of the damage his ship had suffered, had no thought of withdrawing permanently from the action. He was able and willing to re-engage with such guns as he had; his inexperienced ship's complement had dealt with the battle-damage like old hands, and Leach was able both to steam and to fight. Admiral Tovey accepted this to the extent of ordering him to leave the shadowing cruiser force and join the main fleet, which was at that time his proper place; and if the ship had not run out of fuel he would have done so. In that case (had Wake-Walker not lost touch with the enemy) her five serviceable guns would have made as substantial a contribution to the final battering of the *Bismarck* as the *Rodney's* guns: for it must not be forgotten that the *Rodney* was in no outstandingly serviceable condition. No-one criticised Admiral Tovey for "withdrawing precipitately" with the *King George V* before the end of the battle, because that ship's fuel supplies in turn had reached rock bottom. No-one criticised the *Repulse* for withdrawing from the search for the same reason. No-one criticised any other unit that had to drop out of the fight through shortage of oil. Why criticise the *Prince of Wales?* And certainly no-one criticised Rear-Admiral Wake-Walker and his force for losing touch with the *Bismarck* twice—until the official history was published a decade and a half later.

Now the language of Admiral Wake-Walker's despatch is the restrained language of the official document: for an official document it is strong language. It appears to suggest the assumption that a newly commissioned ship which was known to be suffering from more than her ordinary share of teething troubles could do no good. Be that as it may, mouth-to-mouth gossip in turn found its way into the ears of ferreting journalists of the baser sort, and remained itching for expression, so that here is what one of them wrote years later, when the despatches on the action were published after the war—under the banner headline, "WHY THE BATTLESHIP 'RAN AWAY.'"

"The honour of seventeen hundred fighting men and the captain they idolized is vindicated.

"For six years their battleship, Prince of Wales, has been branded as a 'coward ship'—a giant which ran away after only ten minutes engagement with the German Bismarck . . .

"This skeleton, which the Navy believed forever buried, is dragged from the Admiralty cupboard in today's issue of the London Gazette."

Some extracts from the official despatches follow, and at the conclusion of them the journalist goes on to say:

"Admiral Tovey's despatches were secret then, and the men of the Prince of Wales *were cruelly misjudged. They were called 'the POWs who ran away' and the rudest words of the Navy's 'destroyer song' (those about 'no futile good') were used in lower deck banter.* Prince of Wales's *officers found themselves coldly treated by some brother officers in the Fleet."*

There was no "cruel misjudgment" of the *Prince of Wales* and her men except by those who should have known better. There was no need to vindicate the honour of the *Prince of Wales*'s fighting men and their captain, because their honour had never been impugned. And the only dragging of skeletons out of cupboards was done (if the mixed metaphor can be overlooked) not by the London *Gazette*, but by the "naval correspondent" who wrote this piece.

The information services must also bear their share of responsibility for all this. For as well as dishing out such information about the war as could be vouchsafed to press and public, it was their job to know what rumours were flying around and to take steps to counteract "despondency and alarm." The ugly rumours about the *Prince of Wales* cannot have escaped their notice——newspapermen must inevitably have asked questions about them. It might be supposed that they would think it important to the war effort—to both civilian and service morale and to feeling

abroad—to clear the reputation of a fighting ship. They could
have done so easily enough without letting any cats out of
bags. Obviously a great many things could not be disclosed
for a variety of different reasons, including Admiral Holland's blunders and the mechanical state of the *Prince of
Wales*'s turrets. Equally obviously, misconceptions in reports prevented the truth about the *Prince of Wales*'s share
in the sinking of the *Bismarck* being known. But there was
still a whole heap that could have been said: the information
services and those responsible for them made not the slightest attempt to say it. Either they were living (as they so
often did) in a rarefied atmosphere of their own, divorced
from the ways and thoughts of ordinary mortals, with which
it was their business to be familiar—or they couldn't see their
way to doing what was necessary, didn't know how, thought
the difficulties too great. Not on this occasion alone the conduct of the information services (to use again that delightful
phrase of the naval reports) "invites consideration." In
plainer language, one wonders what they were for.

"The battleship with her crestfallen crew was dry-docked
at Rosyth for a spell . . . then the *Prince of Wales* went
back to Scapa for the men to begin all over again the
monotonous grind to work, to build-up battle efficiency." So
continues our "Naval correspondent." If the *Prince of Wales*
complement had been told that years later their return home
would have been described in such language they would have
been very surprised, indeed. It is against this background that
the "*Prince of Wales* Mutiny" is alleged to have taken place
and this story also would have surprised many of the *Prince
of Wales*'s complement: in fact it still appears to surprise
survivors at the present day.

Before we go into this legend, let us have a look at how
matters stood with the battleship and her crew. She had returned to Rosyth with her battle scars; her dead had been
buried at sea and her wounded landed in Iceland. The
Bismarck had been sunk and the *Prince of Wales*'s people

were quite confident that they had played their part in her sinking, even if the press and the outside world thought otherwise. They had been in action, they had a tale to tell. The ship was obviously bound for the dockyard and with any luck there might be leave—this the more welcome because while they had been chasing the German Navy, the Luftwaffe had once more been bombarding their homes, especially on Merseyside, where many of them lived; they would be glad enough to reassure themselves that all was safe and well or to cope with their personal tragedies if it wasn't.

They got their leave, but before they did so there was one last "flap". It was only when they arrived at Rosyth that it was discovered that among their souvenirs of the *Bismarck*, they had been carrying with them all the way from the distant Denmark Strait an unexploded fifteen-inch shell, well down in the ship on the starboard side. It was an uncomfortable travelling companion: they were not pleased to discover it nor were they sorry they had not discovered it sooner. Least pleased of all were those who had to mount guard on this unwelcome projectile while preparations were made for its removal. It seemed a funny thing to be guarding an object which might blow you to kingdom come at any moment and they were delighted to see it go. It is one thing to await the arrival of fifteen-inch shells in the heat of battle but quite another to meet them in cold blood in the battle's hangover.

They got their leave: the civilian personnel also departed for their homes, thankfully and not without distinction. It is impossible not to write about the Navy without taking a rise out of "dockyard mateys" and sometimes their presence aboard the battleship has been treated with a touch of flippancy. There is no harm in it, and dockyard mateys everywhere will understand: let us admit that these men had been in a sea battle, whether they had bargained for it or not, and there is no evidence whatsoever that they disgraced themselves.

One of the few people who got no leave was Captain

Leach. He had not escaped unscathed when the compass platform was hit, and when the ship was docked he went into hospital. He had not yet returned when the watches in turn came back from their leave, although he did so not long afterwards, and the men generally seem to have been very well aware where he was and why. This fact is important in taking to pieces the "mutiny" story.

The repairs were completed and modifications made to the turrets. It is difficult to discover whether these modifications cured all their troubles, because the only action in which the ship was engaged during the rest of her life was aircraft action. No doubt there are reports about them hidden away in those records to which official historians alone have access: to the world at large they are still secret documents.

But what is all this nonsense about a "crestfallen crew," about the "monotonous grind" to work-up battle efficiency? Of course there was hard work, gruelling hard work; of course there was also monotony. Both of these were part of the war at sea and the men never looked on either as a punishment peculiar to themselves. Monotony in particular was inseparable from a place like Scapa Flow, to which the ship returned after her repairs were completed. Conditions there had improved considerably since Slinger Wood had first made its acquaintance at the beginning of the war: there was the NAAFI Canteen, there were concerts with stars and radio personalities, and turns given by the lads themselves. Beer was rationed, but there was an occasional air-raid to liven things up. In spite of all these delights it was still Scapa and still not very exciting. But it was good enough for Alf Tudor and Johnny King and Joe Dempsey and Smithy and Jimmy James, and scores like them all over the ship. No doubt they had their grumbles as all service men had, but memory of them in detail has long since disappeared. When the delights of Scapa were exhausted or when their time was up, they would make their way back on board and finish off their amusement there in their own canteen—with Jimmy James and Smithy knocking hell out of the piano and everyone else swearing that they were as good as professionals. They never tired of making their own amusement and wondered at times why they went ashore, because they had better facilities for amusement aboard. Jokes aside, there seems to have been quite a lot of talent on this ship and it never lacked an appreciative audience in the men's spare time. Apart from that there were poker, draughts, crib, quoits and uckers—which landsmen call ludo and never fail to be astonished at the earnestness with which it is played by grown men in mighty ships of war. There was also the ship's cinema. There were sparring bouts for those who liked them as well as those "differences of opinion" which were liable to end in sparring bouts, whether this had been intended or not. There was the mat-making and belt-making business, and this was not confined to old hands like Seddon. Immensely tough young men became immensely serious and absorbed over this pastime, carefully cutting hundreds of identical pieces out of old serge and similar trifles extracted from the rag bag, and pushed home into a backing of potato sack with a home-made wooden implement. The belts were made of coloured twine. Quite a lot of these manufactures found their way home—and quite a lot of them went with the ship to the bottom of the South China Sea.

Men can honestly say with their hands on their hearts, at this distance of time, that there wasn't a dull moment. Of course they're quite wrong and of course there were many dull moments; because it is a most commonplace and elementary thing about the memories of all servicemen that as the years go by recollection of times when people were bored, cold, hungry, and afraid tends to fade and only the memories of good times remain bright and shining, so that to hear such people talking in any pub in the kingdom you would think all wars were a holiday. It is only when there is unbearable and unjustifiable hardship, when men are unfairly treated, that it remains and rankles, and there are no recollections of this sort among the *Prince of Wales*'s survivors. Whatever her troubles or whatever her difficulties, Captain Leach (still with that persevering smile on his face) was running a good ship. But listen to the "naval correspondent's" version of those days at Scapa Flow between the *Prince of Wales*'s refit and the Churchill trip:

"Their idol, Captain Leach, was away from them. He had not told them that he was injured by blast when his bridge was hit. The crew felt that he would not come back. His removal, they thought, was a reflection on the ship and on themselves.

"Then the chalking on the mess decks began. Like the rumours of 'passive mutiny' and reports of 'indiscipline' it was much exaggerated in the Scapa canteen. The chalking was usually nothing more than 'We want Leach.'"

One's first reaction to this stuff is that the journalist who wrote it knew singularly little about the realities of life aboard a big ship, especially a big ship overcrowded with its extra wartime complement. How would it have been possible for anonymous hands to chalk these messages in the mess decks unseen or undetected? It is quite certain that the majority of the men would never have tolerated it—it is equally certain that any such offending scribble, even if it had been possible to make it unseen, would have been expunged long before it came to the eye of authority. Perhaps some joker did write a message on a wall or perhaps there was a joker who had a passing craze for writing messages on walls. Perhaps there was some really discontented man who did such a thing. Men have written messages on walls since the beginning of time—it is one of the peculiarities of the male sex and the remains of them are found both in the ruins of Pompeii and in the lavatories of large modern railway stations. What of it? Suppose it got picked up and bandied about in the canteens ashore? It might even have been retailed for a space with as much gusto as the story about the *Rodney*'s man and the sheep—and seriously believed just as little. A credulous journalist with his ear to the ground might pick it up and, lacking a sailor's robust and elementary sense of humour, prize it greatly and store it up for future use.

It has proved impossible to discover any surviving memory of this alleged chalking on the mess decks, of the so-called "indiscipline" or of the "mutiny" at all. In fairness it could be admitted that there might be other reasons for this. Men might not wish to discredit their ship by admitting knowledge of it. Only a very few men might have had knowledge of it, for a battleship is a very large place in which no single man knows every other man aboard, or is familiar with what goes on in every part of the ship. But if the latter is the cause of the universally professed ignorance of all this, then automatically it is proved that it must have been small and insignificant. And if it is a case of men not wishing to speak ill of their ship, that also shows a spirit in which anything approaching "mutiny" or even "passive mutiny" could not have existed on any appreciable scale. Of course there was "indiscipline." There is "indiscipline" on any ship and in any type of service unit. Slinger Wood on the *Repulse* made more journeys to the Commander's table than he could ever count and so did many of his mates, but no-one has ever written about "indiscipline" on the *Repulse*. If there are well upwards of a thousand men aboard a ship there is bound to be a long series of petty breaches of discipline and petty charges day by day. It means absolutely nothing, and the whole story of the mutiny probably means absolutely nothing likewise.

The reader must not run away with the impression that the whole of the press is being damned out of hand for the faults of a section of it. Nothing would be more unjust to the legion of newspapermen who were trying to do a job of work reporting the war in spite of tremendous difficulties. These newspapermen were much too busy trying to get their hands on genuine news to waste time in this way, even if they had been inclined to. We shall meet one of them later—O'Dowd

Gallagher, who was the only British journalist on the spot when the *Repulse* and the *Prince of Wales* were sunk. He was there because with a true journalist's "hunch" he correctly divined what a proffered assignment was likely to be, in spite of its being cloaked in security and mystery, and in spite of other journalists having turned it down. He deserved his "scoop" (to use a word more common in lay circles than in Fleet Street) and he went on to write a first-class book called *Retreat in the East*, which has had nothing like the recognition it deserves. This is factual, realistic reporting, full of guts and fire. It is the kind of reporting which a nation at war deserved; and the muck-rakers would have done well to take a lesson from Gallagher and men like him.

When Leach came back to the ship he was wearing the ribbon of the D.S.O. The high days of the *Prince of Wales*'s summer were approaching. She was soon to be the glamour ship, Churchill's Yacht.

CHAPTER
7

IN THE MEANTIME THE "REPULSE" WAS HAVING, QUITE UN-
expectedly, a moment of glamour of her own. Her arrival
at Conception Bay, Newfoundland, short of fuel as she was,
was complicated by the fact that there was no oiler available,
and she had to steam around until one arrived from St. John's
in the morning. Her stay here was very brief, but the men
were allowed a run ashore to a little town called Wibama,
and there, the local inhabitants really did them proud. They
walked or hitch-hiked the four miles in from the jetty: on
the return journey they rode in triumph upon all manner of
transport that ranged from big, shiny American cars to
horses and carts. They were loaded with gifts of all descriptions and Marine Garner has a distinct recollection of one
rating staggering back aboard with an enormous bag of sugar
on his back. It might seem a funny thing to give a sailor,
but when you think of the amount of hot, sweet kye that
was consumed in those long, dreary watches at the guns,
and the amount of scrounging and thieving that went on to

keep it as thick and as sweet as it should be, the gift was pretty appropriate and extremely useful.

From there the ship went to Halifax, Nova Scotia, for repairs, especially to the forward breakwater and the port and starboard forward HA gun barbettes, that had been so unmercifully pounded by the seas in the vain chase of the *Bismarck*. Here there was a fortnight with plenty of shore leave, wonderful hospitality, lashings of food, football matches for the ship's teams and exactly everything that was needed to make them all feel heroes.

This was just what they needed, and it couldn't have come at a better time. In the glow of it all they felt very kindly about the *Rodney*, which after all those months of abuse, swinging at a mooring above her mound of food tins, had after all gone in and helped to sink the *Bismarck*. In fact they were very proud of *Rodney*: in spite of all the bellyaches they were both West country ships and the *Repulse*'s men had a lot of friends and towneys aboard her. They were very proud of her, but they didn't propose to show it.

A few days after they had arrived at Halifax, who should show up but the ruddy *Rodney* in person, to make fast at the next berth, bursting with pride and very full of herself. Do you suppose that she got a hero's welcome from the *Repulse*? In almost any war film men would have crowded *Repulse*'s decks and cheered the *Rodney* in till the harbour rang with their cheering and tears ran down their faces.

In point of fact, what happened was that as the *Rodney* slowly inched her way past them towards her berth a solitary voice from somewhere aboard her shouted "Who sunk the *Bismarck*?" And for a retort from the crowded decks of the *Repulse*, there came a great chorus of sheep noises, as though all the flocks in the New World had been herded in the bowels of their ship.

"Baa! baa! baa!" they roared at the tops of their voices until the harbour echoed with sheep noises instead of cheers, and people not in the know must have thought the *Repulse* a shipload of crazy men.

Now as we have already hinted, there is almost certainly absolutely nothing to this story of the *Rodney*'s man and the sheep. Similar stories were told in all the services, wherever men were billeted in desert and unlovely places. They were told about the Army in the Western Desert, they were told about the RAF in Shaibah, and the variants on sheep included camels and all manner of other creatures. For that matter similar legends were probably told in the armies of Xerxes, the armies of Alexander and the armies of Mohammed—albeit with perhaps a little more truth in those barbarous ages.

"Baa! baa!" cried the *Repulse*'s men, and so *Rodney* was acclaimed after her victory and the *Repulse*'s men got any envy they might have felt healthily out of their systems.

The funny thing was that if anyone else baa'd at one of *Rodney*'s men in a pub or canteen, the *Repulse*'s lot invariably went for him.

Of all this jollification and feasting Slinger Wood (who had been robbed of seeing his handiwork on the *Prince of Wales* sailing the high seas) was able to take his full share, because for some considerable time he had been an exemplary character and was quite free from punishment; furthermore he had just passed his twentieth birthday and so was not merely allowed his rum ration officially but also all-night leave to seven A.M. Within minutes of the ship berthing, a motor boat came alongside from the submarine depot ship *Forth,* and the coxswain of it was his brother's mate. From him he discovered that his brother was on the submarine *Thunderbolt* moored alongside the *Forth.* He couldn't get over there quick enough.

Now before this submarine had been the *Thunderbolt* she had been the *Thetis,* and ninety-nine men had died in her when she went down on her trials in Liverpool Bay. She was to go down again and most of the men then aboard her were to die in their turn. Slinger Wood had been aboard submarines before with his brother at Gosport, and in common with most ordinary people not accustomed to them, he didn't like them. No submarine, however, had succeeded in giving him the feeling of horror he experienced aboard *Thunderbolt*. From having been unable to get aboard her quick enough he couldn't get off her quick enough; but he and his brother, together with the happy villains of Mess 46, spent a very pleasant week in Halifax, and his bank book was in a sorry state when he left—a pity because he was saving up to get married.

It couldn't last, of course, but his downfall did not come until the last night ashore—from which he awoke the following morning with a very large hangover, indeed, and he was an hour adrift getting back to the ship. Here he was welcomed with open arms by Regulating Petty Officer Cawte (the same who had been involved in the breathing licence episode long before), and RPO Cawte thought it was time he got back to his normal routine. And so at nine o'clock he traced his well-worn steps to the Commander's defaulters' table, where he was duly lashed up with seven days' number elevens.

As they were sailing that day with a convoy, he reckoned it would just about last him home, and it turned out to be one of the most comfortable voyages in the whole odyssey of Slinger Wood and the *Repulse*; for about an hour before they sailed a draft came aboard from the *Thunderbolt* and the *Talisman* for passage back to England, and in this draft was his brother, on his way back to a course at Gosport. Thus he both escaped the second sinking of the *Thunderbolt* and was able to give Slinger the voyage of his life. Being the senior among the ratings on passage, Slinger's brother was detailed off to look after the men under punishment. The men under punishment had been detailed off to paint out the recreation space, and here occurs one of those paradoxes which bring civilians who try to study the psychology of servicemen close to insanity. The men on passage had nothing to do and were bored stiff; the men under punishment had a great deal to do and would do anything on the face of the earth to avoid doing it. So Slinger's brother and the rest of his party painted out the recreation space and painted it out well and truly, while the men under punishment got their heads down. The Commander, prowling through the recreation space one day, told off Wood senior for using a paint brush himself. What he didn't know was that not a single man painting was a man under punishment, and that not a single man under punishment was painting.

While this was going on, the *Repulse* safely escorted yet another convoy of Canadian troops across the Atlantic and duly arrived at Greenock the day Slinger's punishment ran out, as arranged.

It was now July 1941, and the sands were running out for the *Repulse*, as well as for the *Prince of Wales*. For the *Repulse*, too, there was to be one more brief spell of summer days, splendour, and admiration. Not quite so splendid, or at any rate not quite so publicised to the four corners of the earth as the splendour of the *Prince of Wales*, but still to be a happy and healing memory for the men of the fine ship that was so soon to become H.M.S. *Anonymous*.

There was no portent of sands running out, nor thought of it, among her men. The only thing there was portent of was leave, persistently rumoured by one of those mess-deck buzzes that originate from heaven knows where and that turn out to be true at least as often as they turn out to be false. Slinger, on the strength of it, made all his plans for his wedding and arranged for his brother to be his best man; and the leave duly arrived—ten days for each watch—just as the buzz said it would. It was the last leave these men were to have from the *Repulse*, and the last time many of them were to see their homes.

Wood and those of his shipmates who lived on Merseyside could well have harked back with regret to that homecoming of just about two years previously, when the leave party had burst out of Lime Street Station into the sunlight of a world still at peace, ousting King Billy's Navy and being cheered by Billies and Paddies alike. There were no crowds to greet them now: servicemen coming and going, especially in that port of many convoys, were too common a sight. It was a different Liverpool too, blacked out, shattered by blitz after blitz that had swept away homes and obliterated familiar landmarks. Only a few weeks before this leave there had been a whole continuous week of raids on the dock area and on Bootle, that had wiped out hundreds of homes, damaged thousands more, and lengthened still further the tale of dead and injured in the long-suffering townships on either side of the estuary. Most of the men found it almost impossible to reconcile themselves to a situation in which their homes and their families and all the familiar things and places that had been part of their lives were under the enemy's fire night after endless night, while they sailed the seas in their great, steel ship—weary, it is true, harassed, cold, wet, and uncomfortable, but never meeting German ships or manning their guns in earnest.

Slinger Wood, for better or worse, had other things to distract him. The business of his marriage was complicated —in common with so many other Merseyside marriages— by the fact that he was a Protestant and his wife a Catholic. At some other time he might have taken a happy-go-lucky view of the business and changed his faith to make matters easier; only it so happened that Canon Bezzant, the *Repulse*'s padre, had carried out on the soul of Slinger Wood as efficient an operation as most of the other operations carried out aboard his ship. He had been confirmed and received his first communion in the *Repulse*'s beautiful little chapel; and how could he turn round and tell the chaplain almost in his next breath that he wished to become a Roman Catholic? This difficulty dragged on through most of the leave until it looked as though the couple would have to be married in desperation by the Registrar. With no more than three days to go, however, Father Burke of St. Nicholas's came to their rescue, got them a special licence, and married them in the imposing background of the pro-Cathedral. Their honeymoon consisted of one day's outing to New Brighton. A photograph, now a little dog-eared, shows the wedding party in all their finery standing self-consciously before the dingy background of a typical Liverpool terrace house that belies the smart uniforms of the men and the gay attire of the women. Behind so many of the men of the *Repulse*, of the *Prince of Wales*, of every other ship in the fleet, of every unit in the Army and the Air Force lay this contrast, generations old and still unresolved. For what were these men fighting? One day it might have to be decided, but it was one of those issues that would have to wait. In no time at all the farewells were being said at Lime Street Station.

Pause for a moment, knowing what they could not know, to see the leave-taking of these men who had so long sailed the seas with impunity, but were now to be sacrificed with their proud ship in one of the most unforgiveable blunders of the war. With Slinger Wood in his compartment were seven other men: Marine Bob Bloxham, who was to hear of his fiancée's death at Freetown and was to be killed himself fighting in the jungle against the Japanese after the ship went down; Able Seaman Sid Anton, who went down with the ship; Able Seaman Nudge Keen, who was lost somewhere on the Malayan coast; Stoker John Dykes, ahead of whom lay four grim years in Japanese captivity on the Burma Railway; Boy Howard, who was drowned; Marine Garner and Able Seaman Bob Hewlett, who, together with Wood, were alone to return to that place before the war was over. Five men out of eight to be sacrificed for a blunder.

The train pulled out to shouts of "Look after yourself!" "See you again soon!" and all the trite phrases that cover such departures.

"I don't think those we left behind," writes Wood, "realised that our concern was mostly for them. The amount of damage that we had each seen during our leave was the main topic of conversation on our return journey, and we were all convinced that the safest place in those days was at sea."

There was something to start the buzzes going in full force when they got back to the ship: the stores they were taking aboard included vast quantities of tropical equipment which, it was quite obvious, would not be required in the North Atlantic, even in the summer. The buzz most favoured was that they were going raider hunting in the South Atlantic— a logical conclusion that, for once, turned out to be completely unjustified. They were, in fact, due for another W.S. convoy—a convoy for the Middle East, which they were to escort all the way round the Cape to Durban, and far north through the Madagascar Channel. Captain Tennant told them it would be the largest convoy they had ever escorted, and this did not impress them at first particularly, because they had escorted many convoys and large ones at that. But when they saw the convoy it staggered them. A troopship convoy is always impressive, even to those who are accustomed to ships, for it is only in wartime and in these circumstances that so many really big ships are seen together at sea at one time. A man would not have thought there were so many great liners and cargo liners in the world as there were in this convoy, steaming at speed in orderly ranks, with the destroyer escorts rolling and plunging along far distant on the flanks, and the battle-cruiser herself ploughing her way proud and mighty in the midst of it. It was so vast, it was spread over such an area of sea that it seemed a target the enemy could not possible miss: as all *Repulse*'s convoys did, this convoy, the greatest and the last, reached its destination without the loss of a single ship. Before the ships anchored under the sun-baked, pitiless rocks of Aden, the *Repulse* would have left them on her way back to Durban and thence to Ceylon. She had already been allocated to the Far East: the blunder that was to send her to the bottom of the South China Sea was already half perpetrated.

The day before Slinger Wood made his appearance at the altar of St. Nicholas's, the *Prince of Wales* had put to sea from Scapa Flow on an errand which was a very well-kept secret indeed, and which the German High Command would have given their very eyeballs to know about. In a matter of ten days it would be headline news in the four corners of the world: as late as the morning of sailing, officers and ratings alike were completely in the dark about it, as well they might be. It was obvious to them, from the disruption of the internal economy of the ship that they were to have among them a VIP or VIPs of some sort or other. H. V. Morton tells us that the officers ran a sweepstake on it. Three of them drew outside chances, these being (in order of apparent probability) taking Rudolf Hess back to Germany, taking Mr. Cochran's Young Ladies to Dakar, and taking Winston Churchill to see Roosevelt. Lower deck controversy was so fierce that it swamped all "differences of opinion" over football and boxing: vast quantities of money and rum were involved in it, and even some blood.

So that on the morning of August 4—a morning of poor visibility, with low-lying mist and driving rain, a typical Scapa morning—the ship's company was mustered on deck in a state of suspense and high excitement. The new destroyer *Oribi* was racing towards her at full speed across the turbulent waters of the narrow sea, performing those antics which delight the hearts of beholders and make destroyers the most exhibitionist of ships. Straining eyes made out a great deal of brass, somewhat damp: on the bridge was a man in a peaked cap without any brass whatsoever. He was smoking a cigar. Audibly all over the ship went round the astonished murmur, "It's Winston!"

It *was* Winston, and he was on his way to a secret rendezvous with President Roosevelt at Placentia Bay in Newfoundland, from which was to emerge a declaration which, at the time, seemed beyond all doubt to be one of the most spectacular events in human history—the signing of the Atlantic Charter. With him were all the Chiefs of Staff, a score of very senior officers and civilians, three top-rank journalists, and President Roosevelt's personal representative, Harry Hopkins. They were probably the most valuable and vulnerable cargo any ship had ever carried across the seas in time of war, and their accommodation had involved a major reorganisation and rendered a large section of the wardroom homeless. The *Prince of Wales*, for the nonce, was no longer merely a battleship—she was Churchill's Yacht. Whether the two roles could be satisfactorily combined might remain to be seen, and what effect all this would have on the working-up of the ship was obvious to any experienced observer. For the moment no-one worried about such considerations—nor could they fairly be blamed. It was a tremendous honour, and the *Prince of Wales*'s people felt very proud of themselves.

"We felt," recalls our friend Tudor (now thoroughly settled down and not hankering after destroyers any more) "as though nothing could touch us with him on board."

H. V. Morton had other thoughts. As the great ship put to sea with her three attendant destroyers, *Harvester, Havelock,* and *Hesperus,* as Orkney became a blur in the mist astern and then faded from sight altogether, he thought of another voyage, another mission which was perhaps the only one in history to bear any similarity to this—Lord Kitchener's mission to Russia in the previous war, in the cruiser *Hampshire.* Kitchener and the *Hampshire* were drowned off the coast of Hoy, and the whole mission and the end of it was so fantastic and improbable, that books are still being written about it. How would Churchill's mission end? Everyone of the relatively few people in the secret must have been shaking in their shoes at the thought of all these important and well-nigh irreplaceable eggs in one basket being committed to the battleground of the Atlantic. There can hardly have been one of them who did not feel that both the Prime Minister, his staff, and the service chiefs, would have been infinitely safer being flown across the ocean in small parcels in bombers. It has never been revealed how much argument and battle there was behind the scenes, but it is a practical certainty that more than one attempt was made to dissuade the Prime Minister. It is equally a practical certainty that no-one got any glory for trying to do so. He got his way about taking this ship to Newfoundland, just as he was to get his way later about sending her to Singapore. At least, in this case, it brought her fame instead of destruction. Maybe Alf Tudor was right—maybe nothing could touch them while Winston was aboard!

What lay behind Churchill's choice of a battleship to take him to Newfoundland at this time has much to do with the qualities that endeared him to the British people in those dark and dangerous days. If we understand them, we shall also understand better why he pressed so stubbornly for the dispatch of the *Prince of Wales* to the Far East. He was incurably flamboyant, he loved spectacular gestures; and there was surely a need for them in those grim years. His personal courage was undoubtedly of a high order (later he had to be restrained from appearing on the Normandy beach-heads) and there was a need for the courageous example he always set. Though not over-fussy about his personal dignity, he had a keen sense of the dignity of what he represented, and one of the things he represented was British domination of the seas: therefore he probably could just not see himself being bundled unceremoniously out of the belly of a bomber like a consignment of NAAFI tea. But above all, there was his own curious and highly personal mystical conception of battleships. Most ordinary people feel something of it when they look at a monster ship of war—or rather, felt something of it, because, although capital ships and their ways are referred to in the present tense in much of this book, they are already things of the past. Most ordinary people feel something of it, a lot of people feel it strongly, and people connected with the sea can feel it as an emotion almost as strong as physical love. Churchill's reaction to battleships— complex, obsession, fetish, call it what you like according to your feelings about the man and his works—was of this order. It overrode all reason and flouted all logical considerations. Certainly he knew, as a matter of cold intellectual appraisal, that the *Prince of Wales* was neither unsinkable nor invincible. Had he not himself bitterly campaigned about the defects in her main armament and what he thought was a flaw in her horizontal armour? Inevitably he must have read both Rear-Admiral Wake-Walker's and Admiral Tovey's despatches, though it is to his credit if Wake-Walker's prejudices about the *Prince of Wales* had not influenced him unduly. Weighing the chances, he must have known that she could be destroyed if the U-boats and the Luftwaffe found her out—just as he must have known later that she could not stand up against the entire Japanese Navy if the whole Japanese Navy came out. But intellectual appraisal counted for nothing. The Prime Minister of Great Britain was going to meet the President of the United States, and the pair of them were going to make history between them; and reasoning be damned, the Prime Minister and his entourage would go in a great ship, a mystery larger than life, riding the seas in glory, while all the winds of the heavens in diapason played "Rule Britannia." It was a magnificent conception: it was also a gamble that paid off. The world applauded. Britain's stock went up, and morale at home received a much-needed uplift.

But there was one thing that was utterly and inexcusably wrong about the whole business—the choice of the *Prince of Wales* for the job. We already know too well that she was both a new ship and a new ship in trouble. We know that she was faced with the appallingly difficult problem of "working-up" in wartime in a fraction of the time that would be allotted for the purpose in peace. We know that her working-up had already been interrupted by a major naval action and a spell in the dockyard for battle damage repairs and modifications. We know that, in the unanimous opinion of all competent naval authorities, to interrupt the working-up of a new ship is disastrous. Yet here was the *Prince of Wales* with her internal arrangements completely disrupted, her routine disorganised, her very accommodation turned upside-down, on duty as Churchill's Yacht—or more appropriately Churchill's floating fortress.

> *Although Mr. Churchill was not always visible to the ship* [writes Morton], *evidence of him was bellowed all over the battleship by loud-speaker. Men in the engine room, sailors on the mess decks, Marine sentries and others smiled with delight as they heard unaccustomed orders shouted such as 'Will Mr. Martin please go at once to the Prime Minister on the bridge?' or 'The Prime Minister requests the presence of Brigadier Dykes upon the bridge.' Hearing such orders the crew caught a reflected glory and knew that this voyage was like no other.*

This was all very well for the crew: of course they loved it, and of course they felt the reflected glory shining upon them, but the fact is that this was not what the ship's loud-speaker system was for, any more than the whole business was what the ship was for. To a ship fully worked-up and fully efficient the interruption would have been of little or no consequence. To the *Prince of Wales* it could well have been disastrous. It could, in another major action, have weighed the scales between victory and defeat, between survival and sinking. The fact that she was ultimately sunk by air action with no real chance to defend herself properly has no bearing on the matter, for certainly neither the Prime Minister nor anyone else had any foreknowledge of how the *Prince of Wales* was going to be sunk.

There were other battleships. There were other modern

battleships. There was *King George V*, Admiral Tovey's flagship in the Home Fleet, which had been commissioned months longer than the *Prince of Wales*. There were older battleships, as fast and as well protected for all practical purposes and much more reliable from a gunnery point of view. Why choose the *Prince of Wales?* It is another great tribute to Captain Leach, his officers and his men that the damage to her working-up process caused by this further interruption was apparently kept to a minimum.

There would have been one circumstance in which the choice of the *Prince of Wales* to be Churchill's Yacht could have been considered a brilliant piece of morale building. That circumstance would have been if the journalists' chatter about her had been true—if the morale of her complement had really been at rock bottom, if she had really been branded as the ship that ran away, if there had been "passive mutiny" chalking on the mess decks, and all the rest of it. Here, straight away would have been a master stroke of rehabilitation, a demonstration to her people, and to the rest of the fleet, as well as such outsiders who knew about such things, that they stood as highly in the Prime Minister's eyes as any other ship, that they were worthy to be his guardians and protectors. But this does not hold water. It only holds water if you believe the journalists' gossip and the story of the "mutiny," which the writer categorically does not. And furthermore, the very idea of it is self-contradictory because Churchill cannot be regarded as a complete and utter fool, and only a complete and utter fool would have entrusted himself, the Chiefs of Staff, and other extremely valuable people to the keeping of a palpably mutinous ship. So that not only is the suggestion that the Churchill voyage was an antidote to the mutiny a silly suggestion—it also joins itself to the other evidence to help prove that the mutiny was a legend with the slenderest of foundations.

The funny thing about the Churchill trip is that in spite of their pride at the honour of it, its actual details bulk remarkably small in the memory of survivors. They remember the church service which Roosevelt attended, they remember the Prime Minister and President gripping each other by the shoulder, seeming immensely pleased with themselves and each other and seeming also to be sharing some private joke between them. They remember the quantities of ice cream they got aboard the American ships. Boy Williams remembers getting "some sort of souvenir" but cannot for the life of him remember what it was, and in any case what is left of it lies in his ditty box at the bottom of the Gulf of Siam. Signalman Seddon, that mine of accurate information who would have had the dates and times of things as firmly recorded in his excellent memory as he has so many other things, is unable to help us because he was absent from the ship—having been detailed with a wireless operator from *King George V* to join the tanker *Black Ranger* in a raid on Petsamo and Spitzbergen.

There are very good reasons for their lack of memory—quite apart from the fact that there was a lot of war still to come to them, that a lot of things have happened since and that much time has gone by. For the whole of their time at sea in both directions they were continuously at action stations—Captain Leach, incidentally, was on the bridge himself for the whole of that time. Truth be known, apart from hearing those continual messages coming in over the loudspeakers, apart from seeing him at Scapa, at Placentia, at Iceland, and occasionally in the distance about the ship if they were lucky, they had very little contact with him or with the important people who accompanied him. If, after all, you seek intimate details about visiting personalities at Claridge's or the Ritz, you don't go to the man who stokes the central heating boilers, or oils the machinery that works the lifts.

The story of the voyage itself is quite briefly told. The battleship with her precious cargo and her destroyers set course westward at high speed into a rising wind and a steepening sea. The journalists (and no doubt other more distinguished landsmen aboard who have left no record of their feelings) found that the great mass of steel which had looked so imposing to them in the anchorage could perform the most alarming and disturbing antics. As the day wore on into evening and the weather worsened, speed was reduced to eighteen knots in the hope of being able to keep the destroyer escort in company. Shortly after midnight the attempt was given up: the destroyers were detached, the battleship put on speed again and continued her way across the Atlantic utterly and completely alone. In the midst of all this Mr. Churchill had entertained the wardroom to a showing of one of the films he had brought with him, sitting companionably among the officers in the mess dress of the Royal Yacht Squadron. He had thereafter retired to bed, but the officer of the watch, who was summoned to him shortly afterwards in the Admiral's suite astern, found him less ceremonially attired. He demanded to be taken to the Admiral's sea cabin on the bridge away from the appalling mechanical racket in the Admiral's quarters. There he slept well—so well in fact that he decided to stay there for the rest of the voyage. The following day he admired the airiness of the warrant officers' mess, so presently the warrant officers were evicted and he was given it as his day quarters in lieu of the Admiral's suite. The warrant officers, however, were not offered the latter in exchange.

On Wednesday the storm abated: its place was taken by thick fog into which the battleship still steamed relentlessly, so that those who had been thinking about the *Hampshire* were able to think about the *Titanic* instead. Three Canadian destroyers from Iceland now picked them up and took the place of the original escort. In the calmer weather the journalists and VIPs were able to explore the ship and have its wonders explained to them: these included the marvels of discharging guns by pressing a button which we have already heard about, the fantastic number of loaves produced every day in the ship's bakery, the serving out of spirits, the Captain's Request Men, the inspection of the ship's cats, and other show pieces. The Thursday was uneventful and on the Friday a full dress rehearsal of the ceremonial for the reception of the American President was held; and the film show that night was *Lady Hamilton,* in which Nelson's death scene so affected the Prime Minister that Morton saw him unashamedly wipe his eyes. On Saturday morning, August 9th, they made rendezvous with an escort of American destroyers who took them into Placentia Bay where, amid a great assembly of American ships of war, President Roosevelt awaïted them in the cruiser *Augusta.* The *Prince of Wales*'s crew manned ship, the band of the Royal Marines played "The Star-Spangled Banner," the Prime Minister and his attendant officers stood to the salute and Captain Leach, who had had no sleep for the greater part of a week, appeared on the quarter-deck looking like a tailor's dummy.

If there is perhaps one impression outstanding among those who were there at that moment, it is the contrast between the *Prince of Wales* and the American ships—still in their full peace-time splendour with snowy decks and gleaming brass work. Although the British ship was almost fresh from the dockyard, she looked war-weary and travel-stained in her dark camouflage. It was not the last time she was to sail out of a world at war into a world at peace: on this occasion as well as the one that was to follow it was a world the peace of which was very soon to be shattered. The American ships were not to wear their peacetime dress for very much longer. There was for them to be at least as big a blunder as the blunder that sent the *Prince of Wales* to the China Sea: in fact it was part and parcel of the same blunder and the blunder was being perpetrated at this very moment when American officers were gazing with something like awe at a ship that had been through battle—the blunder of which the price was Pearl Harbour and the loss of the Pacific Ocean.

Shortly after the ship's arrival the Prime Minister and his

staff disappeared aboard the *Augusta:* his talks with the President and the discussions of the Service Chiefs with each other occupied the whole of the time between then and the following Tuesday morning, apart from formal visits and informal occasions. Two completely separate streams of life were being lived in the vast anchorage of Placentia Bay. One, the life behind closed doors of the statesmen and the chiefs of staff battling out their world problems and the complexities of the relations between two allies, one of whom was at war and the other still at peace. The other life was that of the ordinary people who were not concerned in these discussions at all—the Americans and the British, fraternising with each other, yet fraternising through the barrier that divides war from peace. More than one of the British ratings felt that, in spite of the kindness of their hosts, in spite of the gifts that were lavished on them, the barrier could not be passed by the people on either side. Throughout all the days there was immense activity in the anchorage—craft of every description coming and going on all the mysterious errands that are a part of great fleets and great occasions. On one of these occasions there arrived aboard the British ship fifteen hundred cardboard cartons, one for every man aboard her: each carton contained an orange, two apples, two hundred cigarettes and half a pound of cheese, and they were a personal gift from the President of the United States. Half a generation later it sounds an odd sort of gift in a world that has forgotten that cigarettes were things of great value and that cheese was almost price-less. There is no evidence that the President's gift appeared strange or that it was not appreciated. Later, of course, the men also received souvenir photographs.

As night came on the *Prince of Wales* blossomed from a dark, grim camouflaged bulk to a thing of light. She was free of the blackout for the first time since she was a half-formed hulk in the dockyard of Birkenhead.

The Atlantic Charter, which emerged from the discussions

which were going on behind closed doors on the *Augusta*, loomed so large in the eyes of the world at the time and has done since that it is not often realised that anything else was discussed or decided at all. To people in beleaguered Britain, the Charter was a splendid, a shining thing that came upon them suddenly in the midst of the drabness and the weariness of that dreadful year. The writer of this book, still a junior and frustrated NCO in an infantry battalion, bogged down on a parade ground from which there seemed to be no escape in all eternity, vividly remembers the news of it coming over a welfare radio in a sunlit and barren barrack room. Suddenly there was interest and light and hope; suddenly there was a reminder that the world would not be a barrack room forever, although it still might be a barrack room for a very long time. Suddenly there was memory of the things that had been in our minds when at last, after all the dithering and dallying, we went to war; and for a little space there seemed once more some purpose in it all. If, indeed, the Atlantic Charter was a more nebulous document than it appeared to be at the time, let us remember what it meant to us in those days and let us remember also the men who were responsible for it; since presently we shall have to say some hard things about at least one of them. And if the hope of the Atlantic Charter was yet another hope that was to be belied, that is no concern of this book.

Certainly the Atlantic Charter got all the limelight, but very many other things were discussed and one of the things that came in for its fair share of discussion was the Far East —the Japanese menace, which in Churchill's own words lay at that time in "a sinister twilight." It is perhaps not wholly true to say that the seeds of the blunder which put paid to the *Repulse* and the *Prince of Wales* were sown at this meeting —they had been sown long before. Nor is it true to say that the blunder was perpetrated at this meeting. It is, however, true to say that it arose in a large measure out of what was

said and done at this meeting; and what was said and done at
this meeting arose out of some misconceptions which are, in
the light of later events, almost impossible to credit. The
most important of the misconceptions were, perhaps, three
in number: that the Japanese would on no account risk war
with the Western Powers while Russia remained unbroken
and she herself was bogged down in China; that there was
all the time in the world to negotiate with the Japanese in
the face of a steadily deteriorating situation; and that the
Japanese were not in a position to survive a war for long if
by any chance they were so ill-advised as to start one. That
these misconceptions should have existed passes from the
incredible to the fantastic when we are told that the Americans had been in possession of the Japanese war ciphers since
1940.

Japan was in alliance with the Fascist powers of Germany
and Italy: the Berlin-Rome-Tokyo axis had been forged
long before the war. This had been further strengthened by
the Tripartite Pact of September 1940, which committed
the Japanese to enter the European war on the Axis side if
the United States entered it on behalf of Britain. A month
before the Placentia meeting, an agreement with Vichy
France had ceded Japan bases in Indochina from which,
given sufficient force and insufficient interference, they could
control the whole South China Sea. The reaction of the
United Sates had been to impose economic sanctions and,
as the Japanese Fleet was alleged to have only eighteen
months' reserve of oil, these sanctions must bear heavily
upon her. It was the nearest move to war that Roosevelt
dare make; further than that he could not go. And from the
Atlantic Charter meeting Churchill telegraphed a warning,
that any further Japanese moves would mean war. How
impotent a threat this must have seemed from a Britain
fighting a lone battle on the other side of the world! How
impotent it must have seemed to a Japan where, in October

1941, Prince Fumimaro Konoye's government of compromise had been ousted by the war party of General Hideki Tojo, a Japan to whose imperial ambitions the whole of South-East Asia lay wide open, a Japan better prepared and better informed than anyone in the Western hemisphere dreamed! Churchill and Roosevelt could discuss, decide how long they could temporize with Japan, agree in a perhaps uneasy conviction that Japan could not be lunatic enough to pit herself against the West: one and one only out of all the allied statesmen appears to have had the picture of Japan and Japanese intentions in correct proportion in his mind—Jan Christiaan Smuts, perhaps the most intelligent of them all.

Churchill, in his own history of the war, reveals very little about that part of the Placentia conferences which dealt with Japan. What was decided and what was agreed must be deduced from the fact that almost immediately after his return he started the long chain of memoranda and discussions which ended up by the Admiralty's opposition being steam-rollered flat and the *Prince of Wales* sent with the *Repulse* to Singapore.

So with neither thought nor knowledge of how their own very particular fate was involved in what was going on behind closed doors, the *Prince of Wales*'s complement received the President at Church Parade on the Sunday morning. They sang, Morton tells us, a hymn chosen by the Prime Minister, "Onward Christian Soldiers," and one chosen by the President, "Eternal Father, Strong to Save."

> *Now as the voices rose and fell* [he wrote] *a situation that was almost intolerable in its uncalculated emotionalism reached breaking-point. I have seen many poignant, heart-searching ceremonies in my time. I saw the Victory March through London at the end of the last War. I was present in St. Paul's when King George V and Queen Mary returned thanks for victory. I was in Westminster Abbey when the Unknown Soldier was buried. I saw*

the Menin Gate unveiled upon the blasted ramparts of
Ypres. I saw George V carried to his grave. I was in the
House of Commons when a king gave up his crown, and
in Westminster Abbey when another king was anointed.

All these events pulled at the heart in their different
ways, and the scene upon the quarter-deck of a British
battleship in war-time, yet so far from the War, was of
that order too. We from England had come to it fresh
from two bitter years of struggle, years in which some
of our best friends thought our time had come. But it
had not, and we held on alone; and war can be very
lonely at times. The scene before us upon our battleship
that morning was certainly a symbol of unity, might it
not also have been a promise of alliance?

Maybe it was a promise of alliance. Alliance there was to
be, but this ship would never see it. The hymn the President
had chosen, a hymn sung in ships and seamen's churches
and chapels the whole world over, was more terribly appropriate on that quarter-deck than could possibly be imagined.

There was a great deal of photographing, there was a
luncheon, there was a day of anti-climax in which the pressmen were allowed ashore. The day after that, the good-byes
were said, and the *Prince of Wales* sailed out of her world of
peace back into a hostile and U-boat-infested sea. No official
announcement about the meeting had been made to the
world, nor had the curtain of security yet been drawn aside
for the merest fraction, but it was quite unthinkable that
such a show could have been staged without any whisper of
it at all reaching enemy ears; and late on the night after his
ship had left the shelter of Placentia Bay, Captain Leach
received a signal that German Intelligence was without
doubt aware that the meeting had taken place, that there was
reason to suppose it either knew or suspected where. Early
the following morning he spoke to the ship's company over
the loudspeakers. He warned them that U-boat attack must
be expected at any moment and that they must also be

prepared for air attack when they came within range. Yet all that day—a calm day—the great ship, closely hugged by her destroyers, carved her way onwards unscathed through the seas, vibrating to the thrust of engines and screws and leaving her mighty wake behind her. The Prime Minister again had his film show. The following day the weather broke and perhaps this was the salvation of the ship, and of Mr. Churchill, for the U-boat plot indeed seemed to show a concentration right across her course. She was steaming now for Iceland, where she was due to call on the sixteenth for Mr. Churchill to inspect an American base there.

There was no film show that night: Mr. Churchill was indisposed. There was a broadcast instead from London by Mr. Clement Attlee. From it officers and men of the *Prince of Wales* learned for the first time what had been happening at Placentia Bay—at least they heard it made public to the world that the meeting had taken place "at sea." They heard the terms of the Atlantic Charter. They also knew that whether or not there had been any doubt about it before, German Intelligence and the whole world knew about it now. The ship altered course twice that day to avoid reported U-boat packs.

The day after that—Friday, August 15—a large convoy of merchant ships making its way in good order eastwards towards the British Isles at a plodding eight knots, became aware of a large ship escorted by destroyers overhauling them at speed. It was not for them a pleasant or welcome sight. It could have been any one of a number of possible German raiders—the *Scharnhorst*, the *Gneisenau*, the *Hipper*, the *Prinz Eugen*, the very *Tirpitz* herself at large and in pursuit of them. Their escort consisted of corvettes only, and the corvettes appeared to be surprisingly undisturbed by what they saw, for they had been warned by radio. It was no German raider: it was the *Prince of Wales* which in spite of the extreme peril of her situation had altered course yet again on Mr. Churchill's personal insistence to steam right through this convoy at sea. It was one of those flamboyant gestures which the Prime Minister could not resist. Call it folly if you like, for it undoubtedly was; call it madness to expose this precious, irreplaceable ship; call it irresponsible, lunatic to add to the peril in which his own person stood, together with the persons of so many whose loss would have been a crippling blow to Britain's war machine. Call it anything you like: you have to take off your hat to this piece of irrepressible showmanship. It brings back just the faintest of memories of the spirit of those dangerous years, the faintest of memories of why and how Churchill loomed larger than life to a united nation at war. By all logic, Churchill should have been sunk. By all logic, Britain herself should have been sunk months before. Logic made no sense to the English in those years. The *Prince of Wales*—and surely this was one of her glorious moments which are an abiding part of her memory —steamed through the ranks of the convoy at twenty-two knots with Churchill on her bridge, waving and gesturing like old Father Neptune himself; and defying U-boats and all the perils of sea and sky, she turned about and steamed right through the convoy again.

Early next morning they arrived in Iceland and the journalists admired the wild scenery of this rugged land, thrown up for them in a rare burst of sunlight. The ratings were somewhat less enthusiastic: they had seen Iceland before and they had seen a lot of scenery of this kind since their war began. Too much of their time seemed to have been spent in places like Hvalfjord and Scapa. But at least it was a harbour, and they were glad of any harbour. For the last week, continuously at action stations with all the extra vigilance demanded by the hunting U-boats, had tired them very much indeed. The *Prince of Wales* might be a modern ship, she might have all sorts of comforts and conveniences for seamen that had not been thought necessary in previous generations; but nothing could relieve the misery of the watch on the guns in bitter, stormy weather—continuously on the alert, always cold, wet and uncomfortable and desperately short of sleep. Even in ordinary watch-keeping, men slept so deeply and so greedily that they would have to be shaken and pummelled back into consciousness and a man's best pal would shake and pummell as hard as anyone else, grudging every moment of rest snatched by the sleeper and denied to him. "It was torture," writes Alf Tudor, "to see some of the boys struggling and moaning getting out of their hammocks."

But on the guns even the comfort of their hammocks was denied them. They snatched odd hours or fractions of hours cramped up into such space as they could find in a space in which there was little enough room to move about upright, let alone lie down. Hardest hit of them all was the communication number, usually a boy rating who might not be much more than sixteen. With his earphones clamped about his head, it was very difficult for him to rest, and indeed it was better for him not to rest, because if he rested he might drop off to sleep and then anything might happen. The other men used to give the boys a break now and then as far as they could and take over the headphones themselves for a spell. Sandwiches and tea were the most they could expect for food. The petty officer in charge of Tudor's 5.25 turret probably never realised how close he came to assassination, for he always seemed to have managed to provide himself with a small bottle of rum and he drank the lot himself. It must have been well nigh unbearable.

So Iceland was a relief. Something much more important than the Atlantic Charter was afoot in Iceland: the Americans had only a few weeks before landed troops there and were, moreover, themselves escorting convoys of American ships to these shores. It was these troops the Prime Minister was to inspect. It was really the first important move by the United States into the active theatre of war. But inspection and all, the rest was a bare twelve hours: at eight-thirty in the evening the battleship sailed on the last leg of her journey. Throughout the whole of Sunday—a contrast of a Sunday to the brilliance and calm water against which the previous Sunday's church service had been set—she ploughed and buffeted her way onwards towards Scapa. The Prime Minister did his rounds of the ship, was entertained by the gunroom and the wardroom. He attended his last film show. And early the following morning they sailed into their base with their guns firing. Scapa itself did not seem to be impressed: it had seen the coming and going of so many great ships and so many important people that another great ship and another important person (even with the Atlantic Charter and much else beside) was nothing to it. The rain came down as solidly and continuously as it had come down on the morning of their departure—indeed it might never have stopped. In the rain Churchill addressed the ship's company. The ship's company cheered him; and he was gone.

But if Scapa was not impressed, the rest of the world was. A glamour-thirsty people soaked up the story of the ship and her tremendous mission. Heaven alone knows how many pictures of the ship appeared in the days that followed in newspapers and periodicals and magazines, newsreels, and every other conceivable medium—pictures of the ship, pictures of her officers and men, pictures of Churchill and Roosevelt, pictures of the figures of both nations surrounding both Churchill and Roosevelt. Even in the days when the *Repulse* had sailed on her imperial missions bearing the heir to the throne to South America and South Africa amid all the pomp of peace, there can hardly have been a ship so much photographed and so much illustrated, so much written about, talked about, as this ship was now. She had been denied the ceremonial beginnings of other ships, she had had secrecy and blackout for her launching and for her commissioning in place of pride and pageantry. She had been pitchforked into battle in the sub-arctic seas almost before she was really a ship at all and she had been surrounded with a dark and sinister web of nameless and unworthy rumour;

she had been belittled by Admirals and denied credit for what she had done. Now all this was made up to her. She was a glamour ship, she was Churchill's Yacht. Her days were numbered but she was to remain a glamour ship for such span of life as was left to her.

CHAPTER

8

LET US LEAVE THE "PRINCE OF WALES" FOR A MOMENT, triumphant and basking in her glory in the rain and mist of the Orkneys, and the somewhat utilitarian junketing of Scapa Flow, and look at a very contrasting scene on the other side of the world. It is a scene which was presently to provide a better backcloth for the glamour ship than her grim anchorage of the northern isles—a scene to which the *Repulse*, having left Scapa behind forever, was already steaming.

On the other side of the world lay the great fortress of Singapore. It thought itself impregnable and so did most of the rest of the world: in fact it was as impregnable as the *Prince of Wales* was unsinkable—it was as impregnable as a toy fortification of cardboard. It was the focus and the symbol of British naval and commercial power in the Far Eastern seas which it had dominated as long as men cared to remember. It basked in a sunlight far removed from war. It knew neither blackout nor air-raid warnings, nor bombs; it knew nothing of battle-scarred ships, limping home with their dead and their dying, or of decimated convoys struggling in to port. In fact it lay in that sinister twilight of Mr. Churchill's phrase: it was a fool's paradise and a breeding ground for blunders of the first water.

For its defence at sea—and indeed for the maintenance of British naval supremacy in an area where it had been unchallenged for a hundred years—it had two old D-class light cruisers and two old destroyers in the immediate vicinity, two more old destroyers and eight motor torpedo boats at Hong Kong, far to the north on the Chinese coast. These and the naval base were under the command of Vice-Admiral Sir Geoffrey Layton, who bore the imposing title of Commander-in-Chief, China Station. There were also two Australian destroyers in the area; away to the south-east in Australian waters were three cruisers, two destroyers, and one Free French light cruiser. At Auckland there were two New Zealand cruisers, and the Dutch in Java had three light cruisers, six destroyers, and thirteen submarines. At Manila was the American Asiatic Fleet, the name of which was as misleading as the name of Admiral Layton's command, for it mustered no more than three cruisers, thirteen destroyers, and twenty-nine submarines. The main American strength was concentrated on Pearl Harbour, six thousand miles away, and for all practical purposes off the edge of the world: in any case, America was not in the war. It is true that these forces were no smaller in size and fire-power than the forces which had sustained the British overlordship of these seas in the nineteenth century, but circumstances had changed very much: we were no longer asserting ourselves over mediaeval kingdoms armed with antique and ineffective weapons but, in the case of Japan at least, against a people which had thirstily absorbed the mechanical trappings of western civilisation and western war, had equipped itself with a modern fleet and modern aircraft, and enjoyed the facilities for battle practice on the Chinese mainland for the greater part of twenty years.

For the air defence of Singapore, under Air Vice-Marshal Pulford, there were a few squadrons of Brewster Buffaloes —American lease-lend aircraft of short range, poor performance, and inferior armament, quite useless for the Mediterranean or the European theatres of war. There were a few Catalina flying boats.

On land there were no defences at all, bar the narrow strait that ran between Singapore island and the mainland—making the whole elaborate fortress rather like a stage set with one side missing. North of this stretched the jungle of Malaya, held by a few battalions of troops, thin on the ground, badly equipped and badly cared for, insufficient in numbers and weapon-power even to defend effectively the landing grounds on which the Brewster Buffaloes were based. Malaya, as a glance at the map will show, is a long, thin tongue of land, stretching southwards from the mainland towards Sumatra; it is narrowest near its northern borders, where the Kra Isthmus, barely fifty miles across, joins it to Siam and Indochina. It is said that even Mr. Churchill himself was unaware, till the tragedy of the Far East was almost played out, that the defences of Singapore faced seaward only; and no-one at all seems to have grasped the fact that the Kra Isthmus could have been made into a forward defence line for the whole of Malaya and for Singapore.

Any suggestion of fortifying the Kra Isthmus would have raised an outcry in the Foreign Office—any evidence of military preparations around the Siamese border raised an outcry from the Foreign Office, which was convinced that any such moves would upset Britain's diplomatic relations with Siam; and this in itself was part of a nineteenth century attitude based on information which shows no evidence of having been amended since Queen Victoria's reign. It required no maladjustment of diplomatic relations to make the Siamese turn against us: they had already turned against us and were ready to welcome with open arms the

Japanese, the saviours of Asia. The Malayans, confidently reported by people who had known the country for years and honestly and truly should have known better, to be loyal and deeply attached to Britain, were equally ready to welcome the Japanese and the country was riddled with fifth column activities. (Italy had been christened by Mr. Churchill "the soft underbelly of the Axis" and how we all gloried in that luscious and entirely appropriate phrase! Neither he nor any-one else had said anything about the soft underbelly of the British Empire.)

Now there were very good reasons why this area was starved of ships, starved of aircraft and starved of troops. The situation was part and parcel of that "sinister twilight" of Mr. Churchill's. It was inevitable that it should have been starved when the whole weight of war in the western world fell on Britain alone, and something of the situation had been fore-seen in the Admiralty's first appraisal of the war early in 1939. "I am sure," says Churchill himself, "nothing we could have spared at this time, even at the cost of wrecking the Middle East theatre or cutting off supplies to the Soviet Union, would have changed the march of fate in Malaya"——al-though he also said in his Guildhall banquet speech that every preparation to defend British interests in the Far East had been made, and he also said repeatedly that he could not envisage a Japanese attack in force on Malaya. But people on the spot, from the Commander-in-Chief, Air Vice-Marshal Sir Robert Brooke-Popham downwards, did not see themselves being starved, neglected, or ill-equipped. With the very evidence before their eyes, they still regarded them-selves as omnipotent and impregnable. They fell into the most extravagant extremities of self-deception. The Brewster Buffaloes, Air Vice-Marshal Pulford confidently asserted, "were good enough for Singapore." They were not afraid of Japan: five days before Pearl Harbour, Brooke-Popham told correspondents that Japan did not know which way to turn and that Tojo was scratching his head. They regarded war as an unfortunate circumstance afflicting the other half of the world, from which they were happily far removed; they had air-raid precautions of a sort which were so efficient that the night Japanese aircraft first appeared above the city, the man whose job it was to turn off the street lights could not be found. They were not bothered by the establishment of Japanese air bases in Indochina: they thought that the Japanese were "not very good at aircraft."

Yes, the Japanese were "not very good at aircraft." They were short of oil; they had fought themselves to a standstill in China. We ourselves had comforted ourselves with a number of similar illusions about Germany in the period of the phony war. Nobody seemed to understand that what had been phony in the phony war in Europe could be just as phony in the Far East. Because in point of fact there was nothing phony about Japanese war preparations or war plans, and if use had been made among other things of the Japanese war ciphers that had been in American hands for a good twelve months, everyone, including the good-time empire-builders of Singapore, would have known about them. There was certainly nothing phony about the Mitsubishi aircraft at Saigon, the weapons with which they were equipped or the training of the men who flew them.

Lulled by their feeling of false security, the men of Singapore neither protested against their lack of equipment nor asked for the merest gleaning of the supplies that were becoming available for other theatres of war. Warn against the dangers mounting against them they could not, for they had no appreciation of these dangers—at least, there is no evidence that they had. All very fine that they should accept the priority of the Middle East and of supplies for Russia; all very well that they should understand that frittering away of supplies, equipment, and men on half-a-dozen theatres of war at once would, end in no theatre being properly equipped or armed or manned. Was there any need to carry the process further by pretending that they had all they needed, that the defence of the Malay Peninsula and all that depended on it was assured, that there was all the time in the world to reinforce themselves against the rising menace of Japan? For this very pretence lulled the War Cabinet into a state of false security about Malaya and the Far East, and there cannot be the slightest doubt that no-one at home, from the Prime Minister downwards, fully envisaged the true nakedness of Singapore, the true peril of Malaya—and through these—the appalling threat to Burma, India, Australia, New Zealand, and all those territories through which Mr. Duff Cooper's stately (but somewhat rapid and cursory) progress took him in search of material for his report.

Supposing Air Vice-Marshal Pulford had begged for just a few Spitfires, General Percival for a few more troops, and a few tanks, and modern anti-tank guns, Vice-Admiral Layton for air defence for his base; supposing Brooke-Popham, with the whole responsibility for the defence of these vast territories on his shoulders, had really tried to drive his situation home. Who is to say that, in spite of all the other commitments, a little might not have been spared for Malaya? And who can tell what difference that little might have made when the success of the Japanese attempt to establish themselves on the Kra Isthmus hung in the balance, when the ability to keep landing-grounds in the north serviceable, would have extended immensely the range of fighter cover, when the power to reach and attack the Japanese bases in Saigon could have changed the whole course of the war? Singapore might even have become another Tobruk. Certainly the *Repulse* and the *Prince of Wales* would not have been overwhelmed in a calm sea, under the shadow of an empty sky, defenceless, save for their own too-few anti-aircraft guns, against a trained and resolute enemy who found not a single fighter to deflect the torpedo-bombers from their straight and deadly course.

But no—the fortress was impregnable; the Brewster Buffaloes were good enough for Singapore, and the Japanese were not very good at aircraft. Not a voice was raised, not a protest uttered; and so the ships went down and the Far East was lost.

While Slinger Wood of the *Repulse* had been enjoying his one-day honeymoon, while the *Prince of Wales* was steaming hell for leather westward with Churchill on board and her destroyers left far behind, a gentleman called Alfred Duff-Cooper, Chancellor of the Duchy of Lancaster, and ex-Minister of Information, was setting out by air for Singapore with the duty of reporting to the Cabinet on the situation there. In his book, *Old Men Forget*, he tells us something of what he found. He found that there were certain absurdities of organisation, that there was a great deal of overlapping between various departments, but this only occupies a paragraph in his book. How much more space it occupied in his report we do not know though we do know that this report started off with the prescient statement that the Far East was destined to play a far greater role in the future than it had in the past. He extols the happiness and pleasant quarters of his official party and the merits of his Chinese cook, a great artist who would never repeat himself:

> *Diana loved Singapore. Its baroque beauty and bright colours appealed to her. She got on well with the Chinese and the Malays. She began to learn the language and made some progress. She enjoyed the streets and the shops and the people. I suffered for the first time from grandeur. I like, as she does, to wander at will in new cities, explore narrow streets, gaze into shop-windows and sit down in little cafes. But I was too important now to be natural. Such behaviour would have been severely criticised. I should have lost "face" and so would my mission. Indian soldiers stood as sentries at our doors and I could scarcely leave the house except in a motor-car. So I missed much of the fun of Singapore and have often thought that I should like to go back there as a private citizen.*

There can be nothing more expressive of Singapore and everything in it than this attitude and these impressions. Certainly Duff-Cooper could eat delicately and live pleasantly in Singapore. Certainly, when the time came, Admiral Phillips and his staff would be royally entertained there for a brief space; certainly there would be entertainment (albeit of a different sort) for Johnny King, Alf Tudor, and their shipmates of the *Prince of Wales*. While they entertained and enjoyed their civilised life behind their stage-set fortifications, the Japanese pilots were training at Saigon and the war cabinet in Tokyo was adding the final touches to their country's plans for taking possession of its imperial inheritance.

It was in an attempt to defend this rotten and crumbling bastion, this temple of folly and blunder, that the *Prince of Wales* and the *Repulse* were about to be sacrificed. Since this is the story of those two ships and not the story of Singapore (which has been ably and fully written of by O'Dowd Gallagher, Frank Owen and others) it is necessary to say no more. This much however had to be said in order to put into proper perspective the false and utterly unrealistic background of the views of the Prime Minister, the Foreign Office, and all those who supported them in their campaign to get the ships sent out for sacrifice in the South China Sea.

. . . Slinger Wood had come into the mess, last as usual, for breakfast. The mess was like a turkish bath: those wide, airy spaces that had been so extolled by upper-deck observers were not so wide and airy in the latitude of Freetown and beyond. The men spent most of their time down there in their underpants or with towels wrapped round their middles, and when they had a cup of tea most of it seemed to come out again through the pores of their skin. Tempers were easily roused over the most trivial of things.

Most of the boys had already finished their breakfast, but Taffy Mannings was still sitting at the other end of the table and was just about to start on his second cup of tea, when he noticed that the sugar basin was empty. Now one rule in a mess is that whoever takes the last spoonful of sugar fills the basin from a chest at the end of the table, and Taffy thought Slinger had just emptied it; so he slid the basin up the table to Slinger, who was, as a matter of fact, sitting right by the chest, and asked him to fill it.

"Get your lazy self up off your arse and fill it your bloody self," said Slinger, throwing the basin back at him.

Whereupon Taffy Mannings did get his lazy self up off his arse and invited Slinger to accompany him up on to the forecastle. Here they spent the next half hour knocking hell out of each other, to the pleasure and delight of most of the ship's company, including the officers on the bridge. Not for many years have those who patronise the sport of boxing in more genteel circumstances seen such a marathon bout, without rounds or pauses for refreshment. Eventually Wood managed to catch Taffy with a right hook and he slid down the forward breakwater with the silliest of looks on his face.

"I've had enough," he said.

"So have I," said Slinger, and the two of them shook hands with the greatest of good will and returned to the mess deck. Slinger filled the sugar bowl and the pair of them finished what was left of the breakfast. They remained the best of friends and shipmates after this, although they never saw each other again after Singapore.

There may be several things that occur to the reader about this. In the first place he may think what a wonderful world it was in which a man could get his petty spites and irritations straight out of his system just as soon as they came in, and never give them a second thought afterwards. They may also notice how remarkably fit these men must have been and how their method of settling their differences was approved and encouraged by all concerned from the highest to the low. Perhaps we might occasionally remember such things as this when we read stories of brutality in barrack rooms, savagery in base depots and so forth, and when every NCO or petty officer must sometimes feel that there is a pressman hanging at his elbow, ready to report even a word he may say out of place. Yet the *Repulse* and ships like her were pretty good ships: they were certainly not slave ships and their men went to their end in them very willingly.

So through the endless tropical days the great ship steamed, stately in the midst of her vast convoy, ever southwards. Endless days indeed: few who travelled that way can ever forget how endlessly and how idly they followed one another until the whole world seemed to be blue ocean, and a man might have been on a ship for ever and a day. Endless days, with all the petty routine of a convoy: daily gun practice with the anti-aircraft weapons, daily boat-drill for the troopships, jettisoning of rubbish at sundown, mysterious comings and goings by the destroyers—who alone in the world seemed to be free to move otherwise than in a set, predetermined series of patterns and stations—occasional depth-charging, though it seemed quite impossible that any submarines could lurk below the surface of that dazzling sea flecked by flying fish and starred with Portuguese men-of-war. Idle days indeed, watching porpoise and dolphin sporting about the ships. Idle days and sweltering nights in the blacked-out ships, with the thrash and judder of propeller and shaft vibrating endlessly in the confined spaces, while the Pole Star dipped below the sea and the Southern Cross rose higher and higher each night amid the brilliant constellations.

Very far from the war they all felt now—far from the battles they had missed and the battles that were likely to be. For the men on the troopships—certainly there was battle at the end of it, if ever they came to the end of this eternal sea voyaging which drugged their very minds, so that they seemed to know neither past nor future—the *Repulse* was a symbol of strength and security, and one of them told Scouse Garner long afterwards that they felt her presence was safety and a sure shield to them.

On and forever on until the Southern Cross was high in the sky and the days became less torrid; till the seas lost their unending dazzling blue and steepened into the great, parallel rollers that surge forever out of the Antarctic to crash against the southern shores of Africa. On round the Cape, with the escorts burying their bows in the southern seas, and even the battle-cruiser and the biggest of the convoy's ships pitching solemnly and heavily in the steepest waters of the world. On round the Cape and into the Indian Ocean, divided from the war now not only by half a world but by the great continent they were circumnavigating. On the third of October they arrived in Durban.

CHAPTER

9

ALL THIS TIME A BATTLE-ROYAL WAS BEING FOUGHT IN London. It was not a continuous battle: it went by fits and starts, surged up and died down, rather like the Hundred Years' War. The main protagonists were Mr. Churchill and the Admiralty. On Mr. Churchill's side there intervened from time to time the Foreign Office, backed by its nineteenth century dossiers and its notions of gun-boat diplomacy. Of all the blunders that were perpetrated about the two ships the blunders of the Foreign Office are the most fantastic. Added to their views that the loyalty of the Malays was unshakeable and that the Siamese must not be "offended" by establishing forward bases for the defence of Malaya, they stuck hard by the Victorian precept that all it was necessary to do was to "send a ship." Without doing the Foreign Office any injustice at all, its spokesmen appear quite seriously to have believed that one nice, big, modern battleship would make the Japanese cringe in awe and dread, and forego any thoughts they might have had about the conquest of Asia.

Now the Admiralty had not been idle over the Far Eastern question. We may fairly assume that the state of things in the Far East and our negligible strength at sea there had been very much in their Lordships' minds ever since the loss of the French Fleet in the Mediterranean had made any reinforcement of our Far Eastern Fleet impossible for the time being. During 1941, the official historian tells us, the Far Eastern situation had been repeatedly before them and a great deal of thought, discussion, and planning had been devoted to it. With the obvious signs that things were beginning to move faster in the Far East—with the occupation of Indochina, with the American oil embargo, with Churchill's own warning from the Atlantic Charter meeting—the fact that action could not be much longer postponed was very apparent. Since the war plans that were issued in the early days of 1939, the Admiralty's appraisal of situations had been good, and the appraisal they had arrived at over the Far Eastern situation now was good. If use had been made of the Japanese war ciphers which had been in American hands for a year it would have been seen immediately how sound their appraisal was; and the course of action they proposed was very similar to what was actually done as the only remaining alternative when the American Fleet had been bombed out of the Pacific, the *Repulse* and the *Prince of Wales* sunk and Hong Kong and the "impregnable" base of Singapore over-run.

Towards the end of August, however, and before the Admiralty plan was actually put forward for consideration by the War Cabinet, Mr. Churchill made his own first move —albeit at this stage he was only talking in terms of putting a "deterrent squadron" into the Indian Ocean. It should consist, he said, of the smallest possible number of the best ships: he pointed out the endless preoccupation which the existence of the *Tirpitz*, ready for sea in a Baltic harbour, caused the Admiralty and the War Cabinet. A small but very powerful force in or near Japanese waters, he asserted, would exercise precisely the same effect on the Japanese as the *Tirpitz* exercised on us. The *Tirpitz*, he thought, would not sally out from the Baltic while the Russian Fleet was still in being—although how long the Russian Fleet would continue in being was at that stage of the war a very open question, indeed. He proposed, therefore, that we should place in the Aden-Singapore-Simonstown triangle a force consisting of one *King George* V-class battleship with the *Renown* and the *Repulse* and one carrier of high speed.

At the very outset two important flaws must be noted in Mr. Churchill's thinking. The first was his comparison of the effect the *Tirpitz* had on us with the effect that one *King George* V-class battleship was likely to have on the Japanese.

> *It exercises a vague general fear and menaces all points at once* [he wrote]. *It appears and disappears, causing immediate reactions and perturbations on the other side.*

Yet it is as plain as a pikestaff to anyone viewing the situation objectively that the position of ourselves and the position of the Japanese was not comparable in any way. We were on the defensive—we had convoys strung out all over the seas with a bare minimum of protection, overseas theatres of war to maintain which could easily be cut off. One big, fast, heavily armed and armoured ship, breaking out as the *Bismarck* had nearly broken out, could wreak havoc piled on havoc in any direction. And for the selfsame reason the very existence of one such ship, ready for sea in a Baltic port, could keep tied down for watch and defence against that ship forces that could be ill-spared and were sorely needed elsewhere. The Japanese were in a different case altogether. They were on the attack (or about to be), not on the defensive. They could chose their time and place as the Germans had done in the early days of the war, when the *Repulse* and the *Hood* were forever chasing phantoms; and the existence of one powerful ship in any one particular place could do no more than cause them to make an alteration to their plans. They had no tenuous, straggling lines of supply across the ocean to protect, no almost-isolated overseas bases to maintain. Where, then, was the menace to them of one powerful capital ship? In all the annals of naval strategy there cannot have been a more fallacious parallel or a greater misrepresentation of the roles of the attacker and the attacked.

The second flaw was Mr. Churchill's own peculiar conception of the war at sea in general, and of the functions of capital ships in particular. This arose partly from his own romantic conception of warfare and that mystical addiction to battleships we have already noticed. Odd contradiction in a man whose rapid introduction of the convoy system from the earliest days of the war had served his country so well and whose hard-headed grasp of an incredible mass of detail kept both service chiefs and civilian ministers continually on their toes. Yet the fact is that essentially he regarded war at sea not as a matter of studied and premediated moves by balanced forces against one another, but as a series of knightly duels between individual ships——not as a matter of fleet engagements but as a series of almost personal combats. Ruled by his head, he was a brilliant First Lord and an able Minister of Defence; ruled by his imagination, he had about as much appreciation of the proper use of modern naval units as Nelson's seamen with their firebrands would have had of H. V. Morton's push buttons. And in this present case, his imagination was taking charge.

He favoured the placing in position of his proposed force, he said, by the end of October, and of telling the Australians and the Americans of our intentions. He added, however, that there was plenty of time: negotiations with the Japanese might go on for some time, even for the three months envisaged by Roosevelt; and the Japanese might well wait to see how things were going in Russia before committing themselves.

The First Sea Lord's reply was uncompromising. He rejected any idea of employing *King George* V-class battleships in the Indian Ocean or, indeed, away from home waters at all. He pointed out that ships cannot work-up without targets and that there was no possibility of target practice on the way out east; that if working-up is interrupted, a ship rarely recovers; that the ships were intricate, manned by crews of whom more than half had never been to sea before, so that damage in working-up was inevitable and nearness to contractors' yards vital. He then put as counter-proposals the proposed dispositions which the Admiralty had already worked out: the *Nelson* would be based on Ceylon by the end of November, her sister-ship the *Rodney* (of tin can and *Bismarck* fame) by the end of January, the *Renown* by mid-January, the carrier *Hermes* immediately, the *Ark Royal* in April or the new carrier *Indomitable* in emergency. To this nucleus a force of R class battleships would be added, thus forming a balanced and homogeneous fleet. It was not pretended that this would be a *deterrent* force—that is to say, a force capable of meeting the modern Japanese fleet on level terms—but it would fill the need for capital ship escorts in the Indian Ocean and would safeguard supply convoys in that ocean against Japanese cruisers which would be the particular peril of such convoys. And one *King George* V-class battleship would make no difference, because this class had not the speed to run a Japanese cruiser down. Last of all, the Prime Minister's contention that the *Tirpitz* would not venture out of the Baltic while the Russian Fleet was intact was thought to be dangerous, and three *King George* V-class ships were needed in the Atlantic to deal with her if she did break out.

Surely this was a realistic plan. It accepted the fact that if the Japanese came into the war we would not be able (especially while America was not with us) to defend Far

Eastern waters, and would have to fall back on the Indian Ocean. The force the Admiralty proposed would not be able to fight the Japanese, but based on Ceylon it could certainly keep the Indian Ocean safe for a while; and the keeping safe of the Indian Ocean was vital to the defence and supply of Malaya, not to speak of Australia and beyond. As 1942 progressed, strength in home waters and the Mediterranean would increase with the arrival of new ships and older ships from refit. During these months, therefore, the Admiralty hoped to increase their Indian Ocean force at least to seven capital ships, one aircraft-carrier, ten cruisers, and twenty-four destroyers—more if more could be spared. Churchill's proposal had taken no account at all of the need to protect the Indian Ocean and keep the convoys sailing through it. It took, moreover, not the slightest account of one thing that surely should have been taken for granted——that the Japanese knew just what naval forces we had, the extent to which our naval resources were stretched and were most unlikely to be fooled by the appearance of one modern leviathan into thinking that we had an unlimited array of fast super-ships readily available to "appear and disappear causing immediate reactions and perturbations," and so drive them back into the safe shelter of islands or their new base at Camranh Bay in Indochina.

But Mr. Churchill's reply was an indignant broadside. Broadside anyone who disagreed with Mr. Churchill was liable to get, and very frequently these broadsides were justified and did a lot of good, even if they were unreasonable over matters of detail. This particular broadside was not justified; nor was it reasonable, nor did it pay even the slightest regard to the facts of the case at all. He denounced the First Lord's proposed dispositions as inherently unsound. He agreed that the R class battleships were good for convoy defence against the Japanese eight-inch cruisers—but if the Japanese despatched against them one fast modern battleship they would be easy prey. They were floating coffins, he fulminated. These were his very words and he must have forgotten them by the time he agreed that the *Repulse* should accompany the *Prince of Wales* to Singapore, for with her light armour and her piteously few anti-aircraft guns she was much more liable to become a floating coffin than the heavily-armoured R class battleships. A superior force, he insisted, could only be coped with by using a small number of the best fast ships. It was all illustrated by the Admiralty's extraordinary concern about the *Tirpitz*—and so back to the *Tirpitz* he came again with his talk of "vague general fear," "appearing and disappearing" and so on. It is difficult sometimes to read these words without wondering whether the Prime Minister was talking about a real-life battleship or some sort of naval Flying Dutchman. Yet however far-fetched these words of Churchill's about the *Tirpitz* may seem, one must at least give him credit for what he really said and really meant. Captain Russell Grenfell in his book, *Main Fleet to Singapore*, has made it appear that the Prime Minister was using these words about fast modern battle-ships in general rather than about a particular ship. This was not so. Exaggerated as Churchill's assertions were and even with his imagination strongly in charge of him, he never degenerated to the complete lunacy this would imply. There is quite enough to condemn his views and his statements in this matter without attempting to make him look insane —a condition of which even his most biased critics could not have accused him.

There were some rounds in the broadside still to be fired. He was astonished by the First Sea Lord's claim that three *King George* V-class battleships were needed in the Atlantic to contain the *Tirpitz;* and immediately this brought him back to that other old hobby-horse of which he never tired: if three were really needed, this seriously reflected on the weakness of these ships—under-gunned, weakened by the hangar in the middle of the citadel and so on. We know very well that he was right about one of these points and wrong about the other—but right or wrong, he was now trying to have it both ways. Because if these ships were as bad as all that, it was as much folly to demand one of them for the Far East as it was to send the "floating coffins." You cannot in one breath portray a ship as a floating miracle which is going to keep a whole enemy fleet on tenterhooks, and in the next dismiss the same as under-gunned and under-armoured.

Landing safely on all fours on the far side of this Becher's Brook of an argument (the two-edged character of which no-one seems to have spotted) he added a consideration that certainly could not be taken for granted at that time unless something had been agreed on at the Atlantic Charter meeting which has never been revealed: that American dispositions in the Atlantic could now be counted on. For makeweight, he mentioned the power of carriers to slow down a ship like the *Tirpitz* (omitting to notice that the Japanese also had carriers which could slow down a ship like the *Prince of Wales*, and showing that he had only half learned the lesson of the *Bismarck*) and he repeated yet once again that the *Tirpitz* must inevitably stay in the Baltic as long as the Russian Fleet existed.

The last shot of all in the locker shows once more how utterly and inconceivably ignorant were the War Cabinet, the service chiefs, and everyone else about Japanese plans and intentions. He reasserted that he could not feel the Japanese would face the United States, Great Britain, and Russia whilst still preoccupied in China. He was sure Japan was likely to negotiate with the United States for three more months at the very least. The sort of force he wanted in Far Eastern waters would increase Japan's hesitation and prolong her negotiations: a *King George* V-class battleship would increase the one and prolong the other more than anything else.

The tide of battle surged backwards and forwards. It became apparent that the views of the Prime Minister and the views of the Admiralty were completely irreconcilable, and this being the case, there was only one conclusion the battle could possibly have. Churchill could in the last resort over-rule the Admiralty, but the Admiralty could not overrule Churchill. The former in effect is what happened, but the Admiralty fought a long running battle and half of October 1941, had passed without any conclusion being reached—by which time it was already too late for the Admiralty to start the programme it had so carefully worked out for the Indian Ocean on the timing originally set forward.

It was at this point that the Foreign Office intervened with their demand to "send a ship." It had at last awoken to the fact that Japan was a partner in the Axis, was committed by the Tripartite Pact, had moved into Indochina and was showing aggressive intentions. It demanded a show of force in the Far East, and (though heaven alone knows why the Foreign Office was allowed to express opinions on matters of naval strategy—or if it did why its opinions were accorded any weight) supported Mr. Churchill's contention that one modern super battleship would produce a much better effect than a fleet of older battleships. In other words the Foreign Office came down on Mr. Churchill's side, and for some incredible reason was allowed to influence not the sending of "a ship" (for it was obvious that a ship or ships must be sent) but what sort of ship. It is not difficult to suppose that if the Foreign Office had intervened against Mr. Churchill in this or any other similar matter it would have been roundly sent about its business—and quite rightly.

On October 17 Mr. Churchill opened the final stage of his offensive: In the two months that had passed some of his ideas had changed and others become more definitely crys-tallised. It was no longer a case of the Aden-Simonstown-Singapore triangle—that had vanished somewhere in the jungle of thinking and re-thinking—it was a case of Singapore alone with an obvious orientation towards the China Sea and the Pacific rather than towards the Indian Ocean. It was not a case of an unspecified *King George* V-class battleship with a choice of older battle cruisers which might accompany her: the choice had hardened on the *Prince of Wales* and on the *Repulse*, which was just leaving Durban with her great W.S. convoy on the last leg but one of the long, long voyages to Suez Roads. Neither ship had as yet any clue what was in store—even for the *Repulse* there were obviously a number of possibilities and ratings would wait as ratings on warships and soldiers on troop-ships always had to wait until the ship left Aden and they could see whether she turned right or left. Henceforth, in such of the discussion as is left they are always mentioned by name, and so what has been perhaps a rather long preamble comes back to the two ships, whose fate was now indissolubly involved with it.

It is interesting that there are two versions, presumably already on their way down to history, of the manner in which the solution to the long battle was finally arrived at. The first is that of the Admiralty's official history, which says,

> *The discussion ended by the Prime Minister inviting the First Lord to send as quickly as possible one modern capital ship, together with an aircraft carrier, to join up with the* Repulse *at Singapore. He added that he would not come to a decision on this point without consulting the First Sea Lord, but in view of the strong feeling of the Committee he hoped the First Lord would not oppose his suggestion. The First Lord agreed to discuss the matter with Admiral Pound and make recommendations in a few days' time.*

On October 20, according to this account, the matter was re-discussed and the First Sea Lord made one final attempt to get a last hearing for the Admiralty Plan, shifting his argument from the protection of convoys in the Indian Ocean to action against a possible Japanese invasion force, which Mr. Churchill clearly had in mind and which had no doubt been discussed at the previous conference. To such a force, he said, one modern battleship would be no deterrent, for the Japanese could easily detach four battleships to protect any south-bound invasion force; but if the *Nelson,* the *Rodney* and four R-class battleships were at Singapore, they would have to detach a greater part of their fleet. This would uncover Japan to the American Navy on whose support he (the First Sea Lord) relied in the event of a Japanese attack. Notice that the First Sea Lord has also shifted his attention from the Indian Ocean to the South China Sea; notice, at the same time, that the American Navy in the Pacific becomes for the first time a quoted element in the discussion.

It was all in vain. The Prime Minister reiterated that he did not foresee an attack in force on Malaya: it is very important indeed to notice that reiteration because it is made almost as the dispositions of the two ships are to be finally settled. He rather feared commerce raids against which the R class battleships would be useless, and he quoted the supporting opinion of the Foreign Office.

And so the First Sea Lord yielded, but yielded reluctantly and up to a point only: he made a condition of his yielding that the *Prince of Wales* be sent as far as Capetown and that her final destination be reviewed at that point. In spite of this, on October 21 the Admiralty was officially told that the *Prince of Wales* was likely to leave soon for Singapore. On October 31 the Prime Minister told the Dominion Prime Ministers that the *Prince of Wales* was to join the *Repulse* in the Indian Ocean. On November 1 the First Sea Lord reiterated his demand that the battleship's destination be reviewed on her reaching Capetown: on November 5 Churchill repeated his statement to the Dominion Prime Ministers.

That is one account. The other account is in Mr. Churchill's history of World War II, and this is very brief:

> *It was decided to send as the first instalment of our Far Eastern Fleet both the* Prince of Wales *and the* Repulse *and as an essential element the modern armoured aircraft carrier* Indomitable.

This suggests quite clearly that he had made up his mind, and in his later recollection could only remember having made up his mind. He was determined to send a modern battleship and a battle cruiser—later the *Prince of Wales* and the *Repulse*—to the Far East. He had known all along what he wanted, he had been determined to get it and he got it. He always got what he wanted. So many of the things he had wanted had been things that helped to save England—he wanted planes, he wanted tanks, he wanted destroyers from the Americans, he wanted a hundred other vital things and got them—now he got the *Prince of Wales* and the *Repulse* and the result of his getting them was their destruction, together with ruination and the end of British power in the Far East.

For the first time the aircraft carrier *Indomitable* has not merely been mentioned, but mentioned "as an essential element." This shows that originally at least he had some appreciation of the air cover that would be necessary for the ships and in this appreciation he was at least in advance of the Service Chiefs at Singapore. The *Indomitable* was also a brand-new ship—newer in fact than the *Prince of Wales*— and her employment on such a mission was for this reason as questionable a piece of policy as the employment of the other ship. Undoubtedly she would have gone down in the South China Sea with the *Prince of Wales* and the *Repulse*, or if she had been able to save the other two ships from fatal damage by staving off the torpedo bomber attacks, would have been sunk in or around Singapore not many days later— just as they would have been

The lucky chance that saved her did not therefore materially influence the fate of the *Prince of Wales* and the *Repulse*, although perhaps it altered the precise date of their end and the manner in which they met it. On November 3, while working-up in the West Indies, she went aground off Kingston, Jamaica, and damaged herself sufficiently for her repair to be a dockyard job long enough to rule out any possibility of her sailing with the *Prince of Wales* for the Far East. The only two other armoured aircraft carriers of her type which might have replaced her, the *Illustrious* and the *Formidable*, were both repairing battle damage in American ports. So vanished any possibility of serious air cover for the ill-fated ships: they could hope now only for the help of the problematical Brewster Buffaloes which were "good enough for Singapore."

> *It was decided in spite of this* [writes Mr. Churchill, using once more that umbrella-like term which conceals all the pros and cons that must have been argued], *to let the two fast capital ships go forward in the hope of steadying the Japanese political situation and also to be in relation to the United States Pacific Fleet.*

To Stalin he wrote, "We are sending our latest battleship, the *Prince of Wales*, which can catch and kill any Japanese ship in the Indian Ocean." One cannot help seeing a parallel between this and his desperate statement after the invasion of Norway that every German ship in the Skagerrak would be sunk.

To the House of Commons he presently said, "We now feel ourselves strong enough to provide a powerful naval force of heavy ships with the necessary ancillary vessels for service if needed in the Indian and Pacific Oceans." The reader must decide on his own judgment whether this description could possibly be by any stretch of the imagination applied to the *Prince of Wales* and the *Repulse*. Especially when it is on record that the ancillary vessels consisted of four destroyers. Two of these, the *Express* and the *Electra*, came from the Home Fleet and were experienced, battle-scarred, and in reasonable shape. Two of them came from the Mediterranean Fleet which had been asked to spare and detach two destroyers to meet the *Prince of Wales* at Ceylon and quite naturally detached the two destroyers which were in the poorest shape. These were the *Echo* and the *Encounter*: one of them had something radically wrong with her trim, so that when her fuel tanks were full she developed a permanent list; the other is described as having a corrugated bottom due to unduly close contact on some occasion with the sea bed of the Mediterranean. The only thing that could be done with them when they ultimately arrived in Singapore was to put them in the dockyard and substitute for them the Australian destroyer *Vampire* and the small, antique destroyer *Tenedos*, whose endurance was so low that she could not even accompany the ships to the point of their last mission, at which it was planned to detach the destroyers and send them back to base.

Such was the force which was intended to act as a deterrent to a Japanese navy of ten capital ships, ten carriers, six seaplane carriers, eighteen heavy cruisers, twenty-two light cruisers, one hundred and thirteen destroyers, and sixty-nine submarines—homogeneous ships closely linked in type, easy to concentrate and easy to dispose.

In the whole of the war was there any fiction more absurd or more pointless? Especially when we remember that the Japanese cannot possibly have been unaware either of the state of the *Prince of Wales*'s working-up or of her mechanical troubles; were certainly very well acquainted with the fact that the *Repulse* was an old battle cruiser lightly armoured with but six fifteen-inch guns and anti-aircraft guns, both few in number and ancient in pattern. Events were soon to show that the Japanese knew all they needed to know and were already on the other side of the world making their disposition accordingly.

"Every preparation to defend British interests in the Far East and to defend the common cause now at stake has been and is being made." So spoke the Prime Minister at the Guildhall Banquet on November 10. The *Prince of Wales*, the *Repulse*; four destroyers, two of them unserviceable: the cardboard fortress of Singapore; the almost nonexistent for-

ward defence of Malaya and its airfields; the Brewster
Buffaloes—is there any need to go on? Call it blunder, call it
self-deception, call it anything you like—it adds up to the
same thing and the outcome was inevitable.

CHAPTER

10

WHILE ALL THIS ATTACKING AND COUNTER-ATTACKING had been going on, the *Prince of Wales* had not been kept idle sitting on her food tins in Scapa Flow like the *Rodney*. She had, in fact, once more been in action and had distinguished herself. Following on the Placentia trip there had been an interval of that hard and soul-destroying grind to work-up efficiency of which the naval correspondent had spoken so bleakly. It had not been unwelcome to Alf Tudor, Johnny King, and the rest of them after the strain of continuous action stations on the way home across the Atlantic with Mr. Churchill. They had had time ashore to drink their ration of beer in the NAAFI canteen and to punish the piano a little more. Seddon had found leisure for a little more mat making; Cyril Williams and the boys pursued their intense and vivid existence on the boys' mess deck, part of the ship's complement yet a world of their own. For diversion there had been the occasional air-raid and the crews of the high-angle and close-range weapons got in a little more realistic practice than could be provided by drogues.

Whether or not they had been a ship in disgrace, a ship that "ran away," a ship full of discontent and passive mutiny, there was certainly nothing of the sort now. They were Churchill's Yacht, they were the glamour ship, they were probably for this brief space the most publicised ship in the Royal Navy. It was a pity that the security of wartime reduced their cap ribbons to an anonymous "H.M.S.": if they'd been able to walk about under a label reading "H.M.S. *Prince of Wales*," they would have been able to put a swagger to it indeed. As it was they felt pretty good, even in the desert wastes of Scapa.

Before long they were storing ship again, and early one morning they weighed anchor and went to sea to join up with the almost legendary Force H, which operated from Gibraltar, to take a convoy through to Malta. Among their companions were the battleship *Nelson* and the fabulous *Ark Royal*, which had been sunk by Lord Haw-Haw times without number but was still afloat and had, with her planes, scored the next hit on the *Bismarck* after themselves.

Mess 46 and almost anyone else on the *Repulse* would have given the world for such a convoy assignment as this. In those days the Mediterranean was a closed and hostile sea into which no merchantman might sail without the heaviest of escorts, equipped to fight off attack both from the air and on the water. In the midst of it, Malta had been holding out alone for well over a year, and everything Malta needed both for defence and sustenance had to come by sea through the Pillars of Hercules and the gates of hell. The island was not yet in its most desperate straits, but things were bad enough, and its supply convoys had to be got through at almost any price.

The *Prince of Wales* was very well fitted for this sort of job. Her armour was heavy and her anti-aircraft battery, though not completely adequate for modern war, was as good as anything in the fleet. It was, alas, the sort of job for which the *Repulse* was most unsuitable. Her sister ship the *Renown* had been employed on Malta convoys but she had many more anti-aircraft guns than the *Repulse:* nonetheless she had been so employed at very considerable risk for so lightly armoured a ship. Anyway she was already far, far away in the South Atlantic shepherding her W.S. convoy to Durban and feeling the war recede far behind her.

When the *Prince of Wales* cleared harbour, Captain Leach, as usual, told his men over the ship's loudspeakers what they were about: he told them this was the most vital convoy that had so far sailed for Malta and he told them that the convoy must get through. This was exactly the same thing that was said to merchant ships and escorts in every convoy that left for Malta at this period and in every case it was equally true. Every convoy was vital and every convoy had to get through.

The third week of September saw them at Gibraltar. There had been no trouble so far from air, sea, or those unpleasant depths in which the U-boats lurked. On the way the merchant ships had been exercised in evasion tactics and emergency turns and both by way of practice and to give the merchantmen a little encouragement the naval units had done some practice shooting in which the merchant vessels joined with their own anti-aircraft guns. It was all very noisy and very impressive, but no-one had any doubt that things would soon get noisier. By the time convoy and escorts left the shelter of the Rock to steam eastwards on September 24, everyone was pretty well keyed-up and on their toes. This time action had to come.

From the moment of leaving harbour, the *Prince of Wales*, in common with the other ships, was at action stations; but the weather was warm and the air balmy, ideal for a Mediterranean cruise. The redoubtable company of boozers and boxers found it for the time being very pleasant indeed—much more pleasant than being at action stations in the filthy weather that the North Atlantic had put on to greet Mr. Churchill and his Yacht.

It was not very long before the aircraft arrived, and thereafter the memories of most of the *Prince of Wales*'s people seem to be rather hazy about the precise details and sequence of events. On and off, they were under fairly continuous air attack and in action all the way to Valetta. The aircraft came at them in waves, the confusion was prodigious, and the noise immense. Alf Tudor kept on hoping that it would let up for a bit so that he could get out of the 5.25 turret and not only get a breather but also a look round and see what had happened to his own ship and the rest of the convoy. He remembered the *Bismarck* action, when amid all the noise, racket and thunder of the ship's own guns firing, he had been barely conscious that she had been hit more than once and was amazed at the change of scene when he finally got out into the open and was able to survey the damage.

At one point there was a vague general impression that the sky was full of planes, the sea full of bomb splashes, planes falling into the water, and pilots bailing out in all directions. The commentary from the bridge once more served them well and at one point the speaker—it was probably the Captain's secretary—became so excited himself that his voice resembled that of a boxing commentator from the ring-side in a really first-class bout.

The crews of the fourteen-inch guns had no chance of putting the modifications that had been made to the turrets to the test. There was a time when it seemed very likely that the big guns would go into action, although the men themselves were not told about it until afterwards, for units of the Italian fleet did put out and were reported making for the convoy. At what stage they thought better of it was not clear, but they were presently reported on a reverse course, making away from them. They were never actually sighted and not a shot was exchanged.

When Alf Tudor finally did emerge from his turret he

found that the ship looked exactly the same as it had looked before, albeit somewhat less tidy. She had not received a single hit, and in spite of all the noise and bombardment, very little damage had been done to most of the naval vessels and no serious damage to the merchantmen with one exception only. This one merchant ship was set on fire by a bomb, and, having been abandoned by her crew, was sunk by the guns of the escorts. The vital supplies reached Malta, and while, in a strange way, it could hardly have been called a naval engagement because no hostile naval units had been involved, it ranks deservedly as a battle honour on the memorial card issued by Abrahams of Portsmouth in the identical form familiar to all naval men.

The one exception among the escorts was the battleship *Nelson* which suffered damage serious enough to make her a dockyard job, although not a very long one. Had the Admiralty's plan for using her as the earliest instalment of its proposed build-up in the Indian Ocean prevailed, this could have had quite far-reaching consequences: another ship would have had to be found to take her place, although it is unlikely that the Admiralty of its own volition would have sent the *Prince of Wales* or any other *King George* V-class battleship so far from the contractors' yards unless there was absolutely no alternative. Mr. Churchill, however, did not lose the opportunity of adding yet a further shot to his barrage of argument, or any time in pointing out that the damage to the *Nelson* now, in any case, made the Admiralty's plan impossible to carry out.

By the time the *Prince of Wales* arrived back in home waters, her fate as we know had been as good as settled. Presently there appeared aboard her a little man wearing an Admiral's insignia. He was Admiral Sir Tom Phillips, destined to command the new force in the Far East, now for the first time named Force Z. The men, from a respectful distance, sized him up, and Admiral Tom Phillips promptly became Admiral Tom Thumb.

Now Admiral Phillips is another figure about whom there has been a lot of misunderstanding and a lot of nonsense talked both by press and public. In his earlier career he had gained a great reputation as a practical destroyer commander. He had spent the first two years of the war at the Admiralty, first as Deputy and later as Vice-Chief of Naval Staff. In this latter role he had been the right-hand man of the First Sea Lord and a Rear-Admiral. He was appointed Acting Admiral on taking up his new command, thus achieving an unusually rapid step in promotion at the comparatively early age of fifty-three——a momentous step, when it is remembered that the force he was destined to command was intended to be built up to great strength in a comparatively short period; and had events gone otherwise than they actually did go he would have been a figure of considerable importance in the naval scheme of things. But because he had come straight from the Admiralty to his command he was dubbed a "desk Admiral"—the implication apparently being that so far he had fought all his battles on paper and had no qualifications for fighting battles in a ship at sea. It is true that he had up to this moment neither commanded a naval force nor had he even been second-in-command of one, but from that "desk" at the Admiralty he had played an outstanding part in the fighting of the Battle of the Atlantic—which was by far the most important as well as the lengthiest naval operation of the war so far (indeed, it was still going on) and in which the navy had learned almost all its more important operational lessons. He had seen naval command and naval intelligence knit together, grow experienced, and mature from the fumbling early days of abortive sorties and unrewarded chases to the state when a great engagement such as the pursuit of the *Bismarck* could be co-ordinated over an immense area of ocean and brought to a successful conclusion with every unit and subordinate commander falling into the plot exactly as he was intended to do. Here he had learned his tactical lessons, and the only thing that could possibly be said against him is that he had learned them too well: for in his first and last battle in the South China Sea he expected the same instinctive appreciation of the passing-on of intelligence and the consequences of receiving it, as he was used to in the Battle of the Atlantic, and in this he was grievously and fatally disappointed. Of him the Admiralty's official history says that he had "borne an immense burden with unshakeable resolution and had won the complete confidence of the Prime Minister."

It is tempting to say that the Prime Minister rewarded him by sending him to his death with a totally inadequate force under circumstances in which neither he nor his ships could possibly survive; but the reward of commanders in war is often to be sent to their deaths on impossible assignments— it is even the reward of "desk Admirals." There is nothing to suggest in the history or the fate of Force Z that Phillips' appointment was a blunder or that he failed to fulfil the confidence and trust of both the Prime Minister and the Admiralty. We shall find his proceedings workmanlike, his decisions sound, and his understanding of his duty in the face of appalling odds clear and resolute.

"ARE WE SURE THIS MAN HAS MISSED BEING A HERO?"

The year after he was lost off Kuantan, the self-same "naval correspondent" who was treasuring up the story of the *Prince of Wales* mutiny and other similar matters, trumpeted this question in a four-column headline in his paper. In the copy that followed it he told his readers that the Admiralty had already held an enquiry into the loss of the *Prince of Wales* and *Repulse* and that its findings were secret—tidings not very remarkable nor even news. He then went on, without saying so in so many words, to imply that he was fully acquainted with these findings.

Much of what follows after that is either inaccurate or plain balderdash, and most of the remainder is highly inaccurate: all this will be dealt with in its proper place. What is more to the point at the moment is that he here was referring to Admiral Phillips as having become "the centre of the most acutely personal controversy since Jellicoe-Jutland." He pictured the Admiral as already having become a figure of legend. "His critics," he added, "are anonymous but not all of them are unimportant," and after going on at much length in the same vein he declared that if the ships had not been spotted by enemy aircraft and sunk, "Admiral Phillips would have been a hero as famous as Nelson."

No-one would have been more surprised at all this than Admiral Phillips himself. He did not set out to be a hero, any more than any other commander in the fleet doing a service job of work and making decisions as they arose from day to day. He took no spectacular or unconventional risks: he assessed the situation with which he was faced in a straightforward and workmanlike way and took the only decisions he could have taken. He had not the slightest idea of being acclaimed, through some theatrical stroke of naval tactics, the saviour of Malaya or even the saviour of Singapore; and even had he had any such ideas he would have been grossly misleading himself. The whole world knew that Singapore was impregnable: if Singapore had not fallen it would have been set down to its impregnability and not to any heroic achievement by the desk Admiral.

Questions of "heroism" do not usually enter into the deliberations of naval commanders and certainly they did not enter into the deliberations of Sir Tom Phillips—or those of Captain Tennant or of Captain Leach, who both supported the decisions he made. He was a competent naval officer doing the job assigned him to the best of his ability (which was great) and the equipment at his disposal (which was not). There is quite enough high drama in the bare facts of this story without indulging in mock heroics.

On October 25 the *Prince of Wales* left Greenock and behind her the ragged cliffs of the Scottish coast—that had seen the departure of so many ships—faded for the last time. There must have been very little doubt in Phillips' mind, after the instructions and the briefing he had received, that his final destination was Singapore.

There was very little doubt in Mr. Churchill's mind either, as may be seen from the character of the signal which he sent to the Dominion prime ministers. The ship, he told them, would be noticed at Capetown "quite soon," but he gave no hint that her ultimate destination would be open to further examination at that point; and it is obvious that this condition, on which the First Lord had insisted as the price of his reluctantly giving way, had already vanished from both the Prime Minister's recollection and his calculations.

Field-Marshal Smuts, who, like the other Prime Ministers, approved the sending of ships to Singapore, telegraphed a warning to Mr. Churchill saying that he was worried about the division of power in the Pacific between two fleets, each of which on its own was inferior to the Japanese Fleet. He used these significant words: "If the Japanese are really nippy there is an opening for a first class disaster." The Japanese were not being "nippy," and this is the only respect in which that very sagacious old warrior's observation was at all incorrect. They were being extremely deliberate; they were making their dispositions in their own time and with infinite care. Even as the *Prince of Wales* was weighing anchor in the estuary of the Clyde, Japanese ships on the other side of the world were being stored, fuelled, ammunitioned, and made ready to keep a rendezvous in the far Kurile Islands, from whence almost exactly a month later was to sail the carrier force that launched its planes on Pearl Harbour and set the whole of the Far East aflame. At this time also the ships that were to carry the invading forces to the Kra

Isthmus in the neck of Malaya were being detailed for their work, together with the units who were to sail in them and the escorts which were to accompany them. The Mitsubishi aircraft destined for the attack on Singapore and on the *Prince of Wales* and the *Repulse* were rehearsing their roles and making their plans at their airfields at Saigon. All this must have been going on although it was not until December 1 that Tojo's Cabinet made the formal decision to go to war. They were only doing what our own Admiralty had done in the summer of 1939: making their disposition ready for the moment they should be needed.

All these things were being done, and Field-Marshal Smuts was the only allied statesman who expressed any premonition of them. As we follow the *Prince of Wales* on her voyage south, the *Repulse* in her last triumphal progress around the African ports, let us not fail to keep in our minds the progress of those other ships—far, far away, anonymous, cloaked in secrecy, accorded no triumphal receptions but moving with deadly purpose and ultimately to deadly effect, while the nations against whom they were moving remained confident that they had at least three months' negotiation time in hand.

Meanwhile the *Repulse* had already brought her W.S. convoy safely into Durban: standing at the dockhead the Lady in White sang her welcome as the great ships passed one after the other through the narrow harbour entrance. There was always a welcome at Durban, there were always fleets of cars drawn up on the quayside and hospitality unlimited for all who cared to avail themselves of it—at least at this stage of the war. There was also the YMCA, the Victoria League, the Navy League, and, perhaps outstanding among them all, the Jewish Club, to which all denominations as well as all ranks were welcome. The Royal Marine detachment marched through the city with band and drums and made as terrific an impression on their own matelots as they did on the inhabitants. Slinger Wood, in theory, was now short of money—no new experience. He was now a respectable married man, and although his wife was on war work at Rootes Motors' aircraft factory, he had allotted her most of his pay and was only getting ten shillings a fortnight for himself. But it takes more than a trifle like that to bankrupt a lucky and resourceful sailor, and he had done exceedingly well at tombola on the way out. There was quite enough in the kitty for a few good runs ashore in Durban; but for Slinger and the gang of happy criminals round about him there was no conventional progress from Point Docks to town and back again. Stoker Johnny Dykes knew the second cook on the *Mauretania*, which was in the convoy, and the second cook on the *Mauretania* knew a way out of Point Docks which by-passed the naval guard on the gate. So even when these good and dutiful sailors were on duty watch, they would manage to get out for a few pints and the way back from the few pints was usually via the *Mauretania*, where they filled their stomachs to their great satisfaction, and drank a little of the cook's home-brewed beer which—as Slinger recalls with relish at this long distance of time—"certainly had a kick in it."

It was pleasant at Durban in the South African spring. On the long sea-front, the eternal blue rollers of the Indian Ocean reared and spent themselves rhythmically on the beach. There were green lawns and the shade of trees; fresh, clean air in place of the perpetual turkish bath of the sweltering mess decks or the torrid breath of the stokehold air exhausts pouring round the pom-pom deck. There were coloured lights under an indigo sky, brilliant with the southern constellations; there was music and the shuffling of dancers' feet. There was beer. There were even women. The lights of the white buildings along the front blazed out into a sea innocent of war, blackout or alarms. The North Atlantic with its tenseness of men shivering at action stations through grey days and bitter nights seemed to belong to another planet altogether. The terror of great cities cowering in the darkness under the drone of the pitiless bombers and the stuttering thunder of anti-aircraft fire was an unreal nightmare that could never have been. Pleasant days, indeed—— pleasant days and a good reward for those two years of toiling and chasing and shivering and suffering. Who could grudge the men of the *Repulse* or the proud old ship herself this happy respite between her days of exacting service and her end so soon to be?

But even Durban could not last forever: before the *Prince of Wales* had sailed from Greenock the convoy was away again—ship after ship clearing the harbour in quick succession with the White Lady singing "Land of Hope and Glory" to them on their way, to reform and resume their endless steaming through calm seas up the other side of Africa. At last, in the latitude of Mombasa, the *Repulse* left them. She left them triumphantly, and one wonders whether some premonition did not come upon Captain Tennant that this was the last time his great ship would ever take her farewell of a convoy. He dressed her over-all and her people manned ship; so in her pride she steamed up and down the far-strung lines of shipping while the troops on the merchantmen cheered her farewell in admiration and in gratitude. In later years John Garner was to find himself working with a man who had been one of the soldiers in that convoy. He told him how every morning of the voyage they used to look out and see *Repulse* steaming with them; they always felt safe whilst she was there—and indeed there was something to being convoyed by a ship that had never lost a single vessel out of all her charges. So proudly on her summer sea she said good-bye—the ship that was now so soon to become H.M.S. *Anonymous.*

From Mombasa she went to the Seychelles—much like any other tropical port and very little joy for anybody, because no-one was allowed ashore. Then back again to Durban, where the Lady in White welcomed them once more and where Captain Tennant, hearing that Field Marshal Smuts

was in the vicinity, invited him to inspect the ship. He still
has, a prized possession, an autographed picture of the old
warrior and himself walking together down the ranks of the
Repulse's crew. Very fit the men look and very hearty and
beefy, standing to attention with their caps off, their chests
thrown forward and their stomachs held well in; and about
them there is that faint air of challenge which suggests both
that all this business of inspecting is a bore to them, and
that they dare the inspecting personality to find anything
wrong with them.

The sun is shining on this cherished picture, but it had
not been shining for very long. The marines had formed a
guard of honour on the catapult deck, all done up with their
khaki drill pressed to razor sharpness and their equipment
blancoed to perfection. As they waited, drawn up and ready,
for the South African Prime Minister to arrive, there came
upon them a thunderstorm and a downpour. The work of
many hours was ruined: blanco ran allover the place and
their K.D. looked as though it had just come out of the wash
tub. Smuts did his best for them by remarking on their smart
appearance.

After the inspection he spoke to the ship's company and
this speech is remarkably strong in the memory of the survivors. He spoke to them, as he always did, about South
Africa, what a splendid country it was and how good a home
it made. Looking back at these speeches, one feels how
desperately anxious was the old man, seeing so clearly the
shape of things to come, to encourage as many British people
as he could persuade to settle there after the war was over.
Then he spoke of the old days of conflict between British
and Boer, of how those days had passed and how they were
now friends together, an example to the world. Slinger
Wood's thoughts at this moment wandered away to his
grandfather, the Boer War veteran so lately dead—he wondered what the old soldier would have thought had he been
in his grandson's shoes, listening to his old enemy talk peace

and fellowship. And remembering it now in after years, he wonders whether some day his own grandchildren may be getting a pep-talk from some German admiral or general and wondering why the hell nations ever go to war at all . . . Smuts finished up on his earlier theme. He hoped, he said, that some of them would settle in South Africa when they came back.

"But many of you will not come back," he added, voicing suddenly the premonition of doom that he had so far mentioned only in his signal to Prime Minister Churchill. Had he debated the whole matter still further with himself and the more he debated, realised that the Japanese were fully prepared for war and these ships sailing into a trap? Had some further messages passed between him and Mr. Churchill of which we have no knowledge? Or was it just an old man's foreboding and compassion? Whatever it was—and it was the sort of remark not usually made in this kind of speech or under these circumstances—whatever it was, it had become so strong with him that he clearly could not resist just one brief phrase of warning and premonition to men so many of whom were truly doomed. It struck into them, cold and uncompromising, under the blue sky and the warm sun, so very far from war. They all remembered it—Stoker Dick, Marine Garner, Slinger Wood, Slatts, Chicken Howe, Ginger Devine, and all the rest of them. They remembered it as the ship went down and those who survive remember it till this day. Smuts became for them a prophet.

There was at least one function at Durban in which the *Repulse* did not shine so conspicuously. An invitation came to send a team to box against South Africans at the Technical Institute. It might be thought that all those "differences of opinion" (as well as all those beefy chests and biceps evident in Admiral Tennant's picture of the Smuts inspection) might have added up to a team of boxers capable of laying any opposition flat, but the fact is that twenty-four hours-about watch-keeping is not very good training for meeting

men in the peak of condition, fortified by continual practice
in the ring. Young John Garner had boxed in the Division
at Plymouth as a middleweight and when the physical training instructor sergeant, knowing this, detailed him to repre-
sent the ship at that weight he agreed very readily—although
he was not in a position to say no. To the Institute they
went, stripped off, and prepared for the bouts. Before the
eyes of their astonished and crestfallen comrades in the audience, flyweight, bantamweight, featherweight, lightweight,
welterweight all bit the dust in turn. Now came Marine
Garner's turn for the slaughter and in view of what happened to the others, slaughter he was quite confident it would
be; but something had clearly gone wrong and his bout was
not called. They carried on with the other weights until the
end of the programme and the final score was Durban 8,
Repulse 1—the one fight credited to the ship being Garner's
because his opponent hadn't turned up. The ship's company
had to content themselves with fighting the fights all over
again on the mess decks, and here it is safe to say they won a
return match at every weight, just as they had sunk the
Scharnhorst and the Gneisenau, the Bismarck, and the
whole German submarine fleet.

Now through that lovely and peaceful sea they retraced
their course to Mombasa—leaving behind a few, but only a
very few, gentlemen who had taken Jan Smuts so literally at
his word that they decided to settle in South Africa forthwith
and forgot to return to the ship. Time and circumstances
caught up with most of these: Slinger Wood had the dubious
pleasure of escorting one of them to Exeter detention
quarters when he finally gave himself up in 1945. At the
naval base at Kilindini there were a couple of weeks of
intensive gunnery practice, for in that long voyage the ship
had been without targets for practice firing. This made it
quite obvious to the meanest intelligence that they were
headed for the Eastern Mediterranean, where there was
plenty of shooting in progress and where, as a matter of fact,

their old friend H.M.S. *Barham* was to be finally blown up and this time sunk, with great loss of life. If it wasn't obvious to the meanest intelligence, it was certainly obvious to Mess 46, which had all these things properly worked out. But the mess-deck strategists came unstuck in their conclusions after all, because when they left Mombasa they headed due east and so continued across the Indian Ocean to Colombo, and then round the coast to Tricomalee—not a remarkable place but remembered for a football match against the Ceylon Regiment, where the *Repulse's* team were somewhat concerned to find themselves playing in their studded boots against opponents who wore no boots at all. It seemed unfair and unsportsmanlike and, believe it or not, they were even scared of treading on their opponent's feet. Then one of the Ceylonese kicked a dead ball well over the half-way line with one of these same bare feet and they put their inhibitions behind them. *Repulse* won the match 3–1 in spite of a tropical downpour which came down in the middle. It was the last game ever to be played by the ship's team and not long afterwards she sailed to make her rendezvous with the *Prince of Wales*.

The other ship made the voyage from Greenock around the Cape to Ceylon in just over a month. It was for her company also a pleasant and peaceful voyage although Captain Leach worked his men hard at any sort of training the long passage allowed of. They, too, felt the war recede behind them and wondered where they were bound. They too, even on this fine modern ship, found the heat of the tropics a great trial below decks. For them, however, there was something more serious than heat—there were rats. Alf Tudor first made their personal acquaintance one night when he awoke from a very sound slumber on the mess deck, feeling as though someone was running his fingers lightly over his face. Someone, he thought, was playing a joke—probably his pal Johnny King, who was sleeping beside him. So he opened his eyes cautiously, and instead of Johnny King saw the biggest, dirtiest, and blackest rat he had ever set eyes on, crawling all over him. His yell awoke the whole mess and as sailors are no more fond of rats than other people, there was hullabaloo and chase all over the mess deck. Thereafter there were rats on the beams, rats in awkward places, rats all over the place; and presently there was an order that anyone catching a rat would report it and show it to the officer of the watch, dead or alive. The procedure then was that the officer of the watch handed over half a crown and ordered the rat to be thrown over-side. Now, naval officers are trained to have very sharp eyes but naval ratings have their own ways of dealing with such matters: it was quite common for the same rat to be used twice and Alf swears that one of his shipmates got three half crowns out of the same rodent. It is a common practice and an old skill in the navy and it was much more fruitful on this particular voyage than the spotting of mines (for which there was the same reward) for there were no mines about in these latitudes.

Where the rats had come from was a mystery, because there were certainly none in the spick-and-span ship when she was first commissioned——at least there were none in evidence. Maybe a small colony of them had been lying low in one of those deep-down compartments where Slinger Wood and his mate had once passed the rivets, and there bred prolifically until, like the Nazis, they had come out in search of Lebensraum. They were first noticed when the ship came out of dock after the battle damage of the *Bismarck* action had been made good. It was commonly supposed (and it is very much more likely) that they found their way aboard during this particular docking; so the Birkenhead docks were absolved and Clydeside took the blame. It was even stated in some quarters that they were rats with a Scottish accent, but this is undoubtedly carrying the matter too far: Scottish or otherwise, they kept a lot of people busy and served to provide annoyance and sport, according to the occasion on which they were sighted.

For watching in idle moments, however, there were porpoises gambolling endlessly round the ship, and flying fish in their never-ending flights of death: some of these would land on deck, and men would clean them and cure them and varnish them for a souvenir—centrepiece of a grandfather's tale in years to come, perhaps, if only Smuts's premonition were wrong and the Japanese were not "nippy." Now and then, in the course of streaming and retrieving the paravanes, a small shark would find its way aboard. A little enthusiastic butchery on the part of one of the ratings would yield the teeth, and these made a very nice souvenir indeed: the rest of the shark was returned to the sea. Apart from that there were deck quoits and draughts and the eternal uckers— championship games being played on deck with gigantic pieces—not to speak of crib, on which a tot, gambled away in "sippers," could last a goodly time. There was the cinema, with a good supply of films. There were boxing tournaments, with Johnny King and the PTI sergeant as the star turns. There was the recreation room and the piano, still with a bit of hell not yet knocked out of it, and plenty of voices to help it out in a sing-song. There was the canteen, but here there were soft drinks only, so that generally there developed a great thirst and longing for beer. And the mat and belt-making business was still in full swing.

Alf Tudor had a very interesting job: he was 2 i/c side party, which consisted of twelve ratings; and when the petty officer was on other duties, which was often, he tasted the sweets of command. It was then his job to march smartly up to the Commander, salute and report his party present and correct; whereupon the Commander would then give him instructions about his party's work. It was as well that the Commander never took it into his head to check up whether the party was truly present and correct or not; if he had done so, he'd have found most of them smoking in the lavatories, whence Alf presently had to wheedle them out to get on with the job. What matter? The work always got done and there were no complaints; and it is not unlikely that the Commander had as good an idea as anyone else of what went on.

What were the thoughts of Admiral Phillips and Captain Leach in these days, segregated in the loneliness of command? Surely they must have been long and anxious, even without foreknowledge of the movements of those other ships in another ocean. How Leach must have ached for gunnery practice for his crew, for more working-up time, for a hundred opportunities this hurried voyage into the southern seas gave no hope of. Well enough for the men to enjoy—sailor fashion—their summer days, preening themselves on the action they had already seen, on the glamour with which the Churchill trip had surrounded them, their success in the Malta convoy. Well enough for Mr. Churchill to send boastful cables to Stalin——the Captain had to deal with hard realities. And Phillips, with the greatest opportunity of his career before him and the responsibility for a whole new theatre of war at sea, must have wrestled very earnestly with the problem of turning two ships into a fleet.

The *Prince of Wales* was "noticed" at Capetown on November 16, and Capetown went wild over the Glamour Ship, the most powerful modern battleship that had ever entered Table Bay. She was one of the last generation of British ships of war which would get a reception under the shadow of Table Mountain, where so many generations of naval commanders, from Captain Cook and Captain Bligh of the *Bounty* onwards, had thankfully found haven. In all this welcome and crowding and cheering it would have been quite impossible to imagine that in not very many years this would be almost an alien port, the freedom of which could not be taken for granted by ships flying the White Ensign. Surfeited with their weeks of soft drinks in the canteen and their thirst for beer heavy upon them, the ship's company smacked their lips at the promised joys ashore, and their eyes opened with joyful anticipation at the lines of big American cars drawn up on the quay, with amiable hosts and hostesses proffering hospitality. It was all very exciting: the noble quartet of Johnny King, Joe Dempsey, Smithey, and Alf Tudor made their way down the gangway and took their pick.

For a while they were driven round sight-seeing, relaxing in the soft seats of the big car and feeling like the lords of creation. Then at last Johnny King (after all he was a boxing champion and not to be overawed by big cars and well-to-do hosts and hostesses) suggested stopping for a drink.

"Plenty of time," said their host, "you'll get all the drink you'll need when we get home. It won't be long."

So they sat back and possessed themselves in patience a little longer, with thoughts of long, cool tankards rioting in their fevered brains and their lips as dry as parchment.

They got there at last and were made comfortable in a spacious and comfortable living room, while their host and hostess disappeared.

"I hope he's not much longer getting the bottle out," muttered Johnny.

The words were hardly out of his mouth when in came their host, all smiles, bearing a tray of half-pint glasses clinking with ice. They took their glasses, they raised them gratefully, they drank, and pain and astonishment spread over their faces.

It was lemonade.

There was only one thing to be done about it: as soon as they decently could they thanked these good people for their kindness, made their excuses and withdrew. They were offered a lift back into the town which they accepted; the doors of the car were barely closed behind them before they were legging it at their best speed and with grim determination for the nearest pub.

Now Alf Tudor was carrying the kitty, and even under such circumstances as these, a sailor cannot resist a good practical joke. So he told his pals to sit down at a table while he went to the bar for the drinks: and here he bought himself a beer and sent his mates three large lemonades.

"To hell with this!" they said, and it was only the danger of being thrown out of the bar that saved Alf from being torn limb from limb. It was only when they had a few pints inside them that they began to see the joke. By the time they were on their way back to the ship it was uproariously funny. And so they made their way back up the gangway, roaring, and slapping their thighs. Capetown was all right, after all.

Admiral Tom Phillips had other things to think about than beer or even lemonade. As Mr. Churchill's emissary he called upon Field Marshal Smuts. There is no record of their conversation, but it is safe to assume that the shape of things in the Far East was earnestly discussed between them and there is no doubt whatsoever that Smuts once more unburdened himself of the premonitions which he alone among the statesmen appeared to feel so keenly. We do know that he approved of the sending of the ships to Singapore; we also know that he repeated his warning of Japan's position in the balance of power between the naval forces in the Pacific.

The further review of the *Prince of Wales*'s destination which had been promised the First Lord when the ship arrived at Capetown never took place, and at this stage probably no-one had any expectation that it would take place. Churchill had been determined that the ship should go to Singapore. She was on her way to Singapore: she had passed the point of no return, and all the doubts and all the premonitions would not cause her to deviate from the course which had been set for her.

Smuts inspected her as he had inspected the *Repulse*. The weather was kinder and no-one got wet. And so in all her majesty and splendour, before the eyes of the cheering crowds who feasted their eyes on this vision of power and might, she weighed anchor, cleared the harbour, and was gone—a great floating bastion carrying imperial strength into

distant seas. What other eyes were watching among those
cheering crowds? Or was there now any further need for alien
eyes to be watching? Already the Japanese High Command
knew what ships were on their way to Singapore and already
they had been added to the all too slender total of Allied
naval strength in Far Eastern waters for which allowances
would have to be made when the time for striking came.

That time was near at hand. As the *Prince of Wales*
steamed majestically round Africa's rugged last ramparts
against the great southern ocean that batters eternally upon
them, pitching slowly and deeply in the long Cape rollers,
the movements of those other ships on the other side of
Asia were quickening in pace and in intensity. They assumed purpose, pattern. The concentration in the Kuriles
was complete: the troop convoys for flinging into the Kra
Isthmus and into the Philippines were assembled, the air
striking forces were ready and poised. In only a few days,
Tojo would be warning the Japanese Ambassador in Berlin
that the outbreak of the Far Eastern war might be "sooner
than anyone dreams."

So widespread became these movements that they could
no longer wholly escape the notice of the Allied powers——
up to this moment confident in the three months or more
of negotiation that still assuredly lay ahead, comfortable in
the assurance that the appearance of Churchill's latest and
greatest battleship at Singapore would "steady" the Japanese
situation. On November 26, President Roosevelt sent a
warning to the High Command in the Philippines. Its tone
is almost reluctant, a half-admission that time suddenly
seemed to be running out, that the time-table of British and
American preparations was about to be thrown out of gear:

"Preparations are becoming apparent for an early aggressive movement . . . As yet there are no indications of its
strength and character."

It was on the selfsame day this message was sent that
the Japanese carrier force sailed from the Kurile Islands. Its

destination was not the Philippines, but a pin-point in the
vastness of the Pacific Ocean—a pin-point within air striking
distance of Pearl Harbour. From it a blow would be struck
that would truly change the course of the war and of history.
These ships were on a mission that would turn the voyage of
the *Prince of Wales* and the *Repulse* into a futile gesture of
outworn diplomacy, a threat couched in a dead language,
belonging to an antique and superannuated conception of
the balance of naval power in the East. And once they had
sailed, once the whole, complex machine of Japanese agres-
sion stirred into motion, the *Prince of Wales* and the
Repulse were doomed, Singapore, Hong Kong, and the
Philippines were doomed, the Western hold on the outposts
of Asia cracked.

See, then, the great ship, mighty yet only half-ready for
sacrifice, tried in battle yet with her working-up never properly completed, steaming oblivious through brilliant weather
and a glassy sea—the whole of Africa between her and both
the grim North Atlantic and the battle-torn Mediterranean,
the only war at sea her people were yet aware of. Steaming
towards her rendezvous with the *Repulse*, which Tom
Phillips knew of and Captain Leach knew of—but also towards another rendezvous in the morning of a day off
Kuantan, which they did not know of; any more than did
the Lords of the Admiralty, Mr. Churchill, President Roosevelt, or anyone else.

On November 28 she arrived at Colombo and, pausing
only to top up with oil and water, sailed to meet the *Repulse*
at sea off the coast of Ceylon. Sir Tom Phillips left her
temporarily here: he had orders to fly ahead of his force to
Singapore.

So the two ships were in company at last after all the near
misses, and Slinger Wood, from the deck of his own ship,
could at last behold his handiwork at sea. Somewhere deep in
the bowels of this other leviathan that steamed in company
with them were the narrow compartments in which he had

worked on Cammell Laird's slipway in Birkenhead, away on
the other side of the world—the compartments at the
strength and complexity of which he and his workmate had
wondered, the compartments where they had seen the vision
of great ships queening it on a British ocean, that had driven
them to the naval recruiting office at Canning Place. The
thought intrigued him, but what intrigued him and his shipmates still more was what the hell two capital ships were
doing together so far from any theatre of war of which they
knew. The whole thing had got completely beyond the com-
prehensions of the lower deck, and many long and furious
debates were held about it. In the end they decided the only
thing they could possibly decide, and the course their ship
was now shaping confirmed them in it—that they were out
there as a warning to the Japs. For once the mess deck and
Mr. Churchill were in complete agreement.

It remained now to discuss and put in its proper place the
Japanese Navy and the Japanese Air Force, just as the Nazi
naval and air forces had been discussed and put in their
proper places both before the outbreak of war and after.
What did they know? Almost as much, it might seem, as
the people who had sent them there—almost, beyond denial,
as much as the Foreign Office, which had played such a
strong and curious part in their sending. Almost all the units
of the Japanese Fleet were old and obsolete. The Japanese
Air Force was small and such aircraft as it boasted were supposed to be made of rice-paper, wood, and string: it consisted mostly of fighters, with a few squadrons of bombers,
and some Mitsubishi torpedo-bombers. These latter, they
were certain, were similar to our own Swordfish—flying crates
—not a patch, for instance, on the Coastal Command
Beauforts, which they had seen for the first time just before
they left the U.K. and which they had marvelled at for their
speed and performance. They disposed of all these as readily
as they had disposed of the German pocket battleships, the
U-boat fleet and the Luftwaffe—as readily as a nation of wish-

ful-thinkers had disposed of cardboard mines, fighting vehicles rolling on ersatz rubber, and all the rest of it. Very comical, very lower deck: but was it really so different from the too-ready assumptions of the people in high places who ought to have known and could have known better, of the braggarts in the fools paradise of Singapore, of the strategists who were confident that the Japanese "weren't very good at aircraft," of the Air Vice-Marshal who said that the Brewster Buffaloes were "good enough for Singapore?" Both the lower deck and their betters were soon to know otherwise: the lower deck would atone for their ignorance in blood and in the choking death of an oil-covered sea——their betters in the loss of an empire which they did not deserve to keep.

The two capital ships and their four destroyers set course for Malaya. Captain Tennant was the senior captain and now, with Admiral Sir Tom Phillips temporarily absent, was in command. The *Repulse,* therefore, took the lead with the Glamour Ship following on her starboard quarter—the last time that the fine old ship would lead either this or any other naval force. Her days were numbered, but the days of pride left to her were even less. In a very short time indeed now she would be H.M.S. *Anonymous.*

On December 2 they arrived. Before they entered harbour, Sir Tom Phillips rejoined the *Prince of Wales,* which now took the lead, and the *Repulse* followed behind her. Round they came into the narrow waters of the Jahore Strait, and at the naval base everyone who was anyone in Singapore was waiting to greet them. Vice-Admiral Sir Geoffrey Layton was there, Air Vice-Marshal Brooke-Popham, General Percival, Air Vice-Marshal Pulford, Admiral Spooner, and Mr. Duff-Cooper. The latter gentleman, after a truly royal progress through Malaya, the Dutch Indies, Burma, and India, seeing the sights and dining in state, had compiled his report, in which he had recommended the appointment of a Commissioner General for the Far East. Since completing it he had occupied the time with a lightning visit to Australia and New Zealand. It had only been on December 1 that Keswick, his assistant, left for London with the report: it was an ominous and most appropriate day, for it was the very day on which Tojo's Cabinet made its official decision to go to war, so confirming the preparations which had been so amply and thoroughly made. In short it was now certain that before very long there would be no Far East for a Commissioner General to rule over and organise, but Duff-Cooper and the other personalities had no inkling of this. They watched the ships arrive, punctual to the minute. To them they appeared to be the final contribution to the security of the great fortress and the defence of South East Asia. Now there was not only a fortress: there was a fleet. There was not only a fleet but there was the greatest and most powerful battleship in the world, that had fought the *Bismarck* and carried the person of Mr. Churchill himself across the sea. Could anything more be wanted?

The Japanese aircraft carriers were well on their way. Reports of the other ship movements were becoming so persistent that the Admiralty were already seriously concerned about the future and the fate of Force Z. Their concern was not shared by those in Singapore. How many of those who had a right to know about it is difficult to assess, because there is no record of it having been discussed. Vice-Admiral Layton broadcast on the improvement in the situation brought about by the arrival of the ships.

CHAPTER

11

ALONGSIDE THE "PRINCE OF WALES," THE QUAYSIDE WAS like Portsmouth in Navy Week. Cars came and went. People jostled. Up and down her gangways there was a continual procession; she swarmed with visitors and journalists—the latter ferreting valiantly for any palatable bits of non-security information about ship or crew they could lay hands on. They had already discovered Johnny King, and Johnny King was holding court in a manner which was to prove highly beneficial to his messmates as well as to himself. Every European in the town seemed to be anxious to get as close as possible to the floating fortress that had come to make their security complete. The Glamour Ship was in the limelight again.

By contrast the *Repulse* was as innocent of visitors as though she were still berthed in Scapa Flow. No-one appeared to be interested in her—for all practical purposes no-one seemed to be aware that she was there. To begin with, her crew paid very little attention to this. The *Prince of*

Wales was, after all, the Admiral's flagship—inevitably there must be comings and goings, arrivals and departures of official personages and all the other commotion that went with an Admiral's business. And no-one could deny that she *was* the Glamour Ship, Churchill's Yacht, the latest and greatest of battleships: in comparison with the *Repulse*, she bristled with guns of every shape and size. You had to be fair about these things.

Night came. The good-time city blazed with lights. There was no blackout, ashore or afloat. Scuttles were open and pleasant breezes filled the living spaces of the ships: even the ventilating ducts no longer pumped out hot air, and there was no inducement to Slinger Wood or anyone else to lose his temper. The war seemed further away than ever.

Then it came. It came first through the BBC news bulletin, which had brought so many shocks and surprises to the *Repulse*, from the sinking of the *Royal Oak* onwards.

"The *Prince of Wales* and other heavy units," it said, "have arrived at Singapore."

It sounds a small thing, especially at this distance of years. It was not a small thing for a proud ship's company, as proud as the company of any ship in the King's Navy. Had not this ship been the envy of Portsmouth, gleaming from stem to stern and ready to take the King and Queen to Canada? A great number of the men who had manned her then were still aboard her: they remembered the envious looks, the arguments, the bloody noses. Had she not, long before the *Prince of Wales* was launched, laid down or even thought of, steamed majestically into the ports of South Africa and South America, bearing the heir to the King Emperor, while sirens bellowed, guns thundered in salute, craft swarmed round her and the populace ashore went mad? Had her crew not a reputation for gunnery unchallenged in the Fleet? Had they not steamed a quarter of a million miles at war and never lost a single life or merchant ship entrusted to them? Had they not, brief weeks only before, manned ship to take a formal farewell of the last and greatest of their convoys and heard the troops cheer them from ship after ship as they passed? Had they not been feted in Durban, inspected by Field Marshal Smuts? Had they not been the *Repulse*, a ship whose name was known to and admired by all the world? And now they were lumped somehow into that phrase, "other heavy units." They were no longer H.M.S. *Repulse*. They were H.M.S. *Anonymous*. It rankled bitterly.

But there was more to come. Presently it was discovered that the *Prince of Wales*'s men were being allowed leave ashore: there was canteen leave only for the *Repulse*. Then news filtered through that the crew of the *Prince of Wales* had permission to write home and tell their people where they were—after the BBC announcement there was no point in their situation being barred from mention anyway. And this was the unkindest thing of all: *Prince of Wales* could have all the glamour, her men could have all the beer in Singapore and all the floozies on the island—but why should their friends and families be able to have news of them while the friends and families of the *Repulse*'s men could not? They must have been anxious and wondering why mail had been so infrequent, listening, perhaps, to every news bulletin for ill tidings of the ship. Let the proud old ship be H.M.S. *Anonymous* if she had to be, but why should wives, sweethearts, and parents have to pay in heartbreak for the fact that their men were not on the Glamour Ship?

For the first time in all her vicissitudes, the spirits of her crew hit rock bottom. The men who had refused to be discouraged by all the phantom-chases, still remained ready and eager for anything through disappointment after disappointment, felt weary and forlorn. Their bitterness turned to anger. Some of them remember that bitterness to this day. Forever after, even on the rescue ships, even in their return as survivors to Singapore, many of them read into every hardship that was inflicted on them, every shortcoming in the arrangements made for them, preference for the *Prince of Wales*'s men and neglect of themselves. It was a good job the journalists were not bothering themselves about the *Repulse*—otherwise, once again, we might have had a legend of "passive mutiny" about the *Repulse* to cap the famous "mutiny" of the *Prince of Wales*. It would, of course, have been an equally fatuous legend: there was no mutiny or anything remotely like it. There was not a shred of possibility of it aboard as good a ship as the *Repulse*.

Captain Tennant piped all hands and spoke to his crew over the loudspeakers. He told them he was doing what he could for them. He told them he had spoken to the Admiral, and that they could now write home, telling their people where they were. This action—prompt and understanding as always—eased things a lot, and in a matter of minutes, everyone was writing furiously. More than that he could not give them, because he knew the reason for that anonymity and could not tell them. Even had it been possible for him to tell them, the truth would perhaps have hurt them still more. The announcement and the form in which it was made had two purposes: to advertise to the Japanese the presence of the *Prince of Wales* in Far Eastern waters (thereby providing the Foreign Office with that "steadying" influence it so much desired and filling the enemy with those "reactions and perturbations" Mr. Churchill had spoken of); and at the same time to conceal the fact that the "other heavy units" consisted of one twenty-five year old ship with but six main guns, lightly armoured and appallingly deficient in AA defence, together with four destroyers, two of them unserviceable or nearly so.

Logical, indeed, but what hollow logic! What needless humiliation of a fine ship and a splendid ship's company! Could it really and truly have been supposed that the progress of the *Repulse* over half the world had not been reported to the Japanese? Could it really have been imagined that within hours or less of the arrival of Force Z in Singapore the Japanese High Command were not aware of just what ships were there, what sort of ships and with what escorts? There was no need to advertise the arrival of the *Prince of Wales;* there was no need to conceal the presence of the *Repulse*. There was no chance of doing so, let alone need. Singapore Island and the whole of Malaya boasted a better Fifth Column by far than Spain had boasted in its Civil War, or France in 1940: that became obvious enough when the invasion came and should have been obvious before. General Percival himself has owned to the existence of at least one radio transmitter it had never been possible to track down, and where there was one there were undoubtedly others. Had the security forces been ten times the size they were it would have been impossible to guard against such things completely: in the actual state of things there was not a hope of being able to do so. If more evidence be required, it is provided by the manner of the subsequent Japanese attack on the ships, by the fact that the high-level bombers attacked the *Repulse* alone—knowing what ship she was and that her horizontal armour was light, knowing equally that bombs of the weight they carried would make no impression on the *Prince of Wales*. It was just another blunder, another piece of sloppy thinking, another part of the illusion that ours was the initiative to arrange things the precise way we wanted them in Eastern waters and that the Japanese were without a clue. By this blunder and to foster this illusion, a fine ship's company were humiliated before they were sunk, and felt their ship's name besmirched before it was obliterated.

In the end the *Repulse*'s men reconciled themselves to things. They had been in desolate places often enough before, they had wiled away the long monotony of endless days at sea, in fair weather and foul, tensed for action that never came or bored for want of prospect of action. It was hard with the bright lights and the night life of Singapore beckoning, but it was not impossible: at least the war was far away, at least they were released from the blackout and the eternal humid fug that went with it. For them, therefore, such entertainment as they could make among themselves; for the *Prince of Wales* the garish splendours of the bars and clubs wide open to them and eager to take their money. It could not fairly be grudged to them—even some of the *Repulse's* people in all their bitterness had to admit that it could not be grudged. A very large number of them—a much larger proportion of them than of the *Repulse's* crew—were "hostilities only" ratings, making their first long voyage away from the theatres of war in which their brief service had so far been spent. A century of British seamen had been the lords of the nightspots of the ports east of Suez—had drunk, danced, taken their women, been fleeced, knocked on the head, and run riot in their turn. Now in their trail came the last of the last generation: the long, long era in which every cafe in every seaport had been open house to men of the Queen's Navy and the King's Navy was drawing to a close. It was positively the final appearance in these places of the swashbuckling British tar as he had been sung right from the days of Tom Bowling and before. These were the last inheritors—the clerks, the artisans, the civilians in uniform who had taken the place of the press-ganged crews, and the hard-living sailormen of the generations before them.

In another fashion the admirals, the generals, the air vice-marshals, and the civilian dignitaries were also celebrating the arrival of Force Z. There was a great dinner party for the Admiral and the senior officers, attended by all the important people in the city which had received so many important people and had been the scene of dinner parties without number. Everybody, says Duff-Cooper, felt cheerful and confident, and it may be that in the glow of good hospitality and against the traditional background, dignified by all the trappings of British sovereignty on the seas, even those who knew enough for foreboding could feel cheerful and confident together for just this short space, before all the blunders of the century caught up with them, and the particular blunder of those who had sent it there caught up with Force

Z. "There was a sound of revelry by night," adds Duff-
Cooper; and to all who have survived to remember it, that
night's gathering is known as the Waterloo Dinner.

It can have been but the briefest of respite for Admiral
Phillips and for those who were either in his confidence or
in the confidence of the war cabinet and the Admiralty. In
London there was already deepening anxiety about the ships,
and a growing conviction that Singapore was no secure haven
for them under the existing circumstances and under the
menace of the intense activity that was now clearly going on
among the hidden forces of the new enemy. On December
3 the Admiralty was already asking Admiral Phillips if he
could get some destroyers from the American Asiatic Fleet
to take him away, and the Prime Minister himself—who had
campaigned at such length and with such intransigence to
get the ships despatched to this place as a menace and a
warning to the Japanese—read the signal and observed that
the ship's whereabouts should become unknown as soon as
possible. To paraphrase his own description of the function
of battleships under such circumstances, they had appeared
and now it seemed they were about to disappear, but neither
their appearance nor their impending disappearance seemed
to be arousing the "reactions and perturbations" that had
been foretold.

For his part Phillips (although he must have known that
he was almost asking for the moon) had signalled stressing
the urgency for more ships to reinforce him. The *Revenge*
and the *Royal Sovereign* which were on convoy duty in
Indian waters could, he supposed, reach Singapore by
December 20. The *Warspite* would be due at Singapore soon
on her way back to England from the West coast of America.
The *Ramillies* and the *Resolution*—two more of the R-class
battleships the Admiralty had originally proposed to base
upon Ceylon—were still in the U.K. and it would take six
weeks or more to get them there at the best. The aircraft
carrier *Hermes* was also in the Indian Ocean, and some

commentators have expressed surprise that she was not sent to Singapore to make good the loss of the *Indomitable* which should have accompanied Force Z but was prevented from doing so by her grounding off Kingstown. It is true that this would temporarily or superficially have helped to make good the fighter cover for the ships that could not be provided by Air Vice-Marshal Pulford's command. But the *Hermes* was an old carrier, based on cruiser design, and unarmoured. To send her to join Force Z would have been sending her and her fighters to suicide. It is doubtful whether they could have helped, and it is quite clear now that enough ships and men had already been put up for useless sacrifice.

Phillips was also exploring the possible use of Port Darwin in Australia as a base for the ships, and arrangements were already being made for Captain Tennant to proceed there with the *Repulse* in a couple of days' time. In the midst of all this, however, he was still saddled with his duties, as commander of Force Z, of working out plans and proposals for the employment of that force to best advantage in Far Eastern waters and for co-ordinating its movements with the American, Dutch, and other forces. He was unenviably trying on the one hand to safeguard his force against annihilation and on the other laying down plans for its future tactical and strategical employment. About this latter, too, the increasing tempo and menace of Japanese naval and troop movements were changing people's minds. General MacArthur was alarmed (and very justifiably) about the situation in the Philippines and was proposing that the British ships should come to Manila and so be in a position to help repel a Japanese landing there. On December 4, therefore, Phillips flew to Manila to discuss the situation with Admiral Hart, the American naval commander there, and to produce with him the co-operative plan of action between the British, American, and other naval forces which it had been part of his brief to achieve.

We therefore have the following situation, already complex and about to become more complex still: the ships are at Singapore in a position now clearly precarious and becoming more precarious daily—their offensive role is rapidly becoming obscured by the need to provide for their survival. The *Prince of Wales* is having fitted at the naval base the extra Oerlikons which she has brought from Ceylon; the *Repulse* is about to sail with two destroyers, ostensibly on a short training cruise (what further training did this very well worked-up ship's company require?), but actually to explore the possibilities of Port Darwin as a base for Force Z. The two remaining destroyers—*Jupiter* and *Encounter*—are in dry dock for the making-good of the defects they have brought with them all the way from the Mediterranean. Far away in London the Admiralty is frantically endeavouring to do what it can to organise the safety of the two capital ships it had fought a losing battle to save from the situation in which they have now been placed. Admiral Sir Tom Phillips is airborne on his way to discuss strategic naval plans under circumstances in which neither he nor the people with whom he is about to discuss them any longer hold the initiative: at least half the factors which should condition his discussions are unknown and the whole situation is liable to change radically without warning. The good-time city is still carefree by day, blazing with light, and gay with music by night, and in it the men of the *Prince of Wales* are taking their traditional sailors' pleasures as far as their inclinations move them or their pockets permit, while the men of the *Repulse* are making the best of being the men of H.M.S. *Anonymous* with canteen leave only permitted to them.

And the Japanese carrier force, still steaming in complete security down the vast sea spaces of the Pacific Ocean, has now made good the major part of its course towards that pin-point in the ocean from which the aircraft will be launched against Pearl Harbour. The seaborne forces and their escorts for the invasion of Malaya and the Philippines are poised to strike; the Mitsubishi bombers at Saigon (which are not made of rice-paper, wood and string, and which are manned by pilots specially trained in attacks on shipping) are at readiness. The scene is set for that disaster that Field-Marshal Smuts had foreseen and spoken of.

It took no more than two days for Phillips to reach complete agreement with Admiral Hart at Manila. It may, perhaps, be supposed that neither of them had their hearts completely in this planning for future naval strategy in the Pacific, and it may also be supposed that, with the still vague but increasingly threatening intelligence reports coming in, both felt some measure of haste to get the job over and done with. Nonetheless, the document they produced is a competent and workmanlike job and would certainly have worked out very well if only the Japanese had given it time to. Since they did not—since, moreover, we are only concerned with matters of high strategy insofar as they affect the fate of the *Repulse* and the *Prince of Wales*—there is no point in reproducing it in detail here. It is only necessary to say that it started by stressing two points of prime importance: that in the early stages of hostilities the initiative would lay with the Japanese and not with the Anglo-Americans, and that it was vital to prevent the Japanese from penetrating the "Malay barrier." True though the first of these was, it must still have been novel to some people, at least, in London until the events of the next few days made it historical fact; true though the second was, it was still not altogether obvious to the defenders of Singapore, although forthcoming events were to make it also a matter of history. His appreciation of the overriding urgency of this point to the defence of Singapore was a very strong factor in Phillips' subsequent decisions: it has a strong bearing on the fate of Force Z. Almost as a postscript it recorded the conviction of the two admirals that Singapore as a base for Force Z was untenable, and it proposed Manila as the only alternative. But in the outcome, the one turned out to be as untenable as the other.

Phillips brought the agreement back to Singapore with him when he flew in on the 7th, and it was immediately signalled to London. By the time he reached Singapore it was obsolete; by the time his signal reached the Admiralty it was antedeluvian.

For on the 6th the first hard information about Japanese movements became known in London and Washington. Thirty-five Japanese transports, escorted by eight cruisers and twenty destroyers were on the move from Indochina across the Gulf of Siam, with the undisputable object of a seaborne attack on the Kra Isthmus, the "neck" of Malaya. Other Japanese Fleets were also at sea: information about these was vague and certainly included no hint of the movements of Admiral Nagumo's carrier force, which was now within a matter of hours of flying distance from Pearl Harbour.

The first consequence of this news was the recall of the *Repulse*, only a matter of hours at sea on her voyage to Darwin. Her change of course occasioned little surprise to the men who had had so much experience of racing and chasing any more than did the end of weeks of near-peacetime routine that sent them to battle stations. They guessed that some balloon of some sort had gone up somewhere or other, and under the circumstances it could only be a Japanese balloon. They had seen a lot of balloons go up and all too many of them had been imaginary balloons. Nonetheless, as the ship's faithful old turbines, vibrating beneath them, drove her back at speed to Singapore, they re-examined once more the Japanese Fleet, the Japanese Air Force and Japan's chances in general—the obsolescence of the first, the rice-paper planes of the second and the general dimness of the third—and came to the same conclusions as they had come to before. On the afternoon of the 6th they arrived back.

There was no outward sign of flap or balloons going up at Singapore. The carefree city looked as carefree as ever, going about its business and its pleasures. As dusk fell—it was a Saturday night—the bright lights blazed out again. Still in their role of H.M.S. *Anonymous*, denied shore leave, the men of the *Repulse* relaxed, taking what pleasure their ship afforded. The Marines' Band played on the upper deck and most of those who were free to do so sat or lounged and listened to it. Some even danced together. When they turned in, it was to the familiar fug of blackout, with portholes shut, deadlights down and the ventilating trunks pouring out hot air. Singapore might wait until the enemy planes were overhead, but not His Majesty's ships.

The *Prince of Wales*'s people, however, were enjoying their own equivalent of the Waterloo Dinner. Three of the same quartet that had had that famous teetotal reception at Capetown—Johnny King, Joe Dempsey and Alf Tudor—went ashore. Their desires were not teetotal and their intentions far from innocent, but the bars and honky-tonks had already taken toll of their purses, and they had but a few dollars between them. It was time to cash in on Johnny's boxing reputation.

It wasn't difficult. A few words with one of the reporters forever about the place produced introductions to one person and another, and before long they found themselves acquainted with a wide circle, all the members of which had a much better understanding of the tastes of sailors and boxing champions than their Capetown hosts. Presently they were told to go to the "New World," which Alf describes as "a kind of show place and night club entertainment." To the "New World" they went, and found that they were expected; they were royally received, in fact, and escorted to a table. Presently a bottle of whiskey, with glasses, made its appearance on the table.

"All right, boys," the manager assured them, appearing in person, "It's on the house."

"O.K.," they said, and started on the bottle.

The bottle was followed by a book of tickets for each of them, and the tickets made them free of the dancing hostesses, temptingly displaying themselves along the wall and awaiting the pleasure of their guests. They danced. They drank. They danced and drank again. The evening began to go with a swing. It not only went with a swing—it went very fast. It went so fast that before any of them had drunk enough or danced enough, it was long past midnight, and their entertainment was suddenly cut short by naval pickets rounding up the ship's complement and ordering them back aboard. A little unsteadily, perhaps, but no more, they piled themselves into rickshaws and rode back in state. It was a lordly end to a wonderful evening. It could have been more wonderful and it could have gone on longer, but it was good enough and they were well content. It was their last evening ashore in Singapore, and the last night of bright lights for the good-time city.

There was still one day of peace left to Singapore. There was still one day in harbour left to the *Prince of Wales* and the *Repulse*. It was a strange twilight sort of day—the same kind of twilight that had descended on life in Britain between Hitler's invasion of Poland and Chamberlain's declaration of war. There was a difference however: a difference especially for those in the *Repulse* who, in the first days of September 1939, had been at sea off the enemy's coast, aggressive and confident, ready to blow out of the water the first enemy ship that dared poke its nose out of port—whereas now they were made fast to a quay in a place that had only not much more than hours before seemed incredibly far from war and now still showed no consciousness of the presence of it. There was none of the tenseness of those September days in a Britain ready with barrage balloons in the sky, policemen in steel helmets, sandbag barricades going up and every evidence of a determination to do the best in the face of whatever the Luftwaffe had in store. The mess decks of both ships were alive with buzzes of one sort and another—and not only the mess decks. Every hour brought intelligence reports, some of them clear, some of them conflicting, most of them vague, all of them sinister.

The Japanese ships had again been sighted by a Catalina in the Gulf of Siam and a Hudson had been fired on by a submarine. There seemed to be two convoys now, one large and one smaller. Suddenly the sea seemed infested with Japanese submarines on mysterious patrols and still more mysterious errands; above the waters surface craft seemed to be appearing and disappearing in a fashion calculated to cause as many reactions and perturbations as the distressful *Tirpitz* herself. There were rumours of aircraft concentrations at Saigon; indeed, there were aircraft concentrations at Saigon and had been for a long time, but how many people realised even now on this last and fateful day that they were equipped with machines of sufficient range to cover the whole Malay Peninsula, including Singapore itself, and all the waters around it? Sir Tom Phillips arrived back to hurry his signals off to London and then, having freed himself from the problems and proposals of a hypothetical future, turned to the urgent problems of the present which menaced his ships at every turn.

Into this atmosphere of rumour, confusion, and menace burst the news of Pearl Harbour. That other voyage which had at its commencement run parallel in time with the voyage of the *Prince of Wales* and the *Repulse* from Ceylon to Singapore had reached the pin-point that was its objective, undetected and unsuspected from start to finish. The American Pacific Fleet had been reduced from a mighty and dominating assembly of ships of war to a shambles of foundering wreckage, of which the surviving units lacked both cohesion and all pretence of being able to control the seas. In half-an-hour, for all practical purposes, the American battle fleet had been extinguished like a light and the whole balance of power in the Pacific Ocean had been reversed. The supply lines had been cut, Admiral Hart's forces at Manila virtually isolated, the few and elderly British units at Hong Kong placed beyond hope of succour—and the *Prince of Wales* and the *Repulse* were out on a limb in the most dangerous sort of situation it is possible for two capital ships to be in, with insufficient escorts and well-nigh non-existent air cover.

Now the lower deck understood the meaning of Smuts's words to them, which up to that moment had seemed a bit of old man's strange nonsense, an irrelevant piece of sooth-saying without logic or over-much meaning. "Many of you will not come back," he had said, and alone of all the prophets he had been right. The attack on Pearl Harbour did not seem like the work of rice-paper planes tied together with string: from what little they knew of the details it did not seem to have been carried out by men lacking either in skill or in determination. It was obviously time to make a reappraisal, to take much more seriously the little yellow men, their aircraft, their training, and their equipment. They did not know yet about the Japanese troop convoys at sea heading for the Kra Isthmus, nor of the submarine sightings, nor of the aircraft in readiness at Saigon. These things were only known to the Admiral, his staff, the senior officers, the chiefs of the other services. To Admiral Phillips the role that he would be forced to play with his ships was already be-coming obvious. It was a role dictated not by his own wishes or his own views of naval strategy, but by the circumstances themselves. There was only one possible salvation for his ships—precipitate withdrawal either to the Indian Ocean, to Australia, or anywhere out of these waters in which Japan almost in a moment had achieved a position of supremacy that could not be materially affected by the biggest and most powerful capital ship ever launched. And withdrawal the one course that was not open to him.

"The remaining forces of all the nations involved had either to be withdrawn at once or left to fight against im-possible odds to the finish . . . though their last fights made little or no difference to the enemy's progress . . . Once there, the ships had to fight as best they could with what they had, for they were committed to playing their part in the hopeless struggle. It was that requirement which, in the

end, dictated the movements of Admiral Phillips' ships."
So Captain Roskill sums up the situation in the Navy's
official history, and the accuracy of this summing-up cannot
be contested.

CHAPTER

12

SIR WINSTON CHURCHILL HAS RECORDED FOR US HIS thoughts and emotions when he heard the news of Pearl Harbour. Overwhelmingly, out of the tragedy that had descended upon the American Fleet, upon the Pacific and upon the whole of the eastern hemisphere, one thought took possession of his mind. Britain at last was no longer alone: Britain would be saved. No need any longer in the midst of all the preoccupations of war to have to wrestle with the problems of American politics. No more need for deliberations over how far Roosevelt could go or could not go. No need any longer to see the bastions of the free world falling one after another around us and wonder how long we could hold the conquerors of Europe, Asia, and Africa at bay. In the dark days of 1940, when France had been over-run and Britain first stood alone, he had trumpeted his determination to hold on until the New World in God's good time should come to the rescue of the Old. But how often as the long and weary months went on, as disaster followed disaster, as

American neutrality seemed again and yet again unshakeable, must his resolution have wavered and his spirits flagged.

In the light of this, could he perhaps be forgiven for feeling emotions of thanksgiving for a tragedy that had meant the sinking of great ships, the deaths of many men, the pitchforking of yet another nation into the holocaust of war? Could he be forgiven for failing to be mindful of the *Repulse* and the *Prince of Wales*, on whose mission to the Far East he had so stubbornly insisted, steamrollering opposition and doggedly standing his ground until he got what he wanted? Could he be forgiven for failing at this moment to have thought for the fact that, instead of sending these ships and these men to steady the Japanese situation, he had sent the ships to their end and the men to their deaths with no useful purpose served by either?

The reader must judge all this for himself and in due time history will also judge. The fact is that Winston Churchill did not think at this moment at all of the *Prince of Wales* and the *Repulse*. He thought only of the immense change that had come about in the world situation. He slept; and having slept, decided to visit Washington.

It is difficult to synchronise events in London and Singapore without performing a mathematical calculation at every stage: the time difference is very great. The Prime Minister slept, lulled by his overwhelming thankfulness that Britain had an ally. The men in the two great ships at Singapore went to their hammocks once more in the hot and fetid atmosphere of a darkened ship—the atmosphere from which they had been mercifully free for a little space. The sweat ran over their naked bodies in the overcrowded spaces where the ventilators again blew hot air instead of cold. They would toss and turn for a long time: in the end the very heat itself seemed to dope them into sleep. But their awakening was a different one from Mr. Churchill's, for they wakened to the sound of the alarm and the quartermaster's voice rasping in the loudspeakers with the air-raid warning yellow.

Slinger Wood and his mates raced for the guns, almost glad in the midst of wondering what was coming to feel the cooler air above decks on their faces and bodies. The brilliant lights of the city were blacked-out—the only illumination was that of the probing searchlights, brilliant against the dark sky. It seemed, he says, as though someone had thrown a switch and cut every light in the place off at one movement. The journalist, O'Dowd Gallagher, however, has another story, a story of confusion, of lights left burning long after the air-raid had started—even the street lights, because there was no co-ordination, no organisation for the air attack which no-one had seriously believed would come. Confusion there certainly was, and death and destruction, too—more people were killed and injured and more damage done this first night than in any subsequent raid before the city's last agonies descended upon it. At their guns and at their other stations about the ships the men listened to the familiar thump and reverberation, the familiar engine drone coming and going elusively in the obscurity: it had once been so familiar to them and from it they had seemed so far away. They had known it at Scapa Flow and at sea, they had known it in their homes, in crowded cities which Goering's bombers had pounded night after night till even the North Atlantic seemed a safer place by far. Now it had followed them, now they knew that this was no business of rice-paper aircraft and comic-opera crews: just as their superiors now knew that all the intelligence stuff about Japanese aircraft types was out of date and hopelessly misleading. Pulford had said that the Brewster Buffaloes were all right for Singapore: now it was realised in a flash that from the very fact that the attacking aircraft could only be from bases in Indochina—their range and speed was far greater than had ever been suspected—and that the Brewster Buffaloes were no match for them in either. Just as the whole of the Pacific Ocean lay open to the Japanese Fleet, the whole of Malaya and the whole of the Gulf of Siam lay open to Japanese bombers. The legendary defences of Singapore were no defence against them. There was no cover and no protection from them and there was no protection for the two ships save for their own anti-aircraft guns—inadequate even in the case of the *Prince of Wales*, hopelessly and pitifully inadequate in the case of the *Repulse*.

The two ships were undamaged in the air-raid, which appeared to be concentrated on the town rather than on the harbour. It was not a long raid, for the aircraft were operating at extreme range. The all-clear went in the end, and back the men stumbled to their hammocks, to toss and turn or be doped into sleep in the heat until five-thirty came with the quartermaster piping "Lash-up and Stow."

It was strange for them to be about the ordinary tasks of tropical harbour routine on this morning—scrubbing decks, breakfasting, working their part of the ship. It was almost a peace-time routine and it seemed strangely irrelevant to the new circumstances in which they found themselves. They went about their work quietly and soberly; there seemed suddenly to be an absence of buzzes crackling through the mess decks. They had heard nothing since the news of Pearl Harbour and most of their talk was about Pearl Harbour; they realised not merely that the attacks on Pearl Harbour could not have been carried out by rice-paper airplanes, but also that the American Fleet was out of action, leaving them the only operational allied units in Far Eastern waters. As such they must be a priority target for the Japanese. There was no shrinking, no panic: their realisation came quietly and coldly as had come the realisation on another morning, many months before, that *Repulse* might have to face the *Bismarck's* guns alone. There was nothing they could do about it except do as they were told and make the best of it, but it was none the more pleasant for that.

What they did not yet know was that this same night there had been simultaneous attacks on Hong Kong and on the Philippines, that only a few hundred miles to the north of them in that narrow northern neck of Malaya, which could have been a bastion of defence but which virtually had no defences at all, the Japanese transports under the cover of their aircraft and their escort's guns had landed their troops at Singora and Kota Bharu. There southward movement had already begun, and in advance of it, the airfields in Northern Malaya from which alone the short-range Brewster Buffaloes could operate over the Kra Isthmus were being bombed and made untenable. Already the defences were being rolled up like a piece of paper: without air cover, as the ships were without air cover, the slender and ill-equipped land forces were proving totally inadequate to hold the advance which appeared to push on through the jungle that had been hopefully declared impassable, as well as along the roads which were thought to be Malaya's only arteries of communication. And at the same time all over Malaya the Fifth Column was operating ahead of both troops and aircraft. The Siamese, whom the Foreign Office had been so anxious not to alienate from their loyalty to Britain by fortifying the Kra Isthmus, were receiving the saviours of Asia with open arms.

Duff-Cooper didn't know either. He was unhappy. Diana was ill with dengue fever; his report had not yet been acknowledged; no-one told him anything, and he felt he had no right to ask. Sir Tom Phillips and the other service chiefs were too engrossed with the grim situation that was developing to be concerned with him. As the reports came in one after the other, as the picture became clarified and deteriorated at the same time, the only role that the Admiral and his ships could play became more apparent still.

In London there was now the most acute anxiety for the ships. It does not seem to have been realised, even by the Admiralty, that an operational role would be forced upon them transcending even the problem of rescuing them from the impossible situation in which they had been placed. Probably the time for extricating them at all with any hope for their survival had already gone by. Mr. Churchill, at a meeting held the following evening—"mostly Admiralty"— expressed his opinion that they should "disappear amid the innumerable islands." In his own war history he gives this as the opinion of the meeting: "There was," he says, "general agreement about that." There was indeed no agreement of the sort. None of the Admiralty present could possibly have either voiced such a curious opinion or agreed to it. To what "innumerable islands" was Mr. Churchill referring? Even granted innumerable islands, how do capital ships "disappear"? Had the German capital ships been able to "disappear" from the searching eyes of our own aircraft even in the steep defiles of the Norwegian fiords? They would be sought out, photographed, hunted down.

How could capital ships be maintained among such islands? How could they navigate among them—*Repulse* with a draught of twenty-seven feet, *Prince of Wales* with thirty-six? How could they be anything but sitting targets, denied sea-room in which to manoeuvre unhampered? How could they be fuelled? How could their few destroyers, more vital to them now than ever, be maintained at sea? How could they be ammunitioned, provisioned? Capital ships are immense fighting units which, like any other fighting units on sea, land or air, need a long chain of complex organisation to keep them in existence, let alone operational. It was a fine turn of phrase to talk about the ships disappearing amid the innumerable islands: it was an empty phrase, it was impractical, it was unrealistic.

Now Churchill had been First Lord of the Admiralty in peace and in two wars. To Roosevelt he signed himself as "Former Naval Person." Until he was called to a greater destiny in 1940, he had regarded his days at the Admiralty as the happiest and most rewarding of his whole career: he rejoiced in ships, was completely in his element on the bridge of the *Oribi*, bucketing her way across Scapa Flow, or the *Prince of Wales*, flinging herself majestically through the

Atlantic storm or showing her pride and her paces up and
down the great convoy. On these occasions he was the Old
Man of the Sea himself—he looked it, he felt it. And yet in
spite of this one suddenly faces the shattering realisation
that he apparently knew absolutely nothing of ship handling,
of the mechanics of big ships, of their maintenance, of their
employment. There is no alternative to it: the facts admit
of no other explanation. The suggestion about the ships disappearing amid the islands could not possibly have come
from a mind that harboured any practical lore about ships
whatsoever, and that is why it is unthinkable that there could
have been "general agreement" about it.

But after the meeting had broken up he had a still more
extraordinary idea:

"I thought myself they should cross the Pacific to join
what was left of the American Fleet. It would be a proud
gesture at this moment that would knit the English-speaking
world together . . . in a few months there might be a fleet
in being on the west coast of America capable of fighting
a decisive battle if need be."

Once more he thought he would sleep on it and decide
the following morning what to do with the *Prince of Wales*
and the *Repulse*.

It would have at least been as well if some signal could
have been sent to Tom Phillips at this stage, or even earlier,
conveying the information that the Prime Minister wished
him to devote himself to the salvation of his ships rather
than to the defence of Singapore. Such a message alone
would have reopened to the Admiral the one course which
he regarded, in common with everyone else, as closed to him
—to withdraw the ships; and probably had he done so and
been able to extricate them, he would have withdrawn them
either to Port Darwin or Ceylon. No indication was given to
him that the Prime Minister had changed his mind about
the role he was to play. By the time the Prime Minister's
meeting broke up it was probably too late; by the time he

had slept on it it was definitely and irrevocably too late. The policy of sleeping on things which had provided the answers to so many knotty problems put the solution to this one beyond scope of realisation.

But what a still more extraordinary idea! These two ships were to cross the Pacific and join the remains of the United States Fleet, now hastily withdrawing from the shambles of Pearl Harbour to the west coast of America—much as one might sail two toy battleships across the Round Pond. Certainly a grand conception—a magnificent gesture—that Britain, the erstwhile suppliant, should make a gift to the great ally now in distress, that all America should see Britain not yet wholly contemptible, should see her generous and sincere; so the friendship of the English-speaking peoples would be cemented. Can he have paused to think that from Singapore to Pearl Harbour is well nigh six thousand miles, from there again to San Francisco over two thousand more? Over this whole great distance the Japanese were in command of the sea with capital ships, destroyers, submarines and aircraft carriers able to strike at will. There was not a single port at which the two ships could refuel, still less their destroyer escorts, whose endurance was much more limited. The destroyer escort in itself was inadequate. There was no possibility of any air cover whatsoever. How in the name of Heaven could the *Prince of Wales* and the *Repulse* have been got across these vast distances of hostile ocean totally unprotected from air attack, virtually unprotected from underwater attack, and easy prey to a massive concentration of surface vessels—against which they undoubtedly would have given the best account of themselves they could, but by which they must have been overwhelmed in the end? They would never have reached the United States, they would never even have reached Manila, where Admiral Hart's Asiatic Fleet already lay with its supply lines cut and its doom upon it. What was it about battleships that could turn Mr. Churchill's thoughts into such extravagant fantasies incapable of realisation in a hard world of concrete facts and practical realities?

What Sir Tom Phillips had done in fact was to call a meeting of senior naval officers at which he expounded the facts of the situation and the course he proposed to take. He did not intend that this course should be open to confirmation or alteration by any discussion or majority vote at the meeting, for no commander can conduct his operations after the manner of an urban district council, but he felt that both the situation and his proposed action on it were such that all concerned should be thoroughly in the picture on it and all concerned should have an opportunity to voice their views.

He saw in the landings at Singora and Kota Bharu a fearful threat to the "impregnability" of Singapore. He saw it more clearly than many of those better acquainted with these regions saw it themselves, even at this time. He was not impressed by the seaward-facing defences of the great fortress, nor was he impressed by the alleged impassability of the jungle through which the attacking Japanese would have to move and were apparently already moving quite successfully. Experienced in war (albeit not in war on land), he realised that the Kra Isthmus was the fourth wall of Singapore's defences. He realised that the enemy, instead of joining the audience, which was goggling in awe at the bastions so impressively depicted on the hollow stage set, had gone round by the stage door and was taking the whole illusion in the rear, where there were no bastions at all. To him the landings on the Kra Isthmus were the most significant part of the complex and menacing picture that had developed over the previous thirty-six hours; and he thought his ships had just a fighting chance of doing something about it. The uncertain reports had only suggested one enemy capital ship in the area, the old battle cruiser *Kongo*. As long as he could use speed to supplement his barely adequate destroyer protection against submarine attack and be granted some measure of air support, he argued that the sixteen heavy guns of the *Repulse* and the *Prince of Wales* could blast the Japanese out of their beach-head, isolate their troops already ashore and turn the whole situation. If this could be achieved it would save Singapore for the time being and, in doing so, save Sumatra, Java, and the stepping stones to Australia. It would alter the whole of the Pacific situation by forcing the Japanese to concentrate naval forces on the South China Sea—at the best it could affect the outcome of the whole war. He realised that the risks were very great, but they were assessable risks, and he accepted them. It is impossible not to feel that he knew the ships were doomed in any case, if they could not be immediately withdrawn out of the battle area, and thought that if they had to sink they might as well sink to good purpose instead of to none.

In any case, in the words of the subsequent official dispatch, it seemed to him "inacceptable to retain the powerful naval force at Singapore in a state of inaction."

The essence of his plan was to sail the two ships and their escorts that evening on a northerly course up the Gulf of Siam—in other words heading well away from the Kra Isthmus towards Indochina. A day's steaming would bring him into the latitude of the Kra Isthmus; under cover of darkness on the second night he would turn westwards towards it at high speed. During the night the destroyers would be detached and return to Singapore, for their endurance was much less than that of the capital ships and they were poorly protected. At dawn the following morning the two battleships would carry out an intensive bombardment of the beach-heads, eliminating as far as possible both them and any surface craft that might be in the vicinity—including, if possible, the *Kongo*. He calculated that the surprise of the attack and the speed of his ships would be sufficient to protect them from serious damage. He hoped for sufficient fighter support to disorganise any air attacks. And he thought it unlikely, if the element of surprise could be maintained, that any aircraft encountered would be carrying either anti-ship bombs or torpedoes. Having thoroughly beaten-up the beach-head and anything else within range, he would then retire and steam hell for leather for Singapore. There would obviously be an attempt at retaliation by air, but the effectiveness of hastily-organised bomber sorties from the bases in Indochina would be doubtful. There was thus a reasonable chance that the ships would regain their base with insufficient damage to impair their fighting efficiency, and it would be an infinitely more secure base for the time being than when they had left it. Singapore would have a respite to improve its defences and receive reinforcements: there might be time to organise at least something more than token resistance.

Now this was no death-or-glory, wild-cat plan. It was a clear-cut and logical piece of thinking which demonstrated Tom Phillips' qualities as a staff officer and justified the trust that the Prime Minister placed in him. It involved considerable risks, but these risks were assessed and accepted, and the assessment of them was sound. It was exactly what the ships were there to do. The spectacle of them appearing at speed out of the blue, hundreds of miles from where they were supposed to be, deluging the luckless Japanese with fire and slaughter, and retiring again into the blue at high speed before anyone had time to do anything serious about them, was a vision such as Mr. Churchill himself might have revelled in. But it was more than a vision or a pipe-dream—it was a tactical possibility based on the facts of an actual situation. There was no blunder about it: failing a direct order not to employ the ships in the way they had been sent to be employed, but to withdraw them, it was inevitable and unavoidable that they should be used in precisely the way in which Phillips proposed to use them. The blunder was in the ships being at Singapore at all: once they were there, the rest followed.

Those present at the meeting—the Chief of Naval Staff,

the Captain of the Fleet, Captains Tennant and Leach, and the staff officers—unanimously gave their support to the proposals. Tennant, realising that he was the only officer from the *Repulse* present, thought it incumbent on him to speak first, and did so: the others followed in turn. The clarity and logic of Phillips' thinking was as apparent to them then as it is to those who examine it with more time for reflection years later, and their appreciation of it reflects as much credit on them as it does on him. It was supported to the hilt by the Admiralty in the enquiry that followed the sinking of the ships: it has since been supported by Sir Winston Churchill, by the official historian of the war at sea, by Grenfell (whose book, *Main Fleet to Singapore*, is one of the bitterest and most critical of books) and by everyone who has so far written or commented with any authority upon it. The unanimity of opinion about it is of a degree rare in the discussion of naval operations.

Now there were two basic elements on which both the chances of the plan's success and the chances of the ships' survival rested. The first of these was surprise; the second was at least sufficient fighter support at the beach-heads to upset the effectiveness of enemy air-attacks on the spot. Surprise, in turn, demanded effective air reconnaissance sufficiently far ahead of the force to remove any possibility of the merest sighting. Fortified, therefore, by his fellow-officers' support of his plan, Sir Tom Phillips went to the Air Officer Commanding, Air Vice-Marshal Pulford. From him he asked three things: reconnaissance a hundred miles to the north of him the following morning, December 9; reconnaissance ten miles off the coast and a hundred miles round the mid-point of Singora at first light on the following morning, the morning of the beach-head attack, and fighter support off Singora at the same time. The first of these Pulford agreed to provide: it was provided, in the event, by one solitary Catalina. The second he thought he would be able to provide: in the event, it turned out not to be necessary. About the third—at least as vital as the other two —he was doubtful, and Phillips appears to have had considerable difficulty in getting any firm decision out of him. By the time the ships were due to sail (and had to sail if they were to be well clear of the Anamba Islands by daylight), there was still nothing definite, and the Admiral's last action before getting under way was to send ashore an urgent note to Pulford with his Chief of Staff, Rear-Admiral Palliser, who was remaining in charge of the Commander-in-Chief's office at Singapore. It was not until after the ships had sailed that Palliser was able to signal to his chief:

"Fighter protection on Wednesday, 10th, will not, repeat not, be possible."

He added the information that Kota Bharu airfield had been evacuated and that the British seemed to be losing grip on other aerodromes, due to enemy action; that the Japanese had large bomber forces based on Indochina and possibly Thailand, and that General MacArthur had been asked to carry out an attack on them with his long-range bombers from the Philippines. The latter was a fat lot of good, for General MacArthur had his own preoccupations.

It remained for Phillips to decide the composition of the rest of his force. Of the four destroyers he had brought with him, only two, *Express* and *Electra*, were serviceable. Both were veterans of the North Atlantic; it had, indeed, been *Electra* who, racing back from the position away to the north where Vice-Admiral Holland's detaching of his destroyers had placed her, picked up the three solitary survivors of the *Hood*. Lieutenant Commander Cain tells us that one man aboard her, at least, recalled at this point what had happened the last time the *Prince of Wales* went to sea with a battle cruiser. The other two, *Jupiter* and *Encounter*, bequeathed him by the Mediterranean Fleet, were still in dock. He replaced them with the Australian destroyer *Vampire* and with *Tenedos*, a small and elderly vessel whose endurance was so low that she would have to be sent back long before the other three destroyers. These four, therefore, with the *Repulse* and the *Prince of Wales*, made up Force Z.

"On the Monday night during the first dog watch," writes Marine John Garner laconically, "we went to sea."

All this day, while the menacing messages had been coming in, the conferences and discussions going on and the arrangements taking shape for the sortie of Force Z, the men of the *Repulse* and the *Prince of Wales* had continued in the settled way of their everyday ordinary routine. Though they knew nothing either of the deteriorating situation or of the measures that were being taken to counter it, the atmosphere of unreality grew about them. The last news they had had was the news about Pearl Harbour, the last evidence of the danger of Singapore, the air-raids of the previous night. Neither Pearl Harbour nor the air-raids had touched them, but this was sufficient for them to realise that the Japanese were on the move, attacking in every quarter at once and attacking with a speed and efficiency that completely belied anything they had been led to suppose. In the uncertainty and unreality of these hours the traditional picture implanted in their minds of little yellow men, barely more than medieval in their equipment and training, worry ineffectively about the feet of the great white colossus of the West, was turned upside-down. Out beyond the Johore Straits the Japanese Fleet was somewhere at sea while the Japanese Air Force was ranging the ocean. It stuck out a mile that they would have to meet the Japanese Fleet; it stuck out a mile that Singapore might at any moment become another Pearl Harbour. They had forgotten their contempt for the Japanese: they talked no more of rice-paper airplanes similar to the earlier type of Swordfish. In a matter of hours the legend of Japanese invincibility that was to persist so long had been

born, just as the legend of German invincibility was born in
the grim days of the Battle of France.

These men were not despondent or afraid—any more that
is than the bravest of men is afraid in the dark hour of inaction before battle. The men of the *Prince of Wales*, with
the *Bismarck* action, the Atlantic Charter journey and the
Malta convoy behind them, were as strong as ever in their
pride in their mighty and unsinkable ship, and if their morale
had needed any boosting, their reception in Singapore had
been a boost indeed. The men of the *Repulse*, in spite of
their resentment at becoming H.M.S. *Anonymous* and at
the favours showered on the other ship's complement but
denied to them, were still confident in themselves, their skill
and training, their ship, their officers, and their Captain.
They were still ready for anything and the events of the
next thirty-six hours were to put their readiness beyond all
doubt forever . . . No, they were neither despondent nor
afraid but sober and thoughtful in a situation that might
give anyone to think, especially sailors on ships of war.

It was no surprise to them, therefore, that as the day wore
on, orders came to prepare the ships for sea. Aboard each
of them men could see the others preparing likewise and it
was obvious to them that the whole of Force Z, such as it
was, was to sail together. It could only mean that they were
going to seek action with the Japanese Fleet. For once Mess
46 on the *Repulse* had neither arguments to contend over,
possibilites to discuss, buzzes to accept or reject, or wagers
on which to stake their rum: the thing was self-obvious, and
when all was said and done it was the thing they had been
seeking for and combing the seas to find for more than two
mortal years.

Before the *Repulse* sailed she received two passengers, the
English journalist O'Dowd Gallagher and the American
newsman Cecil Brown, who represented the Columbia
Broadcasting System. Gallagher had been offered by the
Services Public Relations Office (which the journalists,

inevitably adding to its initials, knew as ASPRO) a mysterious assignment which would take him away from Singapore for four or five days: no more could be revealed than that. Journalist after journalist had turned it down, including Cecil Brown, because all were quite convinced that the biggest stories of all would break in Singapore at any time and that it would be madness to be away from it. But something had clicked in Gallagher's brain: he had asked a guarded question and received an evasive answer, and knew his hunch was right. The trip could only be on the *Prince of Wales* (naturally he never thought for a moment about the *Repulse*), and it was going to be the biggest story of the lot. He begged and bullied Brown into coming with him for his own good and they were whistled aboard so rapidly that they had neither kit, typewriters, nor any other tools of their trade —Gallagher had not even sufficient ink in his fountain pen. This was fortunate for him, strange though it may seem, because when his fountain pen ran out he went scrounging for ink to *Repulse's* writers and was given the only sort of ink they had, a concoction made up from issue powder supplied by the Admiralty: he filled his fountain pen with it dubiously. When he and his notes were fished out of the South China Sea the fountain pen ink had been washed clean from the paper but the *Repulse's* concoction had stood firm and was quite legible. Over the years the Admiralty has had a great deal of experience in supplying ink to ships for which it has been given no more credit than it has for some other things, and when it came to mixing ink even the *Repulse's* writers knew their job. It is a nice and comforting thought to see efficiency in small details that landsmen have no thought of, and there is a moral in it for those who are inclined to doubt how much the Navy knew about its business.

As a matter of fact, when Gallagher and Brown discovered that they were to sail not on the *Prince of Wales* but on the *Repulse*, they very nearly gave up. It was much more than a

question of the *Prince of Wales* being the Glamour Ship
and *Repulse* being H.M.S. *Anonymous*: if they were aboard
Prince of Wales their despatches could carry the dateline
"Aboard *Prince of Wales* in the Gulf of Siam," whereas if
they were aboard the *Repulse* they would not be allowed to
mention her name and would simply have to say "with the
Eastern Fleet." It was fortunate that they did go after all
because Gallagher has been able to give us one of the only
two journalists' account of the sinking of the ships and, as
has already been said, he deserved his "scoop" for having a
journalist's hunch and knowing his trade. His account is far
from completely accurate in detail for two very good
reasons: he suffered from the same difficulty as the ratings
themselves in that one man in one place on a big ship can
only see so much of what is going on and has to rely on
rumour and surmise for the rest; and he suffered also from
the fact that the part of his notes not written in the *Repulse*'s
good waterproof ink was lost to him. These defects do not
destroy its value: in the age of push-button warfare, when
ships are no longer manned, and missiles are untouched by
human hands, it will serve as an example of the function
and the work of the vanished breed of war correspondent
and of its era, which lasted for a little less than ninety years.

Repulse was first under way. This was her last departure.
Heaven alone knows how many times the well-worn routine
of falling in for leaving harbour had been carried out upon
her decks. It would never be carried out again. What can one
say or feel, looking back over the years at this moment with
all the foreknowledge of her doom that her complement
could not have? Would foreknowledge have made any
difference? Service routine permits of no heroics, nor are long
farewells the habit of fighting men.

"I hope," wrote Sir William Tennant to the author, "you
can make the *Repulse* book a fairly happy one, until she is
sunk, for they were a good, keen and happy ship's company
and even if she went down in battle with her ensign flying,

I suppose it was what we all joined the Navy to do if necessary—so don't let us be too sad!"

So be it. The stiff upper lip, the silent tear, and all the trappings of emotion belong to the world of melodrama, to the lives of secure people with armchairs under their bottoms and dry land under their feet, seeking a spurious thrill as spice for a safe existence. In a world of action they have no place. Certainly let there be anger for the *Repulse*, for the *Prince of Wales* and for all the other ships who fought out their last fights in these seas—anger for their needless sacrifice, for the blunders that led them into it, for the waste of good vessels and good ships' companies their sacrifice involved. Let there be anger by all means, but let there be no tears. Let us just remember that she was a good ship, a happy ship and that she was sunk—and be thankful for her and the kind of men who sailed in her, for all the good work she did, the long convoys she shepherded safely into port, the countless men who felt secure while she was with them. Let us even forget that she went to her end as H.M.S. *Anonymous*.

She was under way first, and then the *Prince of Wales* was with her, slowly overtaking her to take up her position in the van. Mighty and terrible the *Prince of Wales* looked, one of the last and greatest of the breed of battleships, the doom of which was implicit in her own. From her commissioning, she was less than ten months old. Out of that time, allowing for her two months in dock after the *Bismarck* action, for the Placentia trip, and for the long voyage east, she had spent a bare five at sea on the work for which she had been built. Into that time had been crammed the *Bismarck* action, the Atlantic Charter, and the great Malta convoy, and now she was to go down fighting in the South China Sea. A short life for a great ship that had taken so many years to build, but a life with history in it. The men of the *Repulse* looked out upon her and, in spite of all their resentment, admired her: Slinger Wood looked out upon his handiwork.

Aboard her, Admiral Sir Tom Phillips, with all his responsibilities, all his problems, all his too-clear certainties of the situation developing around him . . . Captain Leach with all the difficulties of his too-new ship and company—still not fully worked-up and now never to be—Churchill's Yacht, the Glamour Ship, H.M.S. *Unsinkable*. H.M.S. *Unsinkable* with H.M.S. *Anonymous* astern of her, and astern of them both, falling into station, *Electra, Express, Vampire, Tenedos*.

Along the waterside the folk of Singapore, who had welcomed them so tumultuously only a few days previously in a world of peace, gathered to see them going, waving and cheering as they went. Still half-way between peace and war, these people, in spite of the news of Pearl Harbour and the air-raids of the night before—still believing, in spite of everything, that their fortress was impregnable and that ships could not be sunk. What eyes among them watched Force Z put to sea? It is certain that the departure of the ships was as speedily reported as their arrival had been; and though security about their destination and intentions had been excellent, there is every evidence that before many hours were up the Japanese were searching for them at sea, determined to discover both.

Soon the cheers faded, the people became indistinguishable: at half-past six they cleared the boom, then the land was falling behind them and Singapore Island was going down into the sea. The vibration of turbines and screws increased: the fleet was steaming at seventeen and one-half knots and Admiral Phillips was making a wide sweep round the Anamba Islands, as a precaution against possible mine-laying activites inshore.

Night fell upon them with the ships' companies in first degree of readiness and the eagerly awaited news of what they were about was, as usual, given to them now that harbour had been cleared. Gallagher faithfully copied down the notice that was posted in the *Repulse*'s upper-deck wardroom (still delicately decorated as it had been for the Queen to use as her boudoir on that long ago and far away state visit to the United States), and fortunately he now had the ship's special concoction in his fountain pen, so that both this and Captain Tennant's subsequent message have been preserved for us.

TO THE SHIP'S COMPANY FROM THE CAPTAIN:

We are off to look for trouble. I expect we shall find it. We may run up against submarines or destroyers, aircraft or surface ships.

1. We are going to carry out a sweep to the northward to see what we can pick up and what we can roar up. We must all be on our toes.

2. For two months past the ship has felt that she has been deprived of her fair share of hitting the enemy. Although we have been constantly at sea and steamed 53,000 miles in nine months we have seen practically nothing.

3. There is every possibility that things are going to change completely.

4. There is every likelihood that we shall get a good deal of bombing in harbour.

5. I know that the old ship will give a good account of herself. We have trained hard enough for this day. May each one of us without exception, keep calm if and when action comes—that is very important.

6. Lastly, to all of you, whatsoever happens do not be deflected from your job. When, say, high-angle guns are engaging a high-flying aircraft and all eyes are in the sky, none of the short-range guns on the disengaged side should be looking at the engagement but should be standing-by for a low-dive-bombing or torpedo-bombing attack coming from the other side. Similarly in a surface action at night, provided the disengaged guns look out on the disengaged side they may be able to repel a

*destroyer attack that might otherwise seriously damage
the ship.*

7. For all of us—concentrate on the job. Keep calm.

*8. Life-saving gear is to be worn or carried, or is to be
immediately to hand, not because I think anything is
going to happen to the ship—she is much too lucky—
but if anything happens you have your life-saving gear
handy; that is all you have to think about with regard
to yourself; you are then absolutely free to think of
your duty to the ship.*

Later he amplified it as follows:

TO THE SHIP'S COMPANY FROM THE CAPTAIN:

*We are making for the north-east coast of Malaya and
shall be off the north-east corner at sunset to-night. At
dawn we shall be to the seaward of Singora and
Pattani, where the Japanese landing is taking place.
Though we may, of course, run into Japanese forces anywhere during the day I think it is most probable that
only submarines and enemy aircraft are likely to be
sighted.*

*1. Any time during the night and at dawn the fun
may begin. We must be on the look-out for destroyer
attack tonight. If we are lucky enough to bump into a
Japanese convoy to-morrow at dawn it will be a most
valuable service and seriously upset the plans.*

*2. Having stirred up a hornet's nest, we must expect
plenty of bombing on our return to-morrow.*

*3. That is what the high-angle guns crews have been
longing for. It will be much better than sleeve-target
practice, and I hope the marking will be done for us
by the Japanese aircraft falling into the sea.*

Through the brevity and restraint of these messages there
is an eloquent note of Tennant's relationship with his men
and an eloquent note of the spirit of the *Repulse*. There was
nothing spurious about his use of the term "lucky," nor was
there any overstatement in the suggestion that the high-angle

gun crews had been waiting for an opportunity to show what they could do. It was just for this sort of thing that Slatts and his pom-pom crew had worked and trained with their endless stripping and oiling and cleaning of ammunition; it was just for this that Slinger Wood had slopped about before that in the triple turret with his long-handled mop; it was just for this that they had labelled their gunnery officer Six-Gun Coney long before the war began. They had been all these years waiting for it and apart from the German raiders over the Firth of Forth, the unfortunate contretemps in Scapa Flow and a few other fleeting moments, the opportunity had never come. All the frustration of those missed opportunities in the North Atlantic they would be only too glad to work off against the Japanese.

It was not until a little before eleven o'clock that Palliser was able to signal from Singapore that one Catalina would provide reconnaissance ahead the following morning, that a dawn reconnaissance at Singora the following morning of the 10th was "hoped" for, that fighter cover over the beaches was impossible. Out of Phillips' two essential conditions for the success of the operation, let alone the safety of the ships, one had already gone.

"We must carry on without it," he is reported to have said.

It was possible that surprise still might have been achieved, for the Gulf of Siam at this particular time of year is liable to rain, mist and low cloud ceilings—conditions not unlike those at some seasons in the North Sea, albeit with more comfortable temperatures. He proposed to try and take advantage of these conditions: where Pulford could not provide cover for him, the elements might. In the early hours of the morning he made this signal to his force:

Inform ships' companies as follows:
"The enemy has made several landings on the north coast of Malaya and has made local progress. Our Army is not large and is hard pressed in places. Our Air Force

has had to destroy and abandon one or more aerodromes.
Meanwhile fast transports lie off the coast.
"This is our opportunity before the enemy can establish
himself. We have made a wide circuit to avoid air
reconnaissance and hope to surprise the enemy shortly
after sunrise tomorrow, Wednesday. We may have the
luck to try our metal [not "mettle," as Gallagher quotes
it] *against the old Japanese battle cruiser Kongo or*
against some Japanese cruisers and destroyers which are
reported in the Gulf of Siam. We are sure to get some
useful practice with the H.A. armament.
"Whatever we meet I want to finish quickly and so
get well clear to the eastward before the Japanese can
mass too formidable a scale of air attack against us.
So shoot to sink."

Darkened, the *Repulse* drove on through the night, out
into the Gulf of Siam—to outward eyes a fleeting blur, a hiss
of foam and a heave of sundered waters in the blackness, but
vibrant within with the hum of complex machinery and the
thrust and vibration of turbines and screws. These inner
voices of her own, this audible pulsing of her own life, were
the only sounds: her crew talked in whispers. It might have
been any one of those other departures, any one of those
endless sorties and sea-chases, so familiar was everything
about it, yet there were differences as wide as the world and
as big as the oceans. There was the sweltering heat of the
humid tropical night below decks to remind the men that
seas and continents separated them from the familiar waters
of their other war. There was the unreality that besets
familiar things and routines seen against unfamiliar back-
grounds. There was the certainty of action against forces
whose equipment was unknown, and whose quality could
only be guessed at, though it was clear that both had been
grossly under-estimated——and this certainty itself was unreality in the ship that had known so many certainties and
missed out on them all. But above all, there was a change

of role, a reversal of character. They were now the hunted, not the hunters. They were no longer part of a navy struggling to hold command of the seas, watching to the limits of endurance and dashing frantically hither and thither to contain an enemy who could break out wherever he chose and vanish in the vastness of seaspaces. They were the *Scharnhorst* and the *Gneisenau*, the *Hipper*, the *Prinz Eugen*, the *Bismarck*, breaking out in the darkness and running the gauntlet of watching forces to reach their objective undiscovered. They were the raiders, the phantoms; and where they had once quartered the seas for a blur of German smoke or a glimpse of German upper works, the Japanese would now be quartering the seas for them. This is not imagination or transplanting of thoughts born of after events into minds that could never have conceived them: Donkey Bray said as much to Slinger Wood and his mates and they agreed with him, talking in whispers. From time to time they thought they could hear the drone of aircraft (and who is to say they were wrong, since these were not men given to fearful imaginings?), and were coolly and calmly convinced that these were Japanese aircraft searching for them. For they were sure of what we may accept to have been quite certainly the case—that their sailing had been reported by secret radio to the Japanese before Changi was astern of them.

The main armament, the triples and the high-angle guns were closed up at all-night action stations; the crews of the close-range weapons were in two watches. In the flat outside the captain's sea cabin, Slinger and his friends squatted, whispering. Bob Bloham came up with the information that one of the war correspondents aboard was Hughie Gallagher, the Scottish International, a much more glamourous person in their eyes than Gallagher of the *Express*, reporter. Hughie Gallagher started them on football, and from football the whispered talk fanned out, widened, until it was back again in those fields of half-fantasy where they had beguiled themselves on so many nights of so many other sorties, squatting in this flat or dodging around to keep in the lee of the funnel. Familiarity re-asserted itself. The ship drove on.

It is less easy to put words to the atmosphere in the *Prince of Wales*. They had not known these long sorties, these chases, these endless, patient watches in the gloom. For them there had been the hurried putting to sea after the *Bismarck*, scarcely yet a ship's company at all, the fever-heat and concentration to breaking-point in the helter-skelter passage of the Churchill trip, the continuous action and heady excitements of the Malta convoy. Then there had been the long journey into peace and sunny seas, their triumphal progress into Singapore, the bright lights and excitements of the good-time city which had been denied to the men of the other ship. The savour and smoke of the bars and night-places was still about them, the music was still in their ears. The day between the coming of the war to Singapore and their sailing had telescoped into nothingness for them: so much so that nearly every man who remembers is convinced that they were rounded up by the pickets and put to sea almost immediately. They were much more a ship's company than they had been when they went to meet the *Bismarck*, though they would never attain to the smoothness and unity of the company of the older ship; they were keen, they knew their jobs, but they lacked experience and the leaven of regular seamen among them was small. They had immense confidence in their captain, in Admiral Tom Thumb, in their great, powerful, unsinkable ship—except for the old hands who knew that no ship is unsinkable. Their confidence was of a different order from the confidence of the *Repulse's* crew: confident, nonetheless, they were, eager to get to grips and unafraid.

All through the night the ships hurried on. Dawn found them far from the land and from prying eyes ashore—and it was such a dawn as Sir Tom Phillips might have prayed for. The light came grey: there was mist, with a low cloud ceiling, occasional showers of rain—no day for spotting aircraft and not much of a day even for submarines. At six-thirty in the morning a look-out on *Vampire* momentarily glimpsed, or thought he glimpsed, an aircraft. It was gone before the sighting could be confirmed or the aircraft identified—it may have been an illusion of the mist or a trick played by straining eyes. It was a fair gamble that if it was an aircraft and an enemy aircraft at that, it had not spotted the ships: they could not have been identified in that fleeting moment of time. Phillips decided to disregard it, and the ships drove on, steady on their course, towards their destiny. If only twenty-four hours of this weather could be vouchsafed, the ships could make good his plan, reach the beach-heads undetected, carry out their bombardment and be away again into the mist before the bombers from Saigon could be upon them.

Presently the solitary Catalina found them—with a moment of mounting excitement, a brief interlude of gun-muzzles roving quickly on to it before it was identified. It circled the ships, flashed a message by Aldis lamp; fleeting visitor from a land that never was with fleeting tidings of battles on the moon. Then it was gone again on its lone reconnaissance—one single aircraft, a token almost, to seek safe passage for such precious ships and so many men on whom so much depended.

Alone again, hemmed in by their close horizons and low sky, the ships sped on. From time to time aircraft droned overhead, never sighted: the unseen skies were busy and probably the depths of the sea as well. Half the Japanese fleet might have been around them, for all they knew. The gun crews only left their positions to go to the heads or in relays for their meals. In the light of day they were a strange and motley collection of men, very different from the smart companies which had manned ship for the arrival in Singapore or for leaving harbour. They were dressed for action in whatever clothes of their choice would cover as much of their

skin as possible and reduce the effect of burns—football
jerseys worn with bell bottoms, sweaters, odd coloured
long-sleeved shirts, old flannels, pumps. Lifebelts and tin
helmets were the one thing common to all of them. Perhaps
the only exceptions were the journalists aboard the *Repulse*,
who had come in haste just as they stood in their tropical
shirts and shorts, without another stitch of kit. Someone
lent Gallagher a flash helmet in which he appeared (he was
a portly man) like some strange and uncouth creature from
another world. Aboard *Repulse*, too, there was one casualty
on this day: an officer, Lieutenant Gifford, missed his foot-
ing on the ladder that led to the air defence position and
fell eighty feet to the deck, breaking an arm and ribs. He
was carried to the sick-bay where he lay, far from mortally
injured, but helpless. His ultimate end would have been
kinder had he killed himself on the spot.

As the day wore on, tension mounted. Every hour of daylight behind them was an hour of concealment won, every
hour's steaming undetected so many miles towards their objective made good. It became almost unbearable as the ships
hurried on to the north, their wakes marking the sullen sea
and disappearing. Down to the youngest boy, every man on
battleship, battle-cruiser, and destroyers knew how vital
these hours of concealment were—these hours that would
lead them into the friendly night, in which the big ships,
leaving their destroyers, would turn westward for the beaches
and find at dawn success within their grasp. Four hours to
nightfall in the fickle Gulf of Siam, three hours, two hours,
one.

And with an hour of daylight to go, Sir Tom Phillips'
luck ran out. The luck of the *Repulse* that had made her a
talisman to endless convoys ran out. Shortly before five
o'clock the mist began to recede rapidly, the cloud ceiling
to rise. The sun came through. In a matter of minutes the
sea was clear from horizon to horizon, and in next to no
time, at least three aircraft were shadowing them. Alien air-

craft, sleek, businesslike, twin-engined monoplanes, quite
unlike the stringbags Mess 46 had disposed of so easily. Pur-
poseful and sinister, they circled, out of range. The second
essential element, surprise, was gone, and Sir Tom Phillips
was immediately faced with having to make a decision about
the future of the operation. It was a difficult, a vital decison:
he must now weigh in the balance the immense consequences the operation could have against the certainty that
his whereabouts were known; he must consider whether,
since he had been discovered, the operation had any prospect
of success at all. If some prospect of success still exited
almost any risk was tolerable; if it could not succeed and
the ships must be lost into the bargain, then obviously he
must withdraw. At the worst the ships could be sacrificed
to save Singapore—it would not be the first time in the
war that ships had had to be sacrificed—but to sacrifice
to no end at all was foolhardy and useless, and would leave
Singapore even more defenceless than it already was. He
had to decide, and he had to decide alone and on the spot.
He was Commander-in-Chief: he had no easy access to any
higher authority nor would he expect to have to refer such
a decision at sea to higher authority. Discuss, seek views he
might, but the decision must be his and his alone.

He had a little time in which to make it. His course was
still northward, his real objective somewhere away on his
port bow, to the eastward of him. To the eyes of the searchers
he might be heading for Indochina, might perhaps be going
to attack Carmranh Bay, might even be engaged on some
foolhardy mission to relieve Hong Kong, far away. He had
not proposed, in any case, to turn in towards the Kra Isthmus
before nightfall: between now and nightfall he must therefore make his choice. If he chose still to steam for the Kra
Isthmus and the enemy had already guessed his intentions,
they would be waiting for him. If he decided to withdraw
and turn south he could, at his ships' best speed, make good
many hundreds of miles before daybreak and the enemy

would have to start hunting him all over again. And luck might favour him again with overcast weather for at least part of the day on the morrow.

Whichever decision he was to make, he would have to hold his northward course until dark; and therefore the ships still steamed on between the wider horizons and under the clear, blue sky. No word came yet to the ships' companies and the tension mounted almost to breaking point. It had a curious effect on the crew of Slinger Wood's pom-pom; it induced almost a feeling of lethargy, a lethargy which nothing but action or some change could break. There was nothing more they could do. They had crammed the eight loading trays with as many belts of two-pounder shells as they could get on them. There were boxes of ammuniton stacked all round the gun deck ready for immediate reloading. Everything was checked, oiled, tested, ready—not even one minor detail had been overlooked. There was nothing more to be done and there was no refuge in small talk any more. After dusk action stations they went into two watches, so that they could get their supper, and succeeding the lethargy came a curious depression—almost a predeliction of doom for those who believe in such things—and it is practically impossible to write about this last night on the *Repulse* without imposing one's own after-knowledge of their doom upon the ship and the men. Without discussing it they all "seemed to decide," as Slinger puts it, that it would be a waste of time peeling the potatoes for the following day's dinner. The general feeling was that they wouldn't be there to eat them, although nobody said so. When Slinger finished his supper, he went over to his kit locker and started squaring it up—a gesture which in a serviceman might either mean a relief from boredom or a sense of finality, of being about to leave one station for another. He picked up the wedding photographs which his wife had sent him and paused to look through them yet again. In his ditty box lay an unfinished airmail letter and the letter took his thoughts away to

Merseyside to things at home. He wondered what sort of a Christmas they were expecting and whether they were still looking forward to seeing him home on Christmas leave. Probably they would not yet know that the *Repulse* was H.M.S. *Anonymous*, the other "heavy unit" with the *Prince of Wales*. But the air letter he had sent from Singapore, when at last they had been given permission to write of where they were, would be there any time, and they would know that he would not be home for Christmas. Perhaps the postman was delivering the letters at that very moment: he came about eight o'clock in the morning as regular as clockwork, regular even in the blitz, and the difference in time was such that it would be just about eight o'clock in the morning on Merseyside now. The postman would be delivering letters, his wife would be setting out for work at Rootes' Aircraft Factory, where she was a driller . . . the idea of drilling took his thoughts away at a tangent again and he wondered how many holes he had drilled in the *Prince of Wales* while she was building on the slip at Cammell Laird's. Well, when he got back home he would be able to tell them in Birkenhead how the *Prince of Wales* had made out and how she had knocked hell out of the Japanese; it still could not enter his thoughts either that there was any possibility of him not getting home or that the *Prince of Wales* could fail to knock hell out of the Japanese. Through alarms and excursions he had lived three years in the permanent world of his ships: it was not possible to think of anything other than permanence.

Back to the kit locker. He looked over the Burberry his father had given him for a wedding present. It was a beauty, silk-lined, and it had only been worn three times: he had had several good offers for it, but it wasn't for sale at any price.

Then it was time to return to the gun deck, closed up at first degree of readiness: and suddenly the mood of depression, of doom had worn itself out and the old confidence came back. The ship, he learned, had changed course and now they would be heading for the beach-heads. Of course they would break up the landings and of course they would save Malaya. So they would give the Yanks a little time to regroup their battered forces and get back into the fight. The weight of the Yanks would reassert itself, on our side. When that happened it would be curtains for the Japanese—the war in the Far East would be over and with the combined forces of the Americans and ourselves concentrated against Hitler, the war in Europe too could be over in six months. With this conclusion they settled down to try and get what sleep they could on the steel gun deck alongside the pom-pom. They had already drawn lots for the duties that had to be done throughout the night—one man on the headphones in communication with the air-defence position, one man as extra lookout—and had divided the night into tricks of one hour each. So passed this night, the last night on the ship which had been their home for nearly three years of their lives. In like sort passed the night elsewhere on the *Repulse,* on the *Prince of Wales* and on the destroyers.

Now Admiral Phillips had indeed altered course to the north-west and increased speed to twenty-six knots, as he had previously planned; but he had, in fact, already made up his mind that the risks that now faced him, discovered by the enemy and without prospect of fighter support in the morning, were beyond tolerance. *Tenedos* was due to return to Singapore, for this was as far as her fuel supplies would take her at the speed Force Z had been making: in any case she was the oldest, the slowest, and the most poorly defended of the destroyers. Now he detached her and he gave her a message to transmit by radio to Rear-Admiral Palliser in Singapore in the morning, when well clear of the main force. This message informed Palliser that his chief was calling off the operation and turning south during the night: it asked for all possible destroyer support to meet him at the approaches to Singapore. At about eight o'clock he signalled the other ships that he had decided to keep the remaining three destroyers in company and cancel the operation—"in view of the fact," reads Captain Tennant's report, "that the whereabouts of the Force was actually known to the enemy; it would therefore be improbable that we should meet any convoy in the morning and the enemy would have at least twelve hours to concentrate his airforce to attack us."

Half an hour later course was altered to south-eastwards and speed reduced to twenty knots, to husband the fuel supplies of the destroyers.

"Will this ship never get into action?" Gallagher heard someone say in the wardroom.

CHAPTER

13

THE MERE FACT THAT THE OPERATION HAD BEEN CALLED off made no difference to the degree of vigilance that was now demanded of the ships' officers and men. In fact the very circumstances under which it had been called off made the need for vigilance even greater. It was now certain that they were being hunted: in the morning, wherever they might be, they might expect attack from aircraft, submarines or even surface vessels—for although intelligence had indicated no major enemy units in the area, it could not be depended upon. They were being hunted as surely as the *Bismarck* and the *Prinz Eugen* had been hunted down the Atlantic from the Denmark Strait. But for the *Repulse* and *Prince of Wales* there was no umbrella of air cover to beckon them on into safety, only a handful of Buffaloes and the dubious haven of Singapore. Cloudy weather and poor visibility could save them as it had saved them on their way north. If they could give the Japanese the slip during the night and continue under a low cloud base undetected, in the morning they might yet win back to what safety there was in Singapore. In effect the ships were already doomed: if they were not sunk at sea in the morning, they would be sunk the day after in Singapore, or at sea in whatever direction they attempted to escape from Singapore or wherever the Japanese might find them. Probably this was apparent to Phillips, but it did not absolve him from the responsibility of keeping his force afloat and effective as long as he could. It was not apparent to the men, though they would not have flinched from it if it had been: ignorant of it, they kept their vigil at action stations through the night. They were now to be continuously at action stations until the ships went down.

During the night a further signal came from Singapore. It read as follows:

> TO: C.-in-C., *Eastern Fleet*. FROM: *Chief of Staff, Eastern Fleet*.
> ### IMMEDIATE
> *Enemy reported landing Kuantan, latitude 03 50′ North.*
> T.O.O. 1505Z/9.

No indication of the reliabilty of this report was given, nor had Rear-Admiral Palliser any indication to give. But Kuantan was almost on the return track of the force to Singapore, from which it was a mere one hundred and forty miles distant—within flying distance even for Brewster Buffaloes. It could almost have seemed that the signal indicated a foreknowledge of his decision to return, albeit Palliser could not be informed of this until he received the signal from *Tenedos* in the morning. But in any case the ships would be returning south in the morning after their attack on the Kra Isthmus convoys and landing places—returning at speed.

To Admiral Phillips this message meant a number of things. It meant in the first place an even more urgent threat to Singapore than the Kra Isthmus landings much further north. He knew, and a surviving staff witness has told us that he knew, that from Kuantan there was a road running west-

wards through the jungle which would enable the Japanese
to move quickly and cut land communications with our already hard-pressed forces in the north. Every move in this
game indicates how well Phillips had informed himself of
the situation on land, as well as at sea, and how much keener
was his appreciation of it than that of people who might
have been expected to be more intimately acquainted with
it. If, therefore, there were landings at Kuantan, they must
be, if possible, stopped at almost any cost.

In the second place it gave him an objective after all, and
if he could accomplish this objective, his sortie would not
have been in vain, whatever the consequences for the ships.

In the third place Kuantan was a full four hundred miles
from the airfields in Indochina and, as we have already seen,
within distance of fighter protection of Singapore.

In the fourth place, assuming that his change of course
had not been observed and assuming that he could escape
detection for the rest of the night, Kuantan was a long way
away from the position in which he had last been reported to
the enemy and in a different direction from the direction in
which he was steaming when so reported.

Last of all, it would be understood in Singapore that this
would be his reasoning and that he would make for Kuantan
on receipt of Admiral Palliser's signal, without the need to
break wireless silence by saying so. This anticipation of the
results of receiving information was the lesson he had learned
from the operations in the Battle of the Atlantic: he had
learned it too well, but Singapore had never had the opportunity of learning it.

At one o'clock in the morning, therefore, he altered course
again to 245° and increased speed to twenty-four knots,
with the intention of being off Kuantan in the morning.

"The rest of the night," says the official report on the action, "passed without incident." In other words it passed
with the two capital ships and three destroyers steaming

hard for their new objective with their men at action stations and their look-outs straining their eyes into the night.

Well might they strain their eyes: they were being hunted every bit as hard as the most fearful imagination among them could suppose they were, and the Japanese were straining their eyes too. They had not, in fact, remained undetected as long as they had thought on the previous day. A Japanese submarine had sighted them but remained unseen itself: the Asdics missed it and the eyes of the lookouts missed the tiny feather of its periscope in the overcast weather. This submarine reported them and its report was received: oddly enough the first reports of the aircraft which sighted them later did not reach their base.

Immediately the Japanese saw Sir Tom Phillips' purpose, and they were not deceived by the fact that his ships were on a northerly course. It really required no superhuman intelligence to do so, for in spite of Phillips' attempts to disguise the direction of his objective, the Kra Isthmus landings were after all the only major objective in that area against which such immensely valuable ships would make a sortie involving so many perils. They were convinced the moment the news came to them that Force Z was intent on beating up their beach-heads and their convoys and they were seriously alarmed for both; for although they could now claim naval control over the whole Pacific, they had no units in the immediate area able to contain the *Prince of Wales* and the *Repulse*. There was no likelihood that this situation would be permanent, that the two ships could go on "appearing and disappearing" and arousing "reactions and perturbations" indefinitely. There was no parallel between our situation in the North Atlantic and the situation of the Japanese in eastern waters. In their own good time they could detach units to take care of the *Prince of Wales* and the *Repulse*, but just at this moment their beach-heads were wide open to them, and the programme for the conquest of Asia faced a hitch. No battleship as heavily protected as the

Prince of Wales had ever been sunk by air attack alone; but even the mighty *Bismarck* had been disabled and sufficiently slowed down by air attack for the surface forces to be able to come up and pound her to destruction. It is possible that at this stage the Japanese hoped for no more from air attack on the *Prince of Wales* than had been achieved by the *Ark Royal*'s Swordfish in their attack on the *Bismarck*, and that would be enough for their purposes. The *Repulse*, not nearly so well protected and able to put up nothing like the *Prince of Wales*'s anti-aircraft barrage, they might be able to deal with by air attack alone.

Now, disabling the *Prince of Wales* automatically meant torpedo attack—bombs of the calibre available might cause destruction, loss of life above decks and reduction of her efficiency, but could not possibly sink her. Torpedo attacks called for a minimum of interference from fighter aircraft and, for preference, the attack must therefore be made while the ships were out of range of the Brewster Buffaloes: with the British grip on the northern airfields becoming weaker every hour, the Brewster Buffaloes could only operate within a couple of hundred miles of Singapore itself, and therefore the ships must be attacked while still beyond their range.

The nearest force available to do the job was 22 Air Flotilla, operating with ninety-eight aircraft from Saigon: it was in fact this flotilla which had mounted the air-raids that doused the bright lights of Singapore. It was a unit well suited for the purpose, because it had been specially trained in attacks on shipping; but at the moment when the sighting report came in, its aircraft were bombing up for another raid on Singapore. The raid was immediately called off, but both bombs and bomb racks had first to be unshipped so that the aircraft could be loaded with torpedoes. This took time. It was six o'clock in the evening and daylight was already going before the bombers were ready, yet so seriously did the Japanese view the prospect of an attack on the convoys and beach-heads at dawn the following day that it was decided to attempt a night attack. And so while the ships were changing course and racing back towards the south, straining every nerve for sight or sound of their hunters, the torpedo-bombers were in fact actually seeking them. They failed. One more night of life was vouchsafed to the two capital ships and Singapore was spared the air-raid that had been planned for it. Further search would have to wait for the dawn.

Just as the dawn of the previous day was such a dawn as Tom Phillips might have prayed for, so the dawn of December 10 was a dawn for which the Japanese in turn might have prayed. From end to end of the Gulf of Siam it was bright and clear. There was no sign of rain or mist, not a vestige of cloud to hinder the hunters or to bring succour to the hunted. The watchers on the ships, still at action stations after their long night of vigilance, saw the sun come up like a ball of fire into a tropical blue sky, under which they steamed naked and visible from horizon to horizon. In this dawn the Japanese had already been searching anew for them but failed to find them where they expected to find them, off the Kra Isthmus. They searched far to the south, to their limit of endurance about the latitude of Singapore. They did not find Force Z, but they found little *Tenedos* returning alone and eliminated her before she had time to transmit Admiral Phillips' message to his base. It was in fact a submarine which once more spotted the ships and home the attackers on to their target as they were returning northward.

Force Z was now near the coast off Kuantan and closing it rapidly. On all the ships the men got their breakfast and a bit of a wash to freshen themselves up as best they could. The officers ate a scratch meal, hurriedly. At about half-past six the loudspeakers told the crews about the new operation and, tension mounting again, they watched the land grow clearer as the ships closed in towards it. To Slinger and his mates at this time it appeared that they were going to be passengers at the pom-pom while the big guns and the secondary armament did the work for which they had been waiting so long, for pom-pom shells explode at 3,500 yards and in this visibility there seemed no likelihood of them closing anything within that range. But they were not idle: they had been well warned that their job was to watch the sky for enemy aircraft irrespective of what else was going on and not let their attention be distracted.

So, the *Prince of Wales* ahead, *Repulse* on her starboard quarter, they came close to the shore. The big ships each flew off a Walrus to carry out a reconnaissance, *Express* was sent in to investigate more closely and the rest of the Force passed down ten miles from the coast inside the seven fathom line. The only thing sighted was a small tug in the distance with what appeared to be a string of barges—clearly no invasion force, nor did Phillips seek to draw attention to himself either by closing it or firing upon it. It was about this time that he himself was sighted by the Japanese submarine which reported his new position. It fired all its torpedoes but missed, and once more apparently, remained undetected. The time that elapsed, however, before Phillips actually knew he was discovered afresh, was so little that the matter is unimportant.

There was no sign of any activity on the shore, nothing could be seen from the flagship or the *Repulse*, nothing could be seen by *Express* passing close inshore, nothing was seen by either Walrus. The Kuantan landings were a false alarm. There were no targets after all for *Repulse*'s fifteen-inch guns, which had still never fired a shot in anger and now never would. There was no last chance to discover whether *Prince of Wales*'s turrets had at last left all their "bugs" behind them. As they turned away, Captain Tennant signalled, suggesting that they should investigate the tug and barges and Phillips agreed. He also suggested that his second Walrus should now be flown off on anti-submarine patrol. Both these suggestions were agreed: the Walrus was flown off and the ships turned back towards the barges.

It was now Slinger Wood's turn to do his spell with the

aircraft lookouts in the air defence position—a platform on the top of the foremast in which there were a dozen swivel seats, each fitted with a stand on which there was a powerful pair of binoculars. He climbed the ladder from which Lieutenant Gifford had fallen the day before. Aloft he found Lieutenant Parker in charge with the Warrant Gunnery Officer, Mr. Page: for both of these he had a hearty respect, especially for Lieutenant Parker, whom he had once watched in a boxing match with *Rodney* in Scapa standing toe to toe with a marine almost twice his size, and slugging it out until both were barely able to stand up. Boy MacDonald slid out of his lookout seat and Slinger took his place. Applying himself to the binoculars, he commenced to quarter his sector of the sky from Red 05 to Green 25: giving every ounce of his concentration to the task he forgot the weariness of the night.

He had covered the sector several times and had just started on another sweep when low down on the horizon in the almost indeterminate meeting place of sea and sky he saw the tiniest of small black dots.

"Aircraft in sight," he cried immediately.

He heard the voice of Mr. Page urging him to keep on it. He sensed the midshipman alongside him reading off the bearing and angle of sight and barely had he done so when the order "repel aircraft" sounded through all the ships. Even as the alarm was given the *Prince of Wales*'s radar picked the aircraft up: it had not done so sooner because it was so low on the horizon.

Wood's place was now back at his pom-pom and as he made his way hurriedly back down the foremast ladder he thought once more of Lieutenant Gifford lying in the sick bay with his broken ribs. When he got to the triple gun deck he saw that everyone had donned their anti-flash gloves and hoods so that they looked like some strange order of nun with a touch of Ku Klux Klan in it—except that on top of the head was perched the inevitable tin hat. Behind T-1—

his old gun where he had slopped so desperately with his long-handled mop in his green days of long before and spent so many freezing nights in the northern seas—the spare gun's crew was busy setting fuses on the barrage shells. Everywhere here and as he made his way aft, an air of expectancy had replaced the tension of the day before and an air of alertness had swept away the tiredness of the hours closed-up at action stations. This was the *Repulse* again, ready for anything up to the very end.

Seconds before Wood reached the pom-pom, Scouse Garner had reported to his action station on T-3 gun below. He had had time to equip himself with a tin of "ticklers" from his locker and a few other essentials. Below T-3 again was Y Turret, with the Oerlikon mounted on top of it and its great guns alert but silent, useless against the menace from the sky. Also below, but forward of the pom-pom was high-angle gun R-3, antiquated but efficient in good hands. All were closed up and ready: somewhere below, Stoker Dick was busy with his fresh water pumps that supplied cooling water. He was thinking of his rum ration which was not far off. On the flag deck, assigned to them as their action station because they were least likely to be in the way there, were the journalists Gallagher and Brown, chatting with the signallers and wondering what sort of a party they had let themselves in for. Gallagher had managed to equip himself with a suit of overalls, oil-stained but covering his skin; beneath these, in the pocket of his shorts, was his precious note-book and he continued to add jottings to it from time to time, using his fountain-pen full of the ship's home-made ink and determined to make the best job he could of his uselessness. It is from him that we have the only report of a single-funnelled, two-masted ship that appeared, hull-down, on the port bow of the ships. He examined it through the yeoman's telescope, but it showed no flag or other clue to its identity. Later, he declares, he met its skipper in Calcutta: it was a British freighter on the run from Hong Kong, and when the air-sea battle developed it continued to run, quite justifiably. It is odd that this vessel is not mentioned at all in any of the official published accounts of the action, nor have any of the survivors whose memories form so much of the basis of this book mentioned it. Gallagher felt that the whole force was watching it. In this he was wrong, for the men's attention was on the arcs of their guns and on their other tasks. They were too well-trained in their duties for sight-seeing. His other outstanding impression is of the *Prince of Wales*'s guns, sky-raking at all angles——like chopsticks, one of the signallers remarked to him. And here Alf Tudor, Johnny King, Joe Dempsey, and the rest waited, tensed for the order to open fire at the aircraft they must expect at any moment, following the single spotter plane. Boy Williams was at the same station in his 5.25 turret from which he had watched the *Hood* go down: he thought of the *Hood*, of Blaenau-Festiniog, of his girl friend Betty, to whom he was now engaged and would one day marry. Seddon was on the bridge, his great mat with the *Prince of Wales*'s feathers still unfinished, his thoughts roving back to the old *Albion* and another war, to Fairrie's refinery and the dark years between one war and the next. The Clydeside rats, decimated but still undefeated, prowled undisturbed, unaware that the classic fate of rats in ships was upon them: had they but deserted the ship in a body at Singapore, they might have gone down to history as a sign and a portent, but perhaps their rat intuition had played them false, or else they found the *Prince of Wales* too comfortable a billet.

The legend of the unsinkability of the *Prince of Wales* and their pride in their splendid and famous ship lay strong on many of her men—especially the less experienced men, the men who had been landsmen less than a year before, who still, in spite of all their pride and keenness, were still landsmen just a little in their hearts. Certainly they had known air action——they had known it hot and strong in the Malta convoy, had triumphed over it and not received a major scar. But this wasn't the Malta convoy, or anything like it. There was no *Ark Royal*, no fighter cover for them. Leach knew it was no Malta convoy. It wasn't his business to tell them. Shortly after eleven o'clock his radar picked up a formation of high-flying aircraft approaching from the south, fifty degrees on his starboard bow.

Slinger Wood's mates on the pom-pom had been discussing the phantom landings at Kuantan—the latest and last of all their phantoms—when the new warning crackled from the loudspeakers. They'd decided that the information had probably come from the Japs themselves, and in this they may not have been far wrong. Now they left Kuantan to history. High-flying aircraft were not their job, and they must keep alert for sudden attack within the range of their own weapons, but they saw the aircraft come—nine of them in close single line abreast, faultless in formation. Everything went dead quiet, save for the voices of the communication numbers on the guns, shouting "aircraft in sight!" and reporting bearing and angle of sight.

"This is it!" he heard Dinger Bell say alongside him, and in the same moment their own four-inch high-angle guns and the whole of the *Prince of Wales*'s anti-aircraft battery opened fire together with a tremendous, crackling barrage that seemed to blanket the whole sky. Below the pom-pom, R-3 had gone into action as though at a touch of one of H.V. Morton's buttons, working with the perfect co-ordination that comes of endless training; they seemed to be loading and firing twice as quickly as they had ever done in practice. The destroyers joined in, and now the aircraft seemed to be flying down a lane of shell-bursts that dirtied the sky. They seemed to float in out of the heavens, silent amid the noise of the guns. Their formation was still perfect; their height about ten thousand feet. The time was precisely 11:18 A.M.

Two illusions were dispelled in these moments: one, the legend that the Japanese were "not very good at aircraft," inefficient little yellow men flying rice-paper planes; the other, the idea that the identity of the *Repulse* and the knowledge of her poor protection and slender ack-ack armament could be kept from them by turning her into H.M.S. *Anonymous*. These Mitsubishi 86 bombers looked at least as efficient as our own new Beauforts, and they were being flown with both skill and resolution. In face of the metal that was being poured into the sky against them they kept course, height, speed, and formation. Not one so much as jinked as they continued on towards their target. And their target was the *Repulse*. They knew not merely that one of the ships was the *Repulse*—they knew which of the ships was the *Repulse*. The anonymity which had aroused such bitter resentment in *Repulse*'s crew was a vain expedient. The Japanese knew them as clearly as if no attempt had ever been made to deceive them and they knew this was the only one of the two capital ships vulnerable to high-level bombing. With complete precision, the attack was pressed home on the *Repulse* alone.

For an eternity of minutes, then, the bombers floated in while the ships, steaming ahead furiously continued to hurl every ounce of metal they could into the sky. They seemed to disregard the barrage; well might they, because although the *Prince of Wales* possessed as massive an anti-aircraft battery as any ship afloat, it was still not massive enough, while the anti-aircraft armament of the *Repulse* and the destroyers was wretchedly inadequate. They might strive to throw a curtain of fire across the sky, but it was a curtain with holes in it; and while one fighter might have broken up this formation, the combined fire of all the ships could not budge a single plane a fraction from its course. For an eternity they floated, and then each aircraft released a single bomb.

Hundreds of eyes saw the bombs detach themselves from the aircraft and fall. Seddon saw them from the bridge of the *Prince of Wales*, Slinger Wood saw them. Sergeant "Taff" Wadley, *Repulse*'s marine gunnery instructor spot-

ting from the deck above T-3, which was not in action because the elevation was too great, saw them and yelled to
the marine gun crew to take cover. They did so—in the only
cover that seemed to be available to them, which happened
to be the ready-use magazine in which the ammunition
brought up from below was stored. It was only afterwards
that they realised the inappropriateness of their shelter and
still were able to laugh about it. Then the racket of guns
was drowned in the detonation and blast of a couple of
thousand pounds of high explosives, and to the watchers on
the other ships, *Repulse* disappeared in a mighty curtain of
upflung water and smoke from which it seemed impossible
that she should ever emerge. It was the Norway campaign
all over again. And just as she had done in the Norway
campaign, the ship presently shot out from it, still at speed
and still on an even keel; but black smoke poured from her
and she seemed to be afire. Wasn't that the way *Hood* had
gone—first a hit, then fire, then disruption? The watchers
waited for the end and many of her own people thought
the ship was finished. The smoke was belching black from
the air-vents behind the pom-pom that had supplied comforting hot air in the North Atlantic and torrid blasts when
they were less welcome. Surely this meant that the bombs
had gone through the armour deck and that there was havoc
in engine and boiler rooms? Gun crews not in action were
ordered to the assistance of the damage control parties and
to help with the wounded. They obeyed at the double: T-3's
crew had a couple of hoses down from the catapult deck in
no time. There was a dreadful mess, hammocks and gear all
round the foremast, smoke and acrid fumes: there were
casualties from below—burned stokers.

Actually the damage was quite superficial: the ship was
barely scratched. The bombs were no more than 250-
pounders. One was a near miss on the starboard side abaft
the bridge, five were near misses on the port side, and one,
and one only, hit the ship. It struck the catapult deck port

side, penetrated the upper deck and the main deck by the marines' barracks, the torpedomen's mess and the torpedo tubes, and burst in a fan chamber near the torpedo office, where the torpedo writer was trapped. Here it started a fire, but it did not penetrate the horizontal armour or cause any damage whatsoever below. The near-miss loosened rivets and caused leaks in number three dynamo room. Certainly there were a number of casualties, mainly from burns, and most of them were stokers, but they were men on duty in the torpedo flat and elsewhere above decks, not below. One of them, for instance, was Stoker Dick who had just come up from the port engine room and was making his way along the deck when something hit him very hard on the head. He woke up in the sick-bay and although he has a scar to this day as a souvenir, his injury was not serious: but it nearly caused him to be drowned along with other casualties. He followed the rest of the action by ear. As for the smoke pouring from the engine room air-vents behind Slinger Wood's pom-pom, the explanation is quite simple. The air might be coming from the engine and boiler rooms, but the smoke was coming from no further than the fan chamber above the armoured deck where the bomb had actually exploded. The ship continued to steam and manoeuvre at high speed for the rest of the action and this can be taken as positive confirmation that no material damage was suffered below.

The sky was clear now—the planes had gone and the guns for the moment had ceased to fire; and in this interval the *Repulse*'s damage control parties, aided by the disengaged guns' crews, went to work on the dynamo room and the fire as though they were on a peace-time exercise. The dynamo was taken off the board, the leaks caulked, the space pumped out and the dynamo put back. The fire by the torpedo office was put out. When the crew of T-3 had finished swamping what was left of their possessions in water, they turned to to help the wounded, but found the situation in the sick-bay well under control and unskilled assistance not in demand.

So they returned to their gun deck, where presently there came to them the ship's padre, Canon Bezzant, making his rounds and proffering a drink of water, padre-fashion. They asked him whether he couldn't make it champagne, but water was all the good man had to offer and they drank it, finding themselves now in high spirits. By the time the next attack came in all the material damage from the bomb burst, such as it was, had been put right, and even damaged lighting had been replaced.

There was now a respite of nearly half an hour, though few of the survivors remember it as so long. Events have telescoped in their minds; the action seems to them shorter than it was in fact and unbroken by any pause. The ships steamed on. Was this all they were going to get? Or was it just a foretaste? Was whatever was coming next going to be as easy to deal with as this first attack? Ships' crews wondered what fighter planes would come to their succour and when they would appear, but the sky was empty even of Brewster Buffaloes. It was at 11:44 that the *Prince of Wales*'s radar picked up another large formation of aircraft coming from the south: not many moments later, they were visible to the naked eye. They were flying low. So low were they flying that Seddon, on the *Prince of Wales*'s bridge, wondered why they didn't open up with the fourteen-inch guns on top of everything else—it seemed impossible to miss. Low flying bombers could only mean one thing—torpedo attack. Very well, they would see what Jap torpedoes were made of.

Now the barrage broke out anew—broke out with an even greater racket and clamour than before, for these low-flying planes were within the reach and range of every weapon the ships possessed, Oerlikons, the pom-poms and all. But the torpedo bombers, infinitely more vulnerable than the high-altitude bombers which had preceded them, nonetheless kept on their course just as resolutely and unshakeably as the high-altitude bombers had done, and this time the *Prince of Wales* was their target.

Straight into the teeth of the anti-aircraft fire they came, to drop their torpedoes and zoom across the battleship's very decks before they could recover and rise clear. Two of them, savaged by the close-range guns, all but crashed into the ship: narrowly clearing her they plunged into the sea on her disengaged side and disintegrated. Captain Tennant saw the torpedoes fall: he noted, almost with professional detachment, that the Japanese launched them both from a greater height and a greater distance than our own Swordfish did: the torpedoes nonetheless ran true——they also ran shallow and their tracks were clearly visible through the water. They were as coolly and accurately aimed as the bombs had been. For years the crews had trained for this moment; for years the back-room boys had worked on their weapons and given them tools as good and even better than the navies of the West could boast.

Heeling over to her helm while her guns still blazed, the *Prince of Wales* turned towards the torpedo tracks streaking towards her. She was not quick enough. One torpedo struck her. One torpedo only, but it wrought unbelievable havoc. It destroyed H.M.S. *Unsinkable*.

It struck her in the stern, the Achilles heel of any ship. It raised a tremendous fountain of water—greater, Tennant says in his report, than the column thrown up by any of the subsequent torpedoes. There was a lot of black smoke about with it, which puzzled him and has continued to puzzle him ever since. It was as though a small magazine or something of the sort had gone up, but survivors he questioned at Singapore afterwards could throw no light on it. Explosion of some sort, however, there was, quite separate and distinct from the strike of the torpedo: Cyril Williams, working in P-3 turret, which was almost above where the torpedo hit, felt first a thud and shudder as though the fourteen-inch guns had opened up: that was the torpedo. Then there was a great blast and concussion, as though something had exploded in the waist of their ship. It threw P-3's crew down like nine-

pins: shells rolled off the rack and knocked one seaman unconscious. When they got themselves to their feet again,
they found power had failed, so that they could not elevate
or train the turret: they tried to work it by hand, but by then
the ship was already listing and jamming everything.

If the torpedo had done no more than put the battleship's
steering gear out of action and jammed the port propeller
shafts, it would have been bad enough. But what it did was
infinitely worse than that: what it did was fantastic. The ship
was steaming full ahead, and there was something like thirty-
thousand horsepower behind each of the huge shafts. Under
the complex change of stresses caused by the explosion, the
port outer shaft sheared at the A-bracket and bent. All this
happened in an instant, before anyone could close throttles
or think of closing them: in the next instant the bent shaft
had sliced the massive bottom of the ship as one might slice
a can with a tin-opener. Then it jammed, reducing the
engine-room to a shambles, the machinery to scrap, and
spreading death and destruction through the vitals of the
ship: the frustrated power of her own turbines disembow-
elled her. This may well have been what Williams felt as an
explosion in P-3. Water poured in a torrent through the gash
made by the shaft, overwhelming men where they were
wounded or trapped. B Engine Room, Y Boiler Room, the
port Diesel Room, and Y Action Machinery Room were
flooded. The warning telephone system failed. Radio and
radar ceased to function. There was no power to either of
the after groups of 5.25 inch guns. The ship listed thirteen
degrees and speed dropped to fifteen knots: she was never
under complete control again. It was the *Bismarck* story
once more—with a few additions. And the *Prince of Wales*—
H.M.S. *Unsinkable*, the Glamour Ship, Churchill's Yacht,
the imagined terror of the Japanese Navy, the saviour of the
fortress of Singapore—was as doomed and damned as the
Bismarck had been when the torpedoes from *Ark Royal's*
Swordfish had caught her. The Japanese could take their

time to finish her off. They could bring up more aircraft, they could leave her for surface ships or submarines. They could leave her for an hour or leave her for a week. They could sink her at leisure by any means they wished. She was a sitting target. And the skies were still empty of British planes.

Neither Captain Tennant nor his crew had much time to spare at this point to take all this in, for almost immediately there developed another attack on the *Repulse*. Another formation of Mitsubishis came up over the horizon, and from their low altitude and the manner of their approach, it was apparent that this also was a torpedo attack. It was dealt with as though the ship were on manoeuvres, playing at war upon a summer sea. Amid the racket of the guns, which made the passing of helm orders extremely difficult, with the huge ship tearing along at something like twenty-seven knots, Tennant held on his course until the torpedoes were launched and committed. Once more they ran shallow, with the tracks easily seen: the bridge personnel, steady at their posts, were pointing them out. Then, and only then was the wheel put over: her guns still blazing, her speed unchecked, she slewed madly, steadied to her new course and steamed up the tracks of the torpedoes, "combing" them so that they passed her harmlessly by. It was the supreme test of a perfectly trained, perfectly co-ordinated ship's company, steady as a rock, every officer and every rating, master of his job. It was copy-book-stuff. It was magnificent.

At last the close-range weapons had been freed from the stifling bonds of inaction. The instant before the ship turned, young Brown, the pom-pom's communication number, had yelled, "Aircraft starboard!" Gallagher saw him pounding the gun layer on the back with one hand, stabbing at the plane with a finger of the other. The heel of the ship as she slewed to starboard made training difficult, the eight machine-guns burst into their deafening chatter. The journalist saw, as one sees small things in the midst of mighty

happenings, the black paint on the cone-shaped flash guard
of one of them rise in a great blister: then seven out of the
eight guns stopped and the gun's crew were madly working
to clear them. One was hopelessly jammed, but the other
stoppages were only separated cases, soon dealt with, and
the gun was in action again.

But T-3 had scored a hit. With all the stuff that was flying
about, T-3's survivors are quite confident of the hit and so
are the pom-pom's crew, who were above them. The plane
was coming in on the port quarter, having dropped its
torpedo, but had not yet veered away. Its machine-guns were
blazing, silently amid the noise of the bigger guns. T-3 laid
on it and fired, and the plane disintegrated before the gun
crew's eyes. It was incredibly simple. Corporal McKillen,
Scouse Garner and the other nineteen of them screeched in
triumph like savages, barely able to credit their eyes. Then
another plane swept over, machine-gunning, and several of
the gun's crew were hit. They went below to have their
wounds dressed and their mates never saw them again.

Immediately on the tail of the torpedo attack came another high-level bombing attack, and this again was exclu-
sively reserved for the *Repulse*. The previous one had been
no accident. The Japanese knew which of the ships were
vulnerable to their 250-pound bombs. The bombs were
delivered with the same coolness and the same accuracy as
the first high-level bombs, but Tennant was still twisting
and turning at speed, and the ship was actually under helm
as the bombs fell. There was one near miss on the starboard
side; the others fell just clear to port.

Was this the last of it? Again the battle seemed to peter
out for the moment. The high-level bombers dwindled and
vanished, the guns stuttered and barked into silence. The
pom-pom crew ruefully cleared the empty cases littering the
deck.

"It'll take more than an afternoon to deprime this bloody

lot," said Slinger to Leading Seaman Slatter, thinking of their old Scapa escapade.

It was only then they looked at the *Prince of Wales*, and what they saw struck cold upon them. She was two or three miles away on their starboard quarter. She listed. She seemed to be hardly moving. She had "not under control" balls hoisted. An Aldis lamp flickered from her. The loudspeakers crackled and told them that her 5.25s were out of action. Then *Repulse* was turning and racing back towards her: at this moment, in the quiet of the lull, she seemed almost a dead ship already.

Immediately after the high-level attack had passed over, Tennant had signalled his flagship by radio, enquiring about her damage, but got no reply. Was her radio out of action and if so how long had it been out of action? Had any signal been made to Singapore that Force Z was under air attack? Had the admiral, keeping radio silence as long as he possibly could, been caught out by the unexpected magnitude of the damage before he could make any bombing report at all? He asked his own people what radio signals *Prince of Wales* had made. They replied: "None." On his own initiative, therefore, he broke silence and made an emergency report to Singapore, "Enemy aircraft bombing." It was 11:58, nearly an hour after the first spotter plane had come over and forty minutes after the first high-level attack on the *Repulse*. It was the first signal received in Singapore and the first intimation that Force Z was under enemy attack.

Now he turned towards the other ship and reduced speed to twenty knots, "the better to see her damage and to see if I could be of any assistance." He made further signals by visual means, telling the Commander-in-Chief that his own bomb damage had been got under control and that he had avoided all torpedo attacks. He told him, one imagines, with some little feeling of pride in his ship—he had every right to. He asked whether the flagship's wireless was in action, and whether Admiral Phillips wished him to make any signals to base for him. There was no reply to all this either, though shortly afterwards the Aldis lamp signals seen by Wood and his mates were made from the *Prince of Wales*—to them they seemed to be urgent appeals for help. And Seddon later remembers signalling later to the destroyers to go to the aid of *Repulse*.

Why had Phillips delayed so long reporting the attack? The handful of Brewster Buffaloes that later arrived on the scene were in the air within six minutes of Captain Tennant's signal being received. Had they come earlier they might have been in time to put the torpedo bombers, if not the high-level bombers, off their stroke. Very likely Phillips himself, realist though he undoubtedly was, was caught out by the intensity and efficiency of the attack. Certainly it could not have entered his head that the *Prince of Wales* could be so rapidly and so completely put out of action, and his communications so utterly wrecked in so short a time. Such a thing had never happened under aircraft attack to any capital ship in the North Atlantic or the Mediterranean: the possibility was so remote that it can never have come into his calculations. And so, still reluctant to break radio silence in case breaking it might bring other attackers swiftly upon him from near at hand in this enemy-infested sea and sky, he delayed making any report when the spotter plane was sighted, delayed again when he saw how little effect the high level bombing attack had made on the *Repulse*—for he himself had little to fear from such attacks, however accurately carried out. Then came the unbelievable destruction wrought by the torpedo, and in the instant it was too late: he lacked the means to send any messages to Singapore at all. The failure to deal with visual signals is another matter altogether and not at the door of Phillips. As we shall see in a moment, disintegration was setting in pretty fast in the *Prince of Wales*.

Slinger Wood looked at the ship he had helped to build. He and his mates felt no pity for her—only surprise, indignation, and disgust—for they had no means of knowing of her appalling luck, of how speedily and how irreparably she had been crippled. Their own ship, under-gunned, under-armoured, with nothing like the *Prince of Wales's* equipment for any purpose, had dealt with her bomb damage, shrugged off the torpedoes by dint of speed and skill, downed one, perhaps two, enemy aircraft and was in tip-top shape. While here was the Glamour Ship, the ship that had got all the publicity, all the favours, all the privileges—the ship that had reduced them to anonymity—steaming in circles like a wounded duck, listing heavily, down by the stern. What of her serried ranks of anti-aircraft guns, what of her vaunted unsinkability? What sort of ship *was* this, after all—and what sort of men aboard her? In the attack that was to follow, they thought she had practically ceased to defend herself.

> *I noticed that she only had one Oerlikon gun firing* [writes Slinger Wood]. *These were not power-operated guns, so why the lot (and she certainly had plenty of them) shouldn't have been firing, God alone knows, apart from those that manned them . . . How we could have done with those extra Oerlikons which were silent aboard the* Prince.

The true picture was not so solidly black as this. The Glamour Ship had not ceased to defend herself with what guns she still had—not by a long, long chalk—and she was still to take toll of the enemy. It was not really that *Repulse's* people were so intentionally biased against the battleship that they could believe no good of her, even in this moment of extremity: good seamen and good comrades that they were, they could never have consciously allowed their prejudice to blind them so. Yet it did blind them—the bitter resentment against the other ship that had eaten into them made them more prejudiced than they themselves knew, and against the background of their own completely organised and efficient ship, what was happening aboard the *Prince of Wales* was past their comprehension. The *Prince of Wales*'s men were still full of fight: many of them were still fighting and some of them did not even know their ship was already wounded to the death. The majority of them, their horizons bounded by the confined limits of their own stations, the turrets of their own guns, never knew and still do not know to this day, that they gave any impression of having ceased to fight back. But two things are obvious. In the first place the ship was so crippled that she was no longer able to steam or manoeuvre at the will of those in charge of her, and for the same reason a very large part of her armament was out of action, while the part that was not actually disabled could be neither directed nor controlled. Secondly, the organisation and cohesion of the ship was vanishing. There was no break-up of discipline, there was no surrender, no vestige of cowardice, no element of disgrace. They were still the same keen, well-drilled crew that had blasted their way to Malta and before that taken the onslaught of the *Bismarck* in their stride, hitting hard and effectively in spite of the defects of their cranky new armament and coping with their battle damage in a way that Rear-Admiral Wake-Walker and Admiral Tovey had refused to believe was possible for a newly-commissioned ship on her first active service assignment. Those who survived were to prove their mettle again in the defence of Singapore, in the last-ditch battles in the jungle, in other ships and on other seas. But something had happened which all their discipline, and all their courage could not cope with.

Blasted and battered though the ship had been by the guns of the *Bismarck*, the damage had been no more than a well-organised ship and a well-disciplined ship's company could handle: control was unaffected—the ship was palpably still able both to steam and fight. What had happened below now was quite beyond the scope of any damage control parties, beyond the scope of anything but a dockyard, could the ship have been got to one. It was impossible for a large number of ratings aboard not to be aware that she was mortally wounded and sinking. This in itself was a shattering blow to men who had heard the world call their ship H.M.S. *Unsinkable*, had called her so themselves. Further, there were a great many men trapped below, in the mangled and flooded compartments, and to those in the after part of the ship their yells and screams came dreadfully through the ventilators, sapping and nagging at them for their own helplessness in the face of their comrades' agonies. On top of that the loudspeaker system, as well as the telephones and every means of communication other than by word of mouth had failed. It had been Leach's use of the loudspeaker system, throughout the *Bismarck* battle and the other hectic moments of her short, vivid life, that had proved such a splendid weapon in keeping the crew informed and together. Bereft of all such artificial aids, such means of mass communication, it was inevitable that the ship's lack of working-up time and the interruption of such working-up as she had had should betray themselves. Many of the men did not yet know well (or sometimes know at all) their officers, warrant officers, or petty officers, nor these their men. They did not know who to turn to, how to make good the lack of direction and information that was the very backbone of their ordered lives. Circumstances such as these are the supreme test of a well shaken-down ship's company. The *Prince of Wales*'s company, heroes though they were, never had the remotest chance of surviving such a test, nor should such a test have been inflicted upon them. It was not the admiral, the captain, the officers, or the men who were responsible for the disintegration that was now setting in. What was responsible was the blunder that sent the ship, too little prepared to die, to undergo her supreme trial too soon in a place where she never should have been—the blunder and those who made the blunder.

"Aircraft in sight!"

Another attack was coming in. There was to be no respite.
There is no quarter for a wounded ship. The *Prince of Wales*
was to be battered until she sank. What could be done for
her? Little enough was left serviceable of all her anti-aircraft
fire—the *Repulse* and the destroyers had nothing like enough
to protect themselves alone. There was only one thing that
could be done—to go on firing till there were no more guns
to be fired. To fight until the ships, fighting, sank beneath
them.

The sinister black dots low over the sea were climbing
over the horizon, visible now to those at deck level. Already
the guns were barking and chattering again, but the volume
of sound was noticeably less with so many of the stricken
battleship's guns out of action. Under the threat of the new
torpedo attack, *Repulse* increased speed again until once
more she was creaming and crashing through the water at
twenty-seven knots or more. This was her last and her finest
hour, and she would meet it with dash and with the grace
of a great ship at speed for which she would always be remembered in the hearts and minds of seafaring men. Not
for her the long, slow agony of the crippled bird on the water,
creeping in dying circles till the sea claimed its prey: she
would steam to her doom whole and in one piece and go
down steaming.

The aircraft came on in the face of the barrage just as the
aircraft before them had come, and they were going to do
exactly as the aircraft before them had done; there was a
sameness about it and the very sameness itself was a menace.
The first group of them came in down the *Repulse*'s starboard side to loose their torpedoes at the helpless *Prince of
Wales*. They ran the gauntlet of the close-range and high-
angle guns: the water in the cooling jackets of the pom-pom's
seven remaining guns bubbled and steamed with the fury of
the firing and one of the aircraft again was first mangled by
tracer bullets and then blasted out of the sky: they saw the
very face of the airman as he went and thought savagely that

he had not put on his funeral robes in vain. It was fruitless. One aircraft stricken—so many still remaining. Three torpedoes in quick succession hit the *Prince of Wales*—one right forward, one abreast of B turret, and one once more in that vital place right aft. The starboard outer shaft was jammed now in addition to both the port shafts, so that one propeller only turned and her speed dropped still further. There was more damage below the waterline, too: water poured into her hull on the starboard side so that she seemed to right her list and settle almost on even keel, but in doing so she was ominously lower in the water. She was beginning to sink by the stern. Any ship less strongly constructed would have been at the bottom of the sea long before; any ship less strongly constructed could not possibly have lasted for a whole hour more of agony as the *Prince of Wales* was to last. The strength and complexity of those underwater compartments on which young Wood and his mate had worked were now evident—yet all that strength, all that complexity, all the ingenuity that had devised the system of compartments and all the integrity of the workmanship that went into them could do no more than prolong her life by that single hour.

The sky was still full of planes. The tempo of the attack seemed to be increasing rather than diminishing. Once more a group of aircraft came in on *Repulse's* starboard side. Once more Tennant played his waiting game and once more when the torpedoes were committed he put his helm over and steamed through the tracks of them. Already he had combed a score of torpedoes in this way and it seemed that the swift old ship, doubling and turning in response to every feint of the attacking aircraft would go on combing them forever. There was contempt, almost arrogance, in the way she turned and shrugged the torpedoes away. Let this indeed be the last picture of her, as fine a picture as there could be of any ship——riding the sea, at speed, intact, superior in wit and efficiency to her enemies.

For in the very moment of her triumph, as she combed

the new attack, her fate came upon her. It was not for nothing that Air Flotilla 22 had been specially trained in ship attacks: they knew all about ships combing torpedoes and how to deal with them. Even as the *Repulse* steamed down the tracks of the torpedoes that had been launched on her starboard side, three aircraft came in on the other side. They were flying straight for the *Prince of Wales*. It looked as though the flagship was destined for a further battering: the guns turned on them, barking and chattering, but failed to stop them. But when they were a little before the *Repulse*'s port beam and perhaps a mile away, they wheeled, turned straight for her and launched their torpedoes. Once more the shallow tracks were apparent, streaking through the water towards the ship but this time there was absolutely no action that could be taken to avoid them. They could not be combed: she was still combing the torpedoes launched in the previous attack on a bearing almost at right-angles to the new one. If she turned now these first torpedoes would strike her; if she held her course she would be struck by the new ones. And so Tennant held his course: he had no option. He and all the others with eyes to spare watched the tracks approaching the port side—watched them for a good minute and a half. Two passed astern, the third struck her amidships with a tremendous roar and concussion and an upheaval of the ocean that deluged the decks and the gun crews. Momentarily she seemed to try to lift herself out of the water, then she steadied again and continued on her course, still on an even keel, her speed undiminished. For so old and so lightly armoured a ship she had stood the explosion extraordinarily well: if she could stand up to torpedoes like this could she not still survive?

There was little scope for such illusions. The respite was very short. Almost immediately more torpedo-bombers appeared. The sky seemed full of them and now they were no longer in formation—they appeared to be coming in every conceivable direction at once. There could be no question of even attempting to comb these attacks—there could not even be any question of the guns being able to concentrate upon all these targets at once. For a matter of moments there was a sort of air circus around the ship and then the torpedoes launched from different directions began to strike her in rapid succession. First one smote her right aft abreast the gun room on the port side, and in a moment it became apparent that she was no longer answering her helm. Her rudder was jammed but her shafts and propellers were intact. She continued to race through the water but she was no longer under control—she could do no more torpedo dodging. The next again caught her on the same side aft and almost in the same instant she was struck abreast the port engine room and on the starboard side of E boiler room. Before even the first results of this bombardment could be seen or felt, before the upflung water had ceased to rain down on the decks, almost before the echoes of the explosions had died away Tennant knew that the ship had had more than she could stand. He knew the ship intimately—he knew precisely what she could do and what she could not do, what she could take and what she could not. A less resolute commander, loving his ship and hoping against hope that she might survive, could well have wasted precious seconds and minutes waiting for the full effect of the torpedo damage to be seen. The ship was still at speed, her guns were still blazing—for all the eye could tell she might have, by some mysterious dispensation, remained whole below the waterline. Tennant knew that it could not be so: he knew also that precious lives depended on the speed with which men could get up from below and get clear of the ship before she sank. Every second the decision was put off would waste some of those lives. He did not put the decision off. He ordered stations to abandon ship. His Commander J. W. C. Dendy, in fact, is sure that he issued the order before the last torpedoes actually struck home: even as he did so, and as the first men came pouring up on deck, the ship, still forging furiously ahead, began to list to port and settle by the stern.

> When the ship had a 30 degree list to port, I looked over the starboard side of the Bridge and saw the Commander and two or three hundred men collecting on the starboard side. I never saw the slightest sign of panic or ill discipline. I told them from the Bridge how well they had fought the ship and wished them good luck. The ship hung for at least a minute and a half to two minutes with a list of about 60 degrees or 70 degrees to port and then rolled over at 12:33.

The factual, restrained phrasing of Tennant's report conveys no picture of the fine ship's end. Listing more and more to port and at the same time settling further and further by her stern she continued to drive on through the water, her speed only diminished by the greater resistance of her sinking hull. Lower and lower she sank and the list increased, then the starboard screws, still revolving madly, were out of the water: so she remained for a little, then she turned turtle and sank rapidly by the stern. Only the survivors were left, flotsam on the face of the water—the survivors and a great spreading stain of oil.

Within minutes of her disappearance, another wave of high-level bombers came over but found that their target was no longer afloat. *Prince of Wales* opened up at them with her three remaining 5.25s, S-1, S-2, and P-1, and the pom-pom: they loosed their bombs at her in default of the more vulnerable target—coolly and accurately as all the bombs had been loosed. These bombs straddled the ship, though they could not pierce the armoured deck or do her any more serious damage than she had already suffered, but they caused casualties and superficial damage, and added to the confusion on the ship's decks. Still afloat, the ship was now nonetheless like a punch-drunk boxer: she could not yet die but she could no longer defend herself, and there was nothing that could be done for her. The *Express* came alongside the quarter-deck on the starboard side and Captain Leach ordered all wounded to be transferred to her and all men no longer required to work his ship to pass over. Very shortly afterwards he gave the order to abandon ship. The destroyer hung on courageously alongside the sinking hulk, a situation of great danger, while men poured across on to her decks. Just as Tennant's quickness in ordering his men up from below saved hundreds of lives on the *Repulse,* so the tenacity and skilful handling of the *Express* saved hundreds of lives from the *Prince of Wales.* She continued to hang on while the battleship's list increased further and further—until it became suicidal to remain alongside an instant longer. Indeed, at the very moment she went astern to get clear, the bilge keel of the dying ship rose up beneath her and all but capsized her. Then at last, the long agony over, *Prince of Wales* heeled over quickly to port and sank at about 1:20 P.M.

It was at this very moment that the squadron of Brewster Buffaloes which had taken off from Kallang six minutes after the receipt of Captain Tennant's air attack signal, arrived over the scene. There was not a single Japanese aircraft in the sky: on the sea were three destroyers, one battleship sinking, masses of survivors in the water, and the great ugly stain of oil creeping wider and wider.

One of the first people to move when the order to abandon ship was given aboard *Repulse* was her Commander: he had work to do. For the whole of the action he had been incarcerated in the tiny compartment in the lower conning tower on the Captain's strict orders to stay there and not go chasing about with his damage control parties. "If I get knocked out," he had said, "I want you there to take over." He had heard the torpedoes strike but, of course, had seen nothing: he, too, knew just how much the ship would stand. He got himself out up the "tube" and emerged on to the upper deck where the several hundred men mentioned by Tennant in his report were collecting. They saw the Captain come to the wing of the bridge: he waved them over the side, and they went. The ship was moving fast and many of them were buffeted as they went in. Commander Dendy, like so many of the others, heard the screws race by, found the water green and clear and not unpleasant. When he came to the surface the ship was already going: the quarter deck was awash. An Australian midshipman, who had strapped himself to an Oerlikon was still firing madly at anything within sight and so firing, went down with the ship. As she turned turtle the forward starboard triple—Slinger Wood's old gun— came clean out of its mounting and dropped down the funnel. And as she turned over and sank, the great rents made by the torpedoes in her hull were clearly to be seen.

From the air defence position, Warrant Officer Page jumped with the wounded lookout, Boy McDonald, in his arms: he never survived although McDonald was picked up. Lieutenant Parker, diving from the same place, got caught in some rigging and crashed on to the guard rails eighty feet below. In spite of his broken ribs and other injuries, Lieutenant Gifford managed to get himself somehow or other on deck, but was never seen again. Stoker Dick, who was also in the sick-bay nursing his bandaged head, had counted nine thuds and thought he felt the ship start to lay over. Then came Tennant's voice over the loudspeakers.

"Abandon ship," it said, "and may God be with you."

All the casualties who were able to move immediately started to get themselves up on deck as best they could. One man had lost a leg and the doctor had given him a shot of morphia. He was unconscious and had no hope of survival: they left him there to drown in a merciful stupor. They got as far as the recreation space, helping each other as well as they might, while the list of the ship increased. Things were beginning to slide about all over the place, and they had the greatest difficulty in preventing themselves sliding about with them. The door which led from the recreation space to the upper deck was jammed by the list, and momentarily there was panic among the wounded men; but one fellow kept his head, opened the porthole, got through and heaved himself on to the deck above him. Dick followed him, and others came after. He stood on the deck, watching men going over the side in all directions—and then he himself almost panicked, for he discovered he had left his life-jacket behind. Then he got hold of himself and carefully slid down the side on to the torpedo blister. From there he plopped into the water and swam away. He found himself near a writer who had a life-belt and was hugging books in his arms. Dick (who never had much respect for books any way) told him he had better dump them because they were no good: he needed no second telling. Having lightened himself in this way he was able to support Dick for a little while he had a rest. Then he swam round again and bumped into a boat, just awash. It was at this moment that the high-level bombers came over and he and everyone else who saw them thought they were in for a machine-gunning in the water, but the planes passed over them. There is no mystery about this, nor was it any chivalry on the part of the Japanese which caused them to spare these men. They were at the limit of their endurance— they only had enough fuel to unload their bombs and get back to their base. This fact undoubtedly saved a lot of the ship's men from the grisly end which befell so many survivors of so many ships—shot cold-bloodedly in the water without a shred of defence.

Dick clung to his boat for about three quarters of an hour. It enabled him to keep his head above the water and so avoid the choking death which the black, spreading oil fuel brought to so many of his shipmates. Then *Electra* came up, threw ropes over her side. He got hold of a rope and three men promptly got hold of him; so he let go of the rope, swam to a Jacob's ladder, put his foot through a rung and was pulled up, Jacob's ladder and all.

"I was then sick," he wrote later, setting down his experiences.

He was lucky. All around him men were retching themselves to pieces with the corruption and corrosion of the fuel oil—black-faced, red-eyed caricatures bereft of individuality or human dignity. The sea was dotted with lifeless figures still supported by their life-jackets—men who had succumbed to the corroding poison of the oil before the destroyers could pick them up.

Scouse Garner's gun, T-3, had lost communication before the order came for stations for abandoning ship: Corporal McKillen, the captain of the gun, was firing in local control. They heard the torpedoes battering one after the other into the hull and the water thrown up by the explosions deluged them, pounding them, and soaking them to the skin. They felt, rather than saw, her settle slightly, with a trace of list to port; but she was still under way, and they went on firing. Then, quite suddenly, the quarter deck was awash and they saw men in the water as the ship swept by. The list became alarming. Petty Officer Harris, a gunnery instructor, shouted to them to get over the side. They blew their lifebelts up, shook hands all round, and wasted no more time. In front of Garner, as he climbed over the guard-rail, was a lad called Alf Hughes from Wigan, who had joined up with him and served with him right through: they paused long enough to wish each other luck.

Garner's intention had been to get to the armoured belt, and so down to the torpedo blisters and into the sea in the most convenient manner with everything under control; but he hadn't bargained (who would?) for the fact that the ship's sides were coated thick with fuel oil while he himself, in common with most of his mates, was still soaked from the torpedo spray. So once he started to slide, he could not stop himself, and went in just forward of S-3 HA gun like the Big Dipper. As he went down, he heard the thunder of the screws grow to a crescendo as they raced by, was buffeted,

and all but drawn into them: but they passed and the
thunder died, and when he broke surface he was already a
good thirty yards astern of the ship. Only the top of Y Turret
was visible; the bows were already rearing up and she was
already beginning to turn turtle at the same time. She was
still going away from him swiftly and he saw he need no
longer fear being sucked down with her; so he trod water and
watched her go, spellbound and awestricken. For a few moments she seemed to stand vertical, her superstructure level
with the water. Then suddenly she started to slide, and in ten
seconds there was nothing but a bubbling of water and
wreckage—men, Carley floats, and boats everywhere, with
the menace of the oil already welling up and spreading
among them. It was at this moment that the last flight of
bombers came over. He saw men shake their fists at them
and curse them for what they had done to their ship.

For Garner, in common with so many other survivors, his
time in the water has telescoped in memory in exactly the
same way as the action which had preceded it. As he remembers things, it was immediately after the ship had gone down,
and the last of the bombers gone over, that he and those
about him looked round for the *Prince of Wales* and found
her gone. In fact he had already been in the water three
quarters of an hour by then. Similarly, it was at least another
hour, though it seemed like no time, before the circling destroyers came within easy swimming distance: he struck out
for the nearest one, keeping his mouth shut against the fuel
oil all around him, and thought he was doing pretty well
until a man he knew called Lennie Brighton went past him
—it seemed, like a speedboat—pausing long enough to exchange greetings before they went their ways. He missed the
circling *Electra* once, caught her scrambling nets the second
time round, and was dragged aboard in pretty good shape,
apart from being black as a Kentucky minstrel from head to
foot, and as unrecognisable to his friends as they were to
him. He blessed the many hours he had spent in Lodge Lane

Baths, away back in Liverpool, learning to swim—and to keep his mouth shut. Hours were never better spent.

The realisation that the ship was sinking also came slowly to Slinger Wood and the gun's crew of the after pom-pom. They felt the ship lift and shudder to the torpedoes, were deluged with water like everyone else above deck—but the familiar vibration of the engines continued and she was still going full ahead. The gun numbers continued replacing the used belts of ammunition on the trays; then suddenly the guns were becoming unmanageable, the weight of ammunition already on the trays was sliding down and they got the locking bars on just in time to stop everything tumbling off on to the deck. In the same instant came the Captain's voice through the loudspeakers, ordering all hands on deck and wishing them Godspeed. It was a shock. Their minds refused to believe that the ship was sinking. It was quite impossible that the ship should sink.

But there was no doubt about it. The port gunwales were already awash.

"Come on, Slinger," said Leading Seaman Slatter, abandoning his beloved guns, "Let's work our way on to the starboard side. Everyone else is."

Everyone else was, indeed, but something kept telling Slinger not to—he thought the best thing was to get into the water as quickly as possible and swim clear of the suction of the ship when she went down. He didn't realise that an ever greater danger than the suction was the still-turning propellers. He slid down the gun deck and never stopped at the guard rails. Normally they were about thirty feet above the water-line, but now the water was nearly up to them. The next moment, instead of finding himself in the sea and clear of the ship, he found himself being forced inside T-3 gunshield by a trick eddy of the water, churning round the projections of the still-moving ship. For a moment he thought all was up with him—the water was growing darker, his lungs were bursting. With a desperate clutch he got his hands on the top of the gun-shield and with an equally desperate effort heaved himself clear. The moment he broke surface he seemed to get into the reverse half of the eddy, and was borne rapidly away from the ship.

Twenty yards from him, he saw a familiar landmark, the fog-buoy of the Tribal class destroyer *Matabele*. It had got caught in *Repulse's* paravanes more than twelve months before and had adorned the after deck ever since. Now it floated, justifying its existence: Slinger made for it and reaching it, turned to look at the *Repulse*. She was already completely on her side and the propellers were churning a fountain of water and oil a good fifty feet into the air. There were heads drifting down the port side, the heads of men apparently powerless to save themselves from being sucked into the blades. But the churning ceased as the ship turned completely over: then her stern was under, her bows high in the air, she was sliding, sliding, gone . . .

The oil was all around the fog-buoy now and through it there came two men helping a third, a non-swimmer—recognisable as a stoker by the badge on his overalls but apart from that black and anonymous like the rest of them. Others arrived and the fog-buoy began to get a little over-crowded. *Vampire* was picking up survivors, but she was still quite some way away; nearer at hand, however, the captain's barge was floating, empty, and Slinger suggested that the swimmers should make for it, leaving the fog-buoy to the others.

So they set off again through the thick, treacly oil that lay like a carpet on the water, and as they neared the barge a cheer went up. Someone had spotted the Captain, just climbing aboard *Vampire*; and at that, as though by some sort of signal, all those around started singing "Roll out the Barrel" with all the heart and lungs they had left to them. It was lunatic, it was crazy—as men opened their mouths to sing, they swallowed the deadly oil, unable to help themselves—yet it was lunatic and crazy enough to give just a few yards' more endurance to men who could endure no longer, and so if lives were lost by it, an equal number were probably saved.

Slinger and Leading Seaman Hodson reached the barge at the same time, with still sufficient strength left to them to heave themselves and each other aboard. For a little they rested, recovering themselves—then lying flat in the bows, where the gunwale was about three feet above the water, they contrived to give a hand up to other swimmers as they struggled the last few yards to the boat. All alike were filthy, black, and unrecognisable with the oil. Most were done in and able to do nothing but lay on the boat, retching with the oil they had swallowed. P. O. Monaghan alone was able to help Wood and Hodson with their work of rescue. Then a baldy head came alongside: its owner was in a pretty bad way, stripped to the waist and covered with oil. They grabbed his hands but he kept slipping from their grasp—he didn't seem able to help himself.

"You've got to try, pal," they urged him. "We're about buggered ourselves."

The bald-head just gasped and held on.

Now, when the order to abandon ship had been given, the journalist Gallagher discovered that he had overlooked one important matter—he could not swim. Also, he was a portly type and, as is the way with journalists, not over-fit. However, it was a case of drowning if he stayed or drowning if he went—so he went. Either in bravado or playing for time (he never knew which himself) he paused on the torpedo blister to light one of the last two cigarettes in his case and offer the other one to a rating beside him. Then, making sure his precious notebooks were tucked well into the pockets of his shorts, he jumped. For him, too, accustomed though he was to noting things accurately, time telescoped—the *Repulse* and the *Prince of Wales* seemed to disappear almost together. He felt very lonely after the ships had gone and being a non-swimmer, was defenceless against the oil: his eyes burned with it, it was in his mouth, his nostrils and in his hair. He joined three other men holding on to a round lifebelt, all as black as himself but presently lost them again and was once more alone for a spell and in a panic amid the oil. He bumped into a paravane and again became one of a quartet but they upset that also, trying to push it along, and it was in his struggles after this that he came up with the boat in which Wood, Hodson, and Monaghan were doing their best to help survivors out of the sea. He hung on to a thin wire rope at its bows, too weak to help himself and too heavy for the rescuers.

He might have hung there forever—or at least until he was too weak to hang any longer—but Petty Officer Monaghan dived in and managed to give him a boost up from below: between that and the pulling of Slinger and Hodson this particular piece of human salvage was got aboard and dumped on the deck. By now he looked to his rescuers to be in a very sorry state indeed, for with all the oil and sea-water he had swallowed his belly was swollen like a balloon and his khaki shorts seemed to be cutting him in half. Slinger undid them, pulled them off and was about to throw them back into the sea while his mates attempted to squeeze some of the water out of the big man, when Gallagher stopped him.

"Take the books out of my pocket first," he croaked, "and the fountain pen. Take my watch off too. You can have the watch and the pen," he added, "but take my notebooks to the news office as soon as you get ashore."

"Who are you, mate?" asked Slinger.

"Gallagher of the *Express*," said the journalist.

Slinger remembered his whispered conversation of two nights before with Bob Bloham and thought it funny that this bloated and unlikely figure could have been mistaken for Hughie Gallagher, the Scottish International footballer. Bob, however, wasn't there to share the joke.

"Never mind, mate," he said to Gallagher, "you'll soon

be playing at Wembley again," but Gallagher couldn't see
the joke because he didn't know about it and was probably
past appreciating jokes anyway.

Soon after this *Vampire* came alongside and willing hands
helped them up the scrambling nets. They got Gallagher
and those who could no longer help themselves along to the
sick-bay, already crammed with the black, still figures of
exhausted men reeking of the loathsome fuel oil, then made
their way back to the upper deck to see what was still going
on and what they could do. No doubt in fact they did the
same thing that Cain saw so many of the *Repulse*'s people
do aboard *Electra:* almost instinctively, he says, they seemed
to make their way towards what stations were familiar to
them, to give a hand there while the ship's own ratings were
busy pulling their comrades out of the sea. It was yet another test of the training and cohesion of a good ship's
company. Gallagher's watch was still going: it is still going
eighteen years later and is on Slinger Wood's wrist at the
moment this story is being written. It showed ten to two—
an hour and a quarter after *Repulse* had gone down and half
an hour after the final plunge of the *Prince of Wales*. *Vampire* was still circling slowly, searching for further survivors,
with a wary lookout for submarines and more aircraft attack.
But there seemed to be little life left in any of the bodies
that were still floating on the water. The oil had done for
them. They were corpses, simply kept afloat by the air in
their lifebelts. They floated thus on every side, dark protuber-
ances on the stained surface of the sea.

Slowly there gathered together groups of friends that had
survived, messmates recognising each other by peering
intently under the black camouflage, and hazarding a name.
They talked of friends they would see no more, of what their
families would be thinking at home, and how soon they
would be able to let them know they had survived, as the
destroyers joined up and turned at full speed for Singapore,

burdened with the flotsam of what had been the companies
of two fine ships.

Of *Repulse's* complement of 1309 officers and men, 796
survived; 1285 of the *Prince of Wales's* complement of 1612
were rescued: neither Admiral Sir Tom Phillips nor Captain
Leach were among them. Her senior surviving officer was
Lieutenant-Commander Skipwith; Captain Tennant and his
second-in-command, Commander Dendy, found themselves
the two senior survivors of Force Z. Gallagher has suggested
that the *Repulse's* longer casualty list is due to the fact that
she was in action to the end, and that the order to abandon
ship did not reach many men in time. This is probably incorrect: there is ample evidence that in the compartments
aft where communication had been lost, word was passed
very rapidly and most who were not already casualties were
able to get clear. But many men did lose their lives in
abandoning ship—sucked down with her, battered and drawn
into the screws and in similar ways still more lost their lives
in the water—not through the exposure of their long wait as
they would have done in northern seas, but because of the
oil that crept over them and poisoned them as they floated
or struggled in the water. The oil probably accounted for
more casualties than anything else.

The long agony of the *Prince of Wales* was the main
thing that made her casualty list smaller. A very large number
of men, indeed, had been able to get over on to the *Express*
while the destroyer courageously hung alongside the sinking
battleship's quarter-deck: these never had to face the hazards
of the sea or the fuel oil at all. Those who did go into the
sea were picked up much more quickly from the very fact
that there were fewer of them, and because the ship was only
steaming very slowly as they went over the side. They were
scattered over nothing like so wide an area as the survivors
of the *Repulse*. The proportion of survivors who lost their
lives in the oil was very much less.

Those who went overside from the *Prince of Wales* tell

very much the same sort of story in general terms as those who did from the *Repulse*—Seddon, Tudor and Boy Williams were all among them—and there comes a point even in the war at sea when repetition becomes monotonous. Beyond all doubt there was much more confusion. Tudor has a general impression of casualities lying around everywhere when he emerged from his 5.25 after the power failed—was quite sure the Japanese were suicide-bombing the ship. He stepped over one prostrate man to find it was his mate Joe Dempsey:

"For Christ's sake, Joe, get to the floats," he said, but Joe did not reply, and at that moment the blast of another explosion sent Alf spinning along the deck: this must have been in the one high-level bombing attack the *Prince of Wales* suffered after the high-level bombers' special target, the *Repulse*, had sunk.

Williams has a dim and flickering memory of an officer with a pistol ordering men over the side—some of the lads, he thinks, said it was the Commander. His more abiding memory is of the dreadful cries and screams of the men trapped below coming up through the quarter-deck ventilators: their agony was the longer for the time it took the ship to sink. Few of the survivors who were in that part of the ship during the sinking find those sounds and the memory of them easy to banish.

Perhaps one of the most publicised descriptions of the men of the two ships in the water is contained in a report by Flight-Lieutenant Vigors, commanding the Brewster Buffaloes that took off from Kallang at 12:15 and arrived just in time to see the *Prince of Wales* sinking. It is worth quoting in full:

> *I had the privilege to be the first aircraft to reach the crews of the* Prince of Wales *and the* Repulse *after they had been sunk. I say the privilege, for during the next hour while I flew around low over them, I witnessed a show of that indomitable spirit for which the Royal Navy is so famous. I have seen a show of spirit*

*in this war over Dunkirk, during the "Battle of Britain,"
and in the London night raids, but never before have I
seen anything comparable with what I saw yesterday. I
passed over thousands who had been through an ordeal
the greatness of which they alone can understand, for
it is impossible to pass on one's feelings in disaster to
others.*

*Even to an eye so inexperienced as mine, it was
obvious that the three destroyers were going to take
hours to pick up those hundreds of men clinging to
bits of wreckage, and swimming around in the filthy
oily water. Above all this, the threat of another bombing
and machine-gun attack was imminent. Every one of
those men must have realised that. Yet as I flew around,
every man waved and put his thumb up as I flew over
him.*

*After an hour, lack of petrol forced me to leave, but
during that hour I had seen many men in dire danger
waving, cheering and joking as if they were holiday-
makers at Brighton waving at a low flying aircraft.
It shook me for here was something above human
nature. I take off my hat to them, for in them I saw the
spirit which wins wars.*

*I apologise for taking up your valuable time, but I
thought you should know of the incredible conduct
of your men.*

Now Flight-Lieutenant Vigors was no raw recruit—as he
himself pointed out he had seen service in the Battle of
Britain and the London blitz—but nonetheless he allowed
his emotions to run away with him and his emotions led
him into some serious mistakes. The most important of these
is that while he flew around admiring the men who were
waving and putting up their thumbs, the men were, in fact,
shaking their fists at the aircraft which had arrived too late.
Boy Williams, indeed, says that when the fighters first arrived
and flew around with their pilots waving, the men in the
water waved back in sheer relief that they were not Japanese
come to machine-gun them—but the waving soon changed

to fist-shaking. It was not the fault of Vigors nor of any of the other pilots that they arrived too late—any more than it was their fault that they had Brewster Buffaloes instead of Spitfires. In the end the men in the water would admit, in all fairness, that all this wasn't the pilots' fault. But just now they had had their ships sunk under them by planes which had had the sky to themselves: they had seen their comrades die and on one of the ships heard the screams of them dying without being able to help them. And the niceties of just who was to blame for the planes not being there in time were of no particular interest to them.

Of course, men made the best of things in the water—as long, that is, as they had more air than water in their lungs, as long as they had strength in their limbs, as long as the miseries of the poisonous fuel oil were not making them want to die anyway. Of course, there were crazy incidents, like Slinger Wood and the rest bawling out "Roll Out the Barrel" with their mouths full of water and oil. What else could they do? But few of them would have expected to see their efforts at self-preservation trumpeted forth in such emotional and highly-coloured fashion as in Vigors' report —still less handed down to history in this fashion, because that is what inevitably happened. There was never a service document calculated to have a better appeal to the sob-writers. It was a heaven-sent gift for sob-writers. Poor Vigors didn't intend it to be, but it was. And when the accounts of the action were eventually published, the sob-writers gave the Vigors story pride of place. There were many other things about the action more interesting and important, many other things which the survivors themselves would sooner have seen earn the prominence of black type. There are all sorts of morals to it; and perhaps one of them is that even under the stress of the kind of emotion Vigors was understandably feeling, service reports are, on the whole, best couched in the restrained language which is more usual for them.

The wreck of the *Prince of Wales* was located by H.M.S. *Defender* on April 23, 1954. Nearby but not identified—anonymous even in death in the presence of the Glamour Ship—lies the *Repulse*. May the bones of both of them lie quietly in their sea change; for this is the grave of the capital ship—the whole rise, supremacy, decline and fall of which had occupied a space of time not very much greater than the active life of Nelson's *Victory*, already fifty years old when she fought at Trafalgar. Until well past the days of the Crimea, navies had patrolled the seas with steam-driven ships of the line. In the eighteen sixties came the first turret ships and from the dockyards of the Western Powers began to emerge the strange and abominable shapes of monsters whose very ugliness thrilled the landsman but revolted the seaman—often with good cause. These slab-sided, top-heavy gun platforms, low in freeboard and cranky in habit were many a time a menace not merely to their country's foes, but also to those who sailed in them, such as the notorious *Captain*, which capsized off Finisterre in no more than a modest storm. But even as armour thickened, as guns increased in power, range and weight, the needs of the sea asserted themselves and the capital ship became a ship again——a ship of a very different sort, indeed, from the old wooden walls, a new conception of a ship, but nonetheless a ship that could become a new naval tradition, a new embodiment of sea power. It grew in size; it became the dreadnought, the super-dreadnought. It became something only the greatest of powers could afford to build and maintain, and so it became something over the building of which great powers competed, both in numbers and in size: this accelerated its development enormously. It also became the badge, the symbol, and the instrument of Western imperialism's domination of the oceans and continents of the world: its decline and fall were associated in many complex ways with the rise of the factors which undermined that imperialism. The pattern of its fate was being woven before it

reached its full development: before it achieved either the
beauty of the *Repulse* at speed or the awesome majesty of
the *Prince of Wales* or the *Bismarck*, the capital ship was
decadent. Radio robbed it of its ability to surprise and over-
whelm, the submarine of its invulnerability and its freedom
to operate unhampered, without an escort screen. The air-
plane menaced it first as a spotter, then as a bomber of not
very much account against horizontal armour and finally as a
torpedo-bomber. It began to be an integral part of naval
strategy and tactics and to play an increasing part in the
harrying and sinking of capital ships, until in the *Bismarck*
action its ability to cripple and pin down for destruction the
strongest ships great powers could produce was clearly
demonstrated. Still no capital ship had been sunk by aircraft
action alone, and singularly few people appear even to have
supposed that capital ships could be sunk by aircraft action
alone. To too many people—alas, to Churchill himself—they
continued to be a mystical symbol of sea power long after
their capacity for maintaining sea power had vanished. Why,
heaven alone knows: all the forewarning, all the evidence
was there, it wanted only an open mind and the application
of a little logic to appreciate it.

Now, not merely H.M.S. *Anonymous*, the elderly battle-
cruiser, but H.M.S. *Unsinkable* herself, lay at the bottom
of the Gulf of Siam, put there by aircraft-launched torpedoes
and aircraft-launched torpedoes alone. Doom hung over the
capital ship. The Japanese Navy's own two greatest ships
were in turn to be sunk by air attack before their war was
over. In the wake of the torpedo-bomber were to come the
atom-bomb, the hydrogen bomb, new instruments of power
infinitely smaller in size, incomparably greater in destruction
than the fifteen- and sixteen-inch gun turrets which had once
seemed like the organ-pipes of hell. Capital ships would see
their second world war out, diminished in their status as
weapons. They would keep the seas for a little after that, and
then their power and their glory would be gone from the face

of the oceans. Their passing would leave the world poorer as it is always poorer when things die that stir human hearts and emotions—but the better, perhaps, for the fact that some of the darker sides of the imperial majesty they represented had gone as well. Only if the world ceased to breed the kind of men who manned ships like the *Repulse* and the *Prince of Wales*, would the world really be a worse place than it had been before; and there is no evidence of that happening.

CHAPTER

14

THERE WAS YET A LITTLE RESPITE BEFORE THE NEWS OF THE sinking of the ships broke upon a Britain which had had to stand up to so many grievous reverses and endure so many bitter humiliations in the course of that year—the almost unbelievably sinister year 1941. It had not yet even broken upon Singapore or on Mr. Duff-Cooper, who that very morning had just received the news for which he had been longing. It was a telegram informing him that he had been appointed Resident Cabinet Minister at Singapore for Far Eastern Affairs, and authorising him to form a War Council. He had already seen the Governor and arranged with him to hold the first meeting of his Council at 5:30 that evening: he then drove across to the naval base feeling that he was back in the world of great affairs and no longer a tourist. He walked into the office of Sir Robert Brooke-Popham, Commander-in-Chief, Far East.

"I have some news for you," he said to Sir Robert, and told him.

"I have also something to tell you," was the reply. "The *Prince of Wales* and the *Repulse* have been sunk."

They agreed that Duff-Cooper should broadcast the news that evening.

Poor Duff-Cooper! He was to have a few brief weeks of power in this crumbling outpost that had once been the hub of Far Eastern affairs; then, as the Far Eastern empire which he had been appointed to govern, folded up on every side, he was to find himself a man without a job once more. He had tried so hard, he had had such great hopes. It is impossible even in the midst of stark and overwhelming tragedy to resist a sardonic smile at the way in which the relentless march of titanic events constantly outran the little man's struggle to keep up with them.

But there was nothing funny about the awakening of Mr. Churchill to the news. There is not even room for the most sardonic of smiles, for here was tragedy without relief. He has told us the story himself. He had gone to sleep, it will be remembered, lulled by the magnificent vision of the *Repulse* and the *Prince of Wales* steaming triumphantly across the Pacific to cement the Anglo-American alliance forever. He had awakened refreshed and was opening his boxes in bed, according to his habit, when the bedside telephone rang. It was the First Sea Lord. His voice sounded odd. There was a sort of cough and a gulp, and at first Churchill could not hear him quite clearly.

"Prime Minister," he said, "I have to report to you that the *Prince of Wales* and *Repulse* have both been sunk by the Japanese——we think by aircraft. Tom Phillips is drowned."

"Are you sure it's true?" demanded Churchill.

"There's no doubt at all," was the answer.

Churchill put the telephone down, glad to be alone at this moment. As he turned and twisted in bed, the full horror of the news sank in on him. Who among his bitterest enemies, his most unrelenting detractors, could grudge him

a mite of sympathy just at this moment? It was not merely
that the ships were lost, that the Japanese were indisputable
masters of the eastern seas, that Malaya was doomed, Singapore as good as finished, Sumatra, Java, Borneo, New
Guinea, Australia in peril. It was not that the *Prince of Wales*
and the *Repulse* would never sail gloriously majestic into
some west coast American port, White Ensigns fluttering
at their jack-staffs. It was not that Tom Phillips, in whom
he had placed so much trust, was gone. It was not that once
more he must stand in the House and deal yet another blow
at the long-suffering people who looked to him as their leader.
It was more. It was that for all this and for whatever other
consequences the sinking of the ships might have, he was
personally responsible.

Soon after eleven he went down to the House. He knew
he must break the news to the Commons himself. It is to
his credit that he did not attempt to shirk whatever reckoning
there might be.

"The House," he writes, "was very silent and seemed to
hold its judgment in suspense. I did not seek or expect more."

It was a bewildered and bitter public upon whom the
tidings broke, and the little information about the sinking
of the ships that could be allowed to pass through the sieve
of wartime security did little to counter the bewilderment
or assuage the bitterness. Once more the information services
bungled the job and once more the "naval correspondents"
who had never been nearer to a ship than the receiving end
of a pair of binoculars launched their flights of fancy. So
plausible were some of these and so well were they believed,
that we even find them being interpolated into news stories
summarising the true story of the sinking of the ships, when
the official dispatches were at last published several years
after the end of the war.

One of the most persistent—and most persistently revived
—of these is that the *Repulse* and the *Prince of Wales* were
sent to Singapore "because they were the only two ships

available that could get there in time." It is amazing how deeply this particular story was inculcated and how hard it has died: from some forgotten source and on some unimpeachable authority, the writer of this very book discovered it was firmly embedded in the wartime jumble at the back of his mind. One almost is driven to suspect that the information services, so far from bungling or falling down on the job, had found means of implanting in the minds of the nation at large a story which would forestall any talk or thought about blunders, except that one knows that such an operation would have been far beyond both their intelligence and their skill.

The only two ships available that could get there in time . . . It doesn't hold water. It is grossly and wholly irrelevant. In time for what? No-one knew what was going to happen. Not one Allied statesman, with the possible exception of Field-Marshal Smuts, had the ghost of an idea that Japan would enter so early and so decisively into the war—still less that her equipment was so good or her service units so well practised in its use. Roosevelt, right up to the last moment when those ships and troop movements were both past concealment and past forestalling, had been certain and sure of the three months of negotiation left to him. Churchill, up to the very day when the news of Pearl Harbour broke, was unshakeably convinced that Japan would not attack the Allied powers, that it would be suicidal for her if she did. Smuts had talked of possible disasters: "I told your little Admiral," he said to Captain Dendy in South Africa later, "to go there and hide himself, not to go rushing about." But did even he foresee anything so sudden or so complete?

How, then, could the *Repulse* and the *Prince of Wales* have been sent because they were the only ships available that could get there in time for something no-one supposed was going to happen? In a situation where it was believed that the Japanese were going to allow us to get on with our war until we had smashed the western end of the Axis and were able to deal with the eastern end in our own good time, why rush ships?

The Foreign Office indeed had wanted ships—not further to forestall any known movements on the part of the Japanese but to "steady" a situation which they read against the background of their Victorian conception of power in the Far East. Singapore had wanted ships—not to stave off disaster from its very doorstep but to perfect the impregnable defences which would keep war far, far away from it for all time. No-one had wanted ships because they had any conviction that the Japanese were ready and poised for attack. In assessing the blunders that were made and the responsibility of those who made them, we must underline first the folly and the failure of both those who persisted in opinions that were not supported by any vestige of fact and those who should have supplied the facts that might have changed these opinions. The British and American intelligence services had both fallen down on the job. Neither had any excuse for falling down, for the Japanese war ciphers had been in American hands for a year without the slightest use being made of them. Even without them is it conceivable that the very existence of aircraft of the character and quality of the Mitsubishi bombers, or the efficiency of the torpedoes with which they were aimed, should have remained such a closed book that there was no trace of them in the aircraft recognition manuals nor any information issued to the services at all? Or was it part of the blunder of failing to take the Japanese seriously that no attempt was even made to secure information about their equipment?

Did Phillips blunder? Did he try to be a hero, visualise himself as the architect of a lightning naval victory that would have sent his name down to the history books with all the glory of a Nelson? So much of what was rumoured at the time and so much of what had been written since suggests, by implication, that he led his ships out on a vainglorious adventure which could in theory have been a spectacular success but was in fact bound to be a disastrous failure. Phillips did none of these things. Enough has already been said to make it clear that he took the only decision which the British naval commander in that place could have taken at that time. His decisions were made for him—not by any dreams of sudden glory but by the march of circumstances in the Far East. Once the ships were at Singapore he had no option but to employ them as he did. It cannot be repeated too often that it was not he alone who saw the conclusions to which he was forced—that all the senior naval officers on the spot supported him, that the Admiralty supported him after the event and has supported him ever since. He took calculated risks and when the risks became too great he withdrew, but it was then too late. He made no blunders, his subordinate commanders made no blunders, the men who fought the two ships made no blunders—not even the men of the *Prince of Wales* in the final overwhelming of their ship, the disintegration under stress of disaster of the organisation of a ship's company which had had no time to work itself up to perfection. Blunders indeed there were about the ships, and the *Prince of Wales*'s lack of working-up time was one of them. Blunders there were about the ships' armament and their protection, but even these became irrelevant; while, for instance, better anti-aircraft equipment might have staved off the worst of that particular attack, it could only have postponed the fate of the ships for a matter of hours or even days. Had they not been sunk off Kuantan they would have been sunk in Singapore harbour. Had they not been sunk in Singapore harbour they would have been sunk trying to find refuge either amid Mr. Churchill's innumerable islands or elsewhere, or fighting some other desperate last battle at sea. They would have been sunk just as *Exeter* was sunk, just as *Electra* was sunk, just as all the other ships which fought their desperate last fights in the darkening Far Eastern twilight were sunk. The fact of their being there made it certain that they would be sunk.

But the inevitability of their being sunk is no alibi for those who failed to take what measures they could for their salvation, or for those whose past blunders or blunders in other directions affected what measures could be taken. Indeed, these were people who seemed unable to grasp the full implications of the situation and therefore were quite incapable of realising that the ships were bound to be sunk.

"My God!" said Air Vice-Marshal Pulford that night, "I hope you don't blame me for this. We didn't even know where you were."

Why did he not know where they were? Was no air reconnaissance being carried out over the Gulf of Siam, where so many threats to Singapore were developing—not even with a solitary Catalina? Was no attempt made to reconnoitre Kuantan, only a hundred and forty miles from Singapore, to see if the reported landings there could be confirmed? Surely this would have been a natural—indeed, an essential—thing to do, and if it had been done, the whereabouts of the ships must have been discovered. Was it necessary for Phillips to break radio silence in face of all the potential destroyers of his ships lurking in the air, on the water and below the water, to tell Pulford what he ought to have been intent on discovering for himself? Even in default of any reconnaissance, Phillips expected Pulford and everyone else at Singapore to know where he was—to know that the signal about the landings at Kuantan would automatically send him there. He also, it is true, expected Tenedos to have transmitted his message that morning and so give a sufficiently close clue to his position, not knowing that Tenedos was overwhelmed—but even that was not essential. The official historian suggests that he assumed too great a degree of insight on the part of Pulford and the others involved; but did he? Time and time again in the Battle of the Atlantic, which had brought Phillips to his maturity as a naval staff officer, everything had depended on just this degree of insight, until in the end failure became so rare that its possibility was not reckoned on. Why expect Pulford and those around him to fail when officers very much junior to him could be relied on not to fail in all the rapidly changing situations of a far-flung naval battlefront?

Admiral Sir William Tennant, a just man, insists that it is unfair to blame Pulford; so does Captain Dendy, second senior survivor of the *Repulse*. But Pulford must be blamed, together with Sir Robert Brooke-Popham, his C.-in-C. Admittedly they cannot be blamed for the poverty and paucity of their equipment, for having Brewster Buffaloes and not enough of those, for being short of flying boats for reconnaissance and everything else—although even here the writer has surely not been wholly wrong in suggesting that had they been less ready to accept their poverty and had they been insistent enough in their demands for just a little more, that little more might have been vouchsafed to them. But they need not have been so complacent about what they had. They need not have gone out of their way to proclaim to friend and foe alike that the Brewster Buffaloes were "good enough for Singapore." It has been urged in their defence that they were not complacent, that they were trying to bolster morale, to keep Singapore and Malaya from alarm and despondency. They succeeded. They succeeded too well. Morale in Singapore was not low: it was high—it was impossibly and ridiculously high. It did not require boosting—it required jolting. Pulford's complacency was not morale-building: it was wishful thinking, and the blame of it is inescapable.

When Phillips asked for fighter support for the morning of his proposed bombardment of the Kra Isthmus landing forces, Pulford lacked the resolution to say on the spot that he could not give it. He allowed Phillips to complete his plans on the assumption that at least there was a good chance of getting it. "It's all laid on," said Captain Tennant, when Commander Dendy asked him about air support on his return from the conference at which Admiral Phillips had expounded his plan, and this shows that Phillips at least gave the impression of thinking he could rely on air support. Only after Force Z had sailed and after more than one reminder did Pulford say categorically that fighter support could not be given: it was then that Phillips was driven to taking his gamble on the weather, which almost came off. Had Phillips known from the beginning that there was no possibility of fighter support, he might still have gambled on the weather. On the other hand, he might not. But at least, when the risks were so great and every one of them had to be so finely weighed, surely he could have been spared indecision which, under the circumstances, almost amounted to deception.

Now two reasons are given why Pulford decided he could not give air support to the operation. One was that because of the short range of the Buffaloes, such support would entail their operating from northern airfields, and the northern airfields were rapidly becoming untenable. The other was that he was husbanding his fighters for the defence of Singapore itself. Certainly conditions in the north were becoming difficult and the land forces, right from the beginning of the Japanese attacks, were too thin on the ground and too ill-equipped to maintain their positions. The airfields were under threat: partly, already, they were under bombardment. But in the Battle of Britain, airfields had been kept operational under conditions at least no better than those prevailing up to that moment on the north Malayan airfields—often under worse conditions. In many of the other theatres of war where, in that terrible year, we had fought so disastrously, airfields had been kept operational in well nigh impossible conditions. Pulford had not yet lost his airfields. He was afraid of losing his airfields. Could he not have taken at least as much of a chance with them as Phillips was taking with his precious and irreplaceable ships and men?

As to the second reason—that he was keeping his fighters for the defence of Singapore—Pulford should have asked himself where lay the best defence for Singapore. Phillips

knew: Pulford should have known too. It lay not in contract-
ing the lines of defence until the Japanese were poised for
their leap over the narrow waters on to the island itself, but
in keeping them at bay in the place where they were best
contained, and if possible cutting them off and strangling
them there. That place was the Kra Isthmus, the natural forward defence line of Singapore, and the place where the
Japanese would have to be stopped by some means or other,
if they were going to be stopped at all. If they could be
stopped there, if their supply convoys and their reinforcements could be blasted out of the water, as Phillips hoped
to blast them, then the northern airfields would continue to
be safe, save for air attack from Saigon, and the defences of
Singapore would get a new lease of life. If Pulford wanted
to use his fighters for the defence of Singapore, then there
could not have been a better place to use them than against
the Kra Isthmus; and there could not have been a better way
of using them against the Kra Isthmus than to use them in
support of Phillips' attack on the Japanese landings there.
He did not see it. And in the event, his fighters failed to
defend Singapore. Once the Japanese got themselves thoroughly established, once they were able to operate from the
Malayan airfields, the fighters could not defend Singapore.
At that stage, fighting on level terms with the Japanese, they
were too few in number, too poor in performance and too
weak in fire-power. Then not all the gallantry of the pilots
who, ever-decreasing in numbers, fought out their last battles
as the ships were to fight out their last battles in the South
China Sea, could make any difference. It was too late, and
they were overwhelmed.

The Brewster Buffaloes were not "good enough for Singapore." Neither was Air Vice-Marshal Pulford.

So one could go on indefinitely, describing and detailing
the blunders of lesser men which had a bearing on the sinking of the *Repulse* and the *Prince of Wales*. There is such an
infinity of blunders, they stretch so far backwards from the

event, that a lifetime could be spent tracking them all down and meticulously cataloguing them. But just as the defects and deficiencies of the ships become irrelevant against the one outstanding fact that once there they were bound to be sunk, so the lesser blunders of the lesser men become irrelevant against the greatest blunder of them all—the only blunder which, in the last resort, is really important at all. And it was not committed by lesser men: it was committed by Mr. Churchill.

At the time this history is being written, Sir Winston Churchill is still alive. Living, he has been canonized: his services to his country have been many and his achievements great. But this book is not concerned with any general assessment of his life and career, nor does it presume to pass any general verdict at all upon him as statesman, strategist, or anything else—these are matters of infinitely wider issue. We are concerned with one thing and one thing only—the loss of the *Repulse* and the *Prince of Wales*—and there is absolutely no escape from the conclusion that the prime responsibility for their loss was his. History will judge this quite surely, and will weigh it in the balance when the time arrives for its verdict to be passed in generations to come.

Mr. Churchill blundered. At some points his blunder ran parallel with the blunders of others; at other points he blundered in the face of advice and argument which he would have done well to heed. He was far from alone in his utter and complete under-estimation of the Japanese, his failure to assess either their strength or their intentions, but his responsibility here, in the first place, is greater than the responsibility of lesser men who fell into the same errors. He was almost alone—save perhaps for that unlikely and irrelevant ally, the Foreign Office—in his erroneous and antique conception of naval strategy, his misunderstanding of the uses and limitations of capital ships. Among politicians, service chiefs, and practical men of affairs in high positions, he must have been utterly and completely alone in his time in that curious mystique of the battleship he created for himself—in the way in which he seemed to credit battleships with almost magical powers. Is there any other way of describing his expositions of what one single ship of the highest quality could be expected to do, or his complete disregard of the requirements of working-up or any other practical considerations in the employment of such ships? Not only, to him, could they work miracles irrespective of the size and character of the forces arrayed against them— they could cross vast oceans unescorted and without refuelling, they could disappear amid island labyrinths where there was neither sea-room for them to manoeuvre nor sufficient water for them to float. Often enough, no doubt, the Admiralty would have been glad enough to have had ships capable of such things, had they existed—but they never fell into the error of supposing that they did exist. Lesser men might have dreamed such dreams (and maybe did) without imperilling anybody: when the Prime Minister and the Minister of Defence, able to wield almost dictatorial powers, dreamed them, disaster was bound to result.

For Churchill did have almost dictatorial powers, and furthermore he chose to use them. He wanted the ships sent to Singapore. The Admiralty opposed him. So did everyone in a position to formulate an informed opinion and possessing the right to express it. It was not a question of hidebound traditional strategists opposing a novel conception or an unconventional move: it was a question of hard-headed men, who knew firsthand the conditions and requirements of war at sea in their time, knowing that what they were hearing was a proposal to send ships to certain or near-certain destruction. For a time, Churchill countenanced argument and sent his own broadsides back, as we have seen, changing his ground, repeating arguments in different contexts, reaching the same conclusions by different routes, but nonetheless reaching them. Unflinchingly stubborn, he insisted, insisted, insisted; he accepted concessions without making the slightest concession in return. And when his patience was exhausted, when the Admiralty refused complete and unconditional surrender, he overrode them. He overrode them with so little compunction and with so little abiding consciousness of having done so, that by the time he came to write his own war history, the very memory of their long opposition was gone—for he could never be accused of wilfully misrepresenting facts.

So it cannot be disputed that it was by his personal and undeviating insistence that the ships were sent to Singapore. Once they had been sent to Singapore, they were bound to be sunk. On the day before the ships were sunk he was forced to realise this himself. And instead of taking the most urgent possible action to get Sir Tom Phillips out of it, either into the "innumerable islands" or anywhere else, he indulged himself in dreams—more dreams about his darling, magical, mystical ships—and went to sleep dreaming while the ships were lost.

CHAPTER

15

THE TRAGEDY OF THE FAR EAST WAS NOT YET FULLY PLAYED
out: nor was the tragedy of the two ships which had become
so much part and parcel of it. The ships were at the bottom
of the sea but there still survived sizeable portions of their
companies—in numbers alone sufficient to be a factor in the
defence of Singapore. Deeply laden with their burden of
filthy, oil-stained survivors, the three destroyers *Electra, Express,*
and *Vampire* were racing back to Singapore. On
Electra, as a measure of helping to balance the enormous
and unwonted load, the men of the two ships were separated
—*Repulse* port side, *Prince of Wales* starboard side, marines
aft. Many of the *Repulse's* men, in whom the memory of
H.M.S. *Anonymous* still rankled, were deeply suspicious that
this boded some sort of differential treatment of the ships'
companies even in disaster, and subsequent incidents, great
and small, ashore were interpreted in the same way, although
it could not be fairly suggested that any such differential
treatment was meted out or intended.

Aboard all the destroyers everything that could be done
for the crowded survivors was being done, but some of them
were so badly injured or had suffered so much from the fuel
oil that they were past recovery. Of those not in need of
medical care perhaps the men who had been picked up by
Vampire were the unluckiest, because she was an Australian
destroyer and had no rum. Aboard *Electra*, Stoker Dick got
the ration he had been enjoying in anticipation when the
first wave of aircraft came over. Aboard *Vampire*, Slinger
Wood and those of his cronies who had managed to find
each other thought sadly of what a wonderful thing a tot of
rum would be.

In the course of the afternoon, the journalist Gallagher
sought him out, having made a fortunate and rapid recovery
from the oil; no doubt the energetic and effective artificial
respiration that Wood and Monaghan had applied to him
had got rid of a lot of it. He took possession of his notes
once more and promised to get a message home to Mrs.
Wood as soon as he got ashore. He was as good as his word,
and Mrs. Wood was one of the first of the survivors' relatives
to hear that her husband was safe.

About half-past two, half-a-dozen Brewster Buffaloes came
over again and circled the destroyers for a little time. Pulford
now seemed to be carrying out some sort of air reconnaissance
at last. On the *Vampire* the men felt cheered up a little by
seeing them, but on the *Electra* their appearance only drew
forth more bitter remarks about the fact that they had not
come in time to save their ships. Just before dark the men
who had died after being rescued were committed to the
sea——covered in oil and near-naked as they had been when
they were picked up. Their shipmates, filthy and exhausted
themselves, bade them a last farewell. "We prayed over the
few," writes Slinger Wood, "but our thoughts were of the
many, then on into the rapidly falling dusk raced the three
destroyers."

During the time since Force Z had sailed, the cruiser

Exeter had arrived at the naval base. She, like the *Repulse*, was a West country ship and aboard her were many friends and townees of the *Repulse's* crew. They turned to, to give a hand to the survivors as the three destroyers entered the blacked-out harbour where they had so recently been feted under blazing lights, and came alongside with their sorry load of human salvage, the survivors of Force Z.

Let Wood tell his own story, firsthand, of the moments that followed:

> It was somewhere around midnight when we berthed at Singapore, in the ghostly emergency lighting we made our way off the destroyers on to the carpet of coke and clinkers with which the quay was surfaced and most of us were still barefoot. Halfway across it someone shouted, "Get on my back, Slinger." It was Jan Humphries, former Leading Hand of Mess 48 and messmate of my brother when they had been aboard Revenge together. He was now a Petty Officer on the Cruiser Exeter. Thankfully I climbed on to his back and was carried over to the tables which were laid out with bowls of hot soup and where a number of writers were taking our names and numbers and filling in next of kin forms for us. At the end of the table was a rum tub and it wasn't being served out with a tot measure. Someone handed me a full glass of neaters. Its warming glow seemed to shake off the tiredness, then we made our way up to the naval barracks and the lovely hot showers. Then we were issued with some underwear, tropical shorts, vest and a pair of pumps, then with a couple of packets of free issue cigarettes and another tot of rum.
>
> We made our way into the long, empty dormitories, and in the dim glow of the blue night-lights we could make out rows of single beds complete with mosquito nets. Bob Bloham, Jackie Bristow and myself made our way to three beds alongside each other, wearily we crawled inside the nets. The rum was beginning to have its effect. I started laughing. Bob said, "What the hell

*are you laughing at?" I said, "My ruddy foot's stuck in
this netting and the only person I ever saw getting into
one of these was Dorothy Lamour and I feel just like
her now."*

*I laid my head on the pillow and closed my eyes.
Almost immediately I was forced to open them again.
It felt like someone was jabbing hot cigarette ends into
my eyeballs. It was caused by the oil under my eyelids.
I forced them shut till they were watering, hoping it
would clear the oil. It must have been an hour later
when I finally went to sleep with my eyes wide open.*

Their place of refuge was H.M.S. *Sultan,* the great new
naval barracks, gift of the Sultan of Johore, which had hardly
been completed and very little used. Even H.M.S. *Sultan,*
however, could not altogether cope with such an enormous
influx of men in need of a complete clean-up, and for the
last arrivals the water ran cold. Marine John Garner and
those with him from *Electra* found they simply could not
get rid of the sticky fuel oil at all. They soused themselves
with cold water and wiped the muck off as best they could
on the towels—chalking up another black mark for Singapore
and still with vague thoughts about discrimination against
the men of the *Repulse.* In this one instance, at least, Singapore could not really be blamed and, of course, there was no
distinction between the survivors of the two ships in the
matter of hot water or anything else from now onwards.

The morning brought a pleasant enough awakening for
shipwrecked men. There was relief from intense vigilance,
violent action, and struggle for survival. There was a swimming pool into which they could plunge. A couple of days of
ease lay ahead before they were drawn back into the wheels
of the Far East's tragedy and the tragedy of Singapore.
Captain Tennant addressed what was left of both ships'
companies. He explained to them that he was under orders
to leave for England almost immediately and told them that
he would do what he could for them and get them home as

soon as possible. He was cheered to the echo by his own ship's company and the *Prince of Wales*'s men joined in and cheered him too; and this was the last that many of them saw of him. For the moment Commander Dendy, the second senior surviving officer of Force Z, was in charge of them. Once again in his memory—and he is a man of no foolish prejudices—there stands out the impression of how coherent an entity the *Repulse*'s crew still remained, even with their ship no longer under their feet. They were known to each other, they knew their petty officers and their petty officers knew them—even the leaven of additional personnel who had joined her to make up her wartime complement had been spread so thinly and evenly through the ship that they had been absorbed into the company long before this. It was comparatively easy to arrange and do things for so closely knit a body of men. Inevitably the *Prince of Wales*'s people were less closely knit and less homogeneous as a body. This again was no fault of theirs, but of the people who had sent them there before they had reached that state of close cohesion that marks a thoroughly well worked-up ship's company: they were proud, eager and willing, but it was less easy to organise them, and less easy to do things for them.

In the course of this couple of days' vacation the ships' crews occupied themselves according to taste, opportunity or whatever use they could find for the twenty Malayan dollars given each man by the Sultan of Johore. Inevitably, Slinger Wood found himself sought out by an uncle serving on the Australian merchant cruiser *Kinimbler*, which was in harbour——an uncle he had never even seen. One wonders whether there was anywhere a corner of the world where some member or acquaintance of the far-flung Wood family was not liable to pop up and make things easier at a crucial moment. Slinger and the survivors of Mess 46 sat long in the canteen with the Australians, smoking cigarettes, drinking and yarning while the sun went down. Alf Tudor of the *Prince of Wales* and some of his surviving cronies spent the

day more adventurously but less comfortably. They decided
to go for a walk outside the town, which is a foolish thing
sailors sometimes do, got themselves thoroughly lost in the
jungle and were in trouble when they got back.

Admiral Sir Geoffrey Layton was now back in command
at Singapore. His China Station command had been absorbed into Sir Tom Phillips' command, although he had
only officially relinquished his appointment on the morning
Force Z sailed—the morning of December 8th. He was
actually embarking for home when the news of the sinking
came, and he was prevented from sailing only by a matter
of minutes.

It might have been a good thing for the survivors of the
two ships if in fact he had sailed, because his ideas about
their treatment were very different from Captain Tennant's,
and he lost no time in making them clear. On the second
day after the survivors had landed he piped all hands and
proceeded to address them in his turn; this address put an
end very rapidly to their brief holiday, to their hopes of
getting home and to the sense of security that had been
imparted to them by Captain Tennant.

They were assembled on the parade ground of H.M.S.
Sultan under the open sky. They were told that they need
have no illusions about what the future held or what was
coming to them—they were to forget in particular about early
evacuation from Singapore, survivors' leave or easy postings
home. They were still in an operational unit, he warned them,
and they would go on being in an operational unit, and there
would be no nonsense. In particular, until they were allotted
duties, they would not go wandering about on their own: in
fact, ratings found so wandering about outside the town
would be treated as deserters and shot. Alf Tudor and his
mates could not help feeling that this last warning was directed specially at them and had an uncomfortable impression that the Admiral was looking straight in their direction
when he gave it.

If they had shown themselves thoroughly demoralised and undisciplined, there would have been good cause for cracking the whip, but there is no evidence that they had shown themselves anything of the sort. They had fought their ships to the bitter end, they were conscious of having done as much as they could do with what they had and they were not ashamed of themselves. Now they were being addressed like a collection of criminals or a ship-load of deserters. If anything could be calculated to undermine their discipline or destroy their morale, it was this.

When the draft chits began to go up, as they did very shortly after this, it was seen that he had been as good as his word. Apart from wounded there were practically no home postings or, indeed, postings out of Singapore for either of the two ships. Postings indeed there were: they were for the most part for personnel who had spent the whole of the war so far in Singapore and had seen no active service at all. One of the few exceptions was old Seddon of the *Prince of Wales*, who was packing off to Colombo on the cruiser *Mauritius*.

On this ship, by coincidence, was serving Midshipman Leach, the son of his lost captain, who was in Seddon's own watch. Captain Stephens of the *Mauritius* issued strict orders that the sinking was not to be discussed, but no orders were needed. Seddon, oddly enough, felt badly about all this, but when Singapore fell he realised that he was one of the lucky ones.

When the postings did start coming for the survivors of Force Z they were postings for demolition parties to go up the coast, for armed guards for Changi wireless station, and similar inviting possibilities. The ships were gone and now the companies were beginning to break up. The Far Eastern empire which they had been sent to save was also breaking up, for even in these past couple of days the Japanese had been inching their way relentlessly down the Malay Penin-

sula. Yet what was left of the *Repulse*'s crew came within
an inch of going to sea in one piece as a ship's company
again.

At Surabaya, the Dutch had a cruiser which had just completed a refit. There was no crew for it. Commander Dendy
was sent over by Layton to see if he could come to terms
with the Dutch about taking it over. It was the second mission for which Dendy had been briefed by the Admiral. The
first had been to go to Penang, blow up what he could, do
what he could and come back: fortunately for him the news
of the fall of Penang arrived just in time to prevent his somewhat reluctant departure from Singapore, and so he lived to
fight another day. This seemed a more hopeful assignment.

The cruiser was there all right and fit for service, but there
was an interminable haggle with the Dutch C.-in-C. over the
manner in which she was to be taken over, and the flag under
which she was to sail. Dendy refused to allow his men to
sail under any other flag but their own, and the Dutch made
precisely the same stipulation about the cruiser. To some
minds it may sound silly and odd from this distance, in the
middle of a war. It is not so silly when it is realised that
there was deep distrust of the Dutch command, which
boasted not one single senior officer with battle experience:
this distrust, unfortunately, proved justified in the disastrous
Battle of the Java Sea the following February, when the
Dutch commander failed to keep his force under control, so
that it was split up and most of the surviving naval units in
those waters sunk piecemeal by the Japanese. Maybe Dendy
felt that his men had suffered sufficiently by one series of
blunders to be spared exposure to another. Who can blame
him?

The negotiations fell through altogether in the end. The
cruiser remained in dock, to be sunk by Japanese air bombardment instead of Japanese naval action at sea, and Dendy
returned to Singapore. He found that in any case there was

now no ship's company to take over a cruiser or any other ship. The companies both of the *Repulse* and the *Prince of Wales* had been dissipated completely and posted here, there and everywhere.

Perhaps one of the most coherent groups that still remained were the marines. *Repulse's* marines formed A Company and the *Prince of Wales's* B Company of the 2nd Battalion, Argyll and Sutherland Highlanders—who immediately became known as the Plymouth Argylls. Few of them were to return. They were to bear the brunt of the bitter rearguard action down the peninsula as the Japanese advanced on Singapore with ever-increasing strength and speed: they were to be among the last troops across the causeway and thereafter, cut off and with no further retreat, to give up their lives in desperate last hand-to-hand combats.

The others were divided up in penny numbers—guard duties, demolition parties, postings to other ships, lorry driving, supply and communications duties. There can hardly have been a job of any kind in the last days of Singapore that the men of the two ships did not have a finger in. Boy Williams of the *Prince of Wales* had, perhaps the best bird's-eye view of the situation, for he was given a job in the wireless office, working a decoding machine; so that between air-raids and other excitements, his days became a sort of hour-by-hour chronicle of the onward march of the Japanese through Malaya, and the progress of the Japanese by land, sea and air throughout the whole of the eastern theatre of war.

To him and to all the other men the rottenness of Malaya became rapidly apparent. Their reminiscences are full of stories of Malay naval ratings throwing away their uniforms and changing into native dress, of ack-ack gunners sitting idly at their guns and watching the Japanese come over. How badly all the experts had blundered over the allegedly unshakeable loyalty of the Malays was now plain to see, and plainer still was the size and strength of the Fifth Column, now emerging into the open. Of all the Asiatic peoples, only the Chinese showed any desire or will to resist the Japanese: in February, just before the end, Alf Tudor and some others were driving lorry loads of Chinese volunteers up to help in the defences, and the Chinese were singing and cheering as they drove. They, perhaps, had cause to know that the Japanese were not the saviours of Asia.

Among the scattered survivors of the ships' companies, a steady attrition was taking place—through action, through air raids, through all the many avenues of death that opened up in these twilight days. In the final stages casualties rose sharply: apart from all those lost in the final desperate battles, many drowned in the evacuating ships, a very large number in trying to save civilians.

No figures exist of the total number out of the complements of the two ships who actually got out of Singapore alive. Slinger Wood cannot even remember the name of the ship in which he reached Ceylon; Cyril Williams remembers his as the *Bulan*, remembers also being bombed on the ten-day voyage by a Catalina which had been captured by the Japanese. Tudor got out in a Chinese river-boat called the *Ping Wo*. Let him tell a typical tale of the last days of Singapore. They had delivered the last of their lorry loads of Chinese volunteers:

> We made our way back after dropping the Chinese, looking for a bite to eat and some place for a nap. My mate [McMins from Bolton] suggested dropping in on the Union Jack Club but it was packed like flies, so we made our way elsewhere. Where we were going I didn't know and didn't care, as all I wanted was something for my inside. I was bloody starved. My mate said, "Boy I could eat a cow now." It was while we were walking and roaming around amongst the bomb ruins, we met an oncoming lorry. I was relieved to see it

contained some naval sailors and others. They asked us where we were going. I said I was going to see what I could salvage to eat in regards of food and drink. One chap said, "You had better bloody well jump in the lorry unless you want to walk into Japanese hands, that's where you are heading for." "Good Christ," I said, and jumped in, finding to my joy the lorry well equipped with tin food and biscuits and drove on to Singapore harbour, which by now was getting the full weight of the enemy. The harbour was one ball of orange flame and operations in full swing in regards of evacuation of Singapore. On our arrival we were told to make our own way. There wasn't much time to lose as it was a matter of hours [it was middle of February 1942]. I and my mate manned sampans towed by a small motor boat helping civilians to board ships that were already under steam to make under way. We worked desperately that night. We were on our way with another batch, this was the last batch to board and I and other sailors were told to board a Chinese river boat named Ping Wo. On looking around for my mate McMins there was no sign of him. I later learned his sampan broke tow and was left to drift around the harbour and drifted near the beach to be taken prisoner by the Japanese four hours after we left. I recently met up with McMins in Liverpool one day on his travels from Bolton. On boarding the Ping Wo I met up with Ginger Hayes who I knew well.

It was on February 15, 1942, that resistance in the fabled and fabulous fortress ceased and Singapore surrendered to the Japanese. With its fall British power—and indeed the power of the West—passed forever from the Far East, and all the years of gunboat diplomacy, all the years of swaggering domination by merchant adventurers were avenged. For more than a hundred years the warships of the West had held sway in these waters: under their protective guns generations of greedy men had battened on the seaboard people of the far eastern nations, disgracing the name of Britain, which through them became a synonym for oppression, extortion, and fear. The grossness of their arrogance, the unscrupulousness of their extortions, were but little known or realised in their native land, to which they returned swollen with plundered riches and heavy with ill-gotten gains; and such knowledge of them as there was has long since gone down into oblivion.

In the whole of British history, with all its glories, all its failures, its shining splendours, and its dark places, there is no more discreditable episode than this. In many territories, British trade went hand-in-hand with British conquest and British imperialism: traders, conquerors, and empire-builders, were followed by a strange and dedicated race of civil governors who, albeit alien of race and purpose, won the respect and often the affection of those over whom they ruled, and did no little good. With them, too, came missionaries, doctors, civil engineers, and a host of others. In some areas their achievements were great and in others small: at the most they left a permanent mark on the culture and structure of the peoples over whom they had held sway; at the least they went in the end without disgrace. But in the Far East we had exercised domination without possession, tyranny without responsibility. The merchant adventurers went where they would and traded on what terms they would, openly contemptuous of the wily oriental gentlemen whose only defences against them were subterfuge and evasion. Any attempt to impose the slightest restriction, or curb on their activities, or deny them entry into any place, could bring down hell-fire and thunder in the shape of naval bombardment, followed by burning and looting. Justice was summary, defence by temporising or by oriental wiles was not allowed. "There was obviously no point in wasting time in nogotiation" is a phrase which occurs again and again in such books as *Britain's Naval Power* by Hamilton Williams, published at the end of the last century. This and similar books, widely used as text-books in their time (and, one is tempted to suppose, still lying about in the Foreign Office, historical background to that Department's demand to "send a ship"), portrayed the whole business as a series of glorious naval victories and heroic exploits. Heroic exploits there certainly were and many deeds of high personal courage by men who were only doing the duty laid upon them, and who neither knew nor were responsible for the injustice of what they were doing: it is curious to notice that they often did their duty with unsuitable ships, inadequate equipment, and always under wretched conditions of service, for Victorian Britain bragged of its Navy but hated to waste money on it. The details of these operations have long since vanished from the most traditional of schoolbooks. The names of them read like fairy tales, belonging to another world: the storming of Tycocktow, the Peiho River, the Battle of Fatshan, the capture of the Tagu Forts, the bombardment of Kagosima, the sacking of Shimonoseki, and so on. A few names, such as the Boxer Rebellion, survive: this latter, without the memory that among its prime causes was a justifiable attempt by the Chinese to exclude Indian opium imported by British merchants.

But the peoples of Asia had not forgotten these things, have not forgotten them to this day. The Japanese had not forgotten them. In both the hearts of the Japanese and the hearts of these other peoples who saw them as the liberators of Asia, the helpless, hopeless hate had smouldered concealed for all the years. Now it burst into flame and burned lividly in a holocaust of savagery and atrocity with all the variations and refinements of revenge that will not be sated, but goes on renewing and renewing its impetus like unappeasable lust.

Many of the survivors of the two ships were to endure the full horrors of that revenge; more than a few of them to

succumb to its cruelties. And since we have been talking of
blunders, the blunders of the nineteenth-century gentlemen
who laid the fuel for this fire should not be forgotten; for
these blunders too played their part in the long chain of
causation that led to the sinking of the *Repulse* and the
Prince of Wales.

EPILOGUE

THE MORNING OFF KUANTAN SEEMS BOTH LONG AGO AND far away in the sitting-room of Slinger Wood's home in Liverpool. But the memories of it and of the great ship in which he served still come alive in his talk and in the talk of old shipmates with whom he still meets from time to time. In the rest of his war and the rest of his time in the Navy he is still convinced that he never found another ship quite like the *Repulse*.

It was not until 1943 that he got home to continue that one-day honeymoon. He gravitated in his career as an anti-aircraft gunner into smaller and smaller ships and finally ended his career in MTBs. He is still concerned with ships, but only treads their decks as an alien visitor from the shore, for he is a stevedore on the Liverpool docks.

Times have changed for him and for people like him since those grim days in Birkenhead in the 1930s, when the lack of a few pounds robbed him of his scholarship and his place in the world. The little house is spick and span and com-

fortable: neither his pretty teen-age daughter, nor his up-
and-coming son (who has a twinkle in his eye like his
father's), will want for a shilling or a rag to their backs.
Perhaps at least some of the blunders that were inflicted on
his grandfather and his father and mother have been partly
made good, and his children will have a better chance in
life than he had. To that extent at any rate the service of
such men has been requited and it is perhaps sometimes
worth remembering for a moment that there was a debt
owing to them.

In like manner, most of those whose names have occurred
in the pages of this book have left the sea and the services
behind them. One of the few exceptions is Alf Tudor of the
Prince of Wales, who still sails the sea in tankers; but he has
a cabin and a bunk and all sorts of amazing conveniences
that he would never have dreamed of, even aboard "Churchill's Yacht"; and so life for him too has changed for the better. Marine Garner served in landing-craft and ended up as a
commando. He is a commando still, though only with the
Territorials, and an army battalion of Territorials at that;
but he still enjoys his spare-time soldiering.

Captain Tennant in his report formally signified his readiness for another sea-going command. He never got another
ship—he got promotion instead and next time Slinger Wood
saw him on H.M.S. *Gambia* he was a Rear-Admiral commanding a cruiser squadron. He became in the end Admiral
Sir William Tennant, C.-in-C., West Indies, from which appointment he retired to lead the active and interesting life
which he enjoys today in his native Worcestershire, with
business interests that take him frequently to London.

Amid a great mass of detail about people and what happened to them after the ships were sunk and their companies
divided up, the most extraordinary story of all is that of Boy
Seaman Williams of the *Prince of Wales* whose career reads
like the pages of an adventure book and only differs from one
in that it happens to be true. From the rest camp in Ceylon

after he was evacuated from Singapore he was drafted to the
carrier *Formidable* in the Bay of Bengal, and from there
presently to Force H in the Mediterranean: so he covered
the landings in North Africa including Oran, Mers el Kebir,
and Algiers; then the Sicily campaign, and he was on his
way to cover landings at Naples when Italy surrendered.
From the Mediterranean he went straight to Iceland in October 1943, was with a Russian convoy escort to Bear
Island. Home for Christmas that year, he did a course in
anti-submarine detection and was drafted to the mine-
sweeper *Serene* in Canada. In her he spent four years sweeping the seas of the world clear of moored and magnetic
mines: in the course of these he re-visited Penang and Singapore. In 1945, he was with the first minesweeping flotilla to
enter Hiroshima and Nagasaki after the atom bombs had
fallen on them and from these, acquired another memory
he will never forget. After more home leave and another
torpedo course in mines he joined the destroyer *St. James*
in 1947, had a win on the Pools and painted Plymouth red.
In 1949, he was back in the Far East again, and in April of
that year joined H.M.S. *Amethyst* at Hong Kong, a fit
Leading Seaman. Nine days later he had both his legs blown
off by a Chinese shell in the Yangtse River—"which," he
observes, "after ten and a half years of exciting and interesting times in the Royal Navy, put an end to my naval career."

He married the girl he was courting in his *Prince of Wales*
days, and the pair of them are manager and manageress of a
small hotel in his native Blaenau Festiniog, where he leads
an exceedingly happy and contented life.

"I have no regrets whatsoever," he writes, "and I am not
bitter. I count my blessings and thank God for looking after
me."

Which perhaps makes a fitting end to a book which
inevitably has had at least its share of bitterness.

A Short Bibliography

Supplements to The London *Gazette:*
   38098 October 16, 1947—Sinking of the German Battle-
      ship *Bismarck*
   38214 February 26, 1948—Loss of H. M. Ships
      Prince of Wales & Repulse
Capt. S. W. Roskill—War at Sea 1939–45 Vol. I (History of
   the Second World War, U. K. Military Series, H.M.S.O.)
Sir Winston Churchill—*The Second World War*, Vol. III
Russell Grenfell—*Main Fleet to Singapore*
M. Okuniya & J. Horikoshi—*Zero*
O'Dowd Gallagher—*Retreat in the East*
Cdr. R. Pears—*British Battleships*
Lt. Cdr. Cain—*H.M.S. Electra*
H. V. Morton—*Atlantic Meeting*
Alfred Duff-Cooper (Lord Norwich)—*Old Men Forget*
C. S. Forrester—*Sink the Bismarck!*
Lt. Gen. C. E. Percival—*The War in Malaya*